Ghost Girl

Torey Hayden

Ghost Girl

HarperElement
An Imprint of HarperCollins*Publishers*
77–85 Fulham Palace Road,
Hammersmith, London W6 8JB

The website address is: www.thorsonselement.com

and *HarperElement* are trademarks of
HarperCollins*Publishers* Ltd

This book produced for Premier Direct Group plc 2007
First published in the US by Little, Brown and Company, Inc. 1991
This edition HarperElement 2006

Torey Hayden asserts the moral right to be
identified as the author of this work

A catalogue record of this book is
available from the British Library

ISBN-13 978-0-00-780473-3

Printed in the UK by CPI Bookmarque, Croydon, CR0 4TD

This book is based on the author's experiences. In order to
protect privacy, names and some identifying characteristics,
dialogue and details have been changed or reconstructed.
Some characters are not based on any one person but are
compostire characters

The names of people in this book have been changed for reasons of privacy.

Ghost Girl

Chapter One

There were 152 miles between the city and Falls River and from there another 23 miles to Pecking. All of it was prairie, wide flat, and open, interrupted only by the interstate. There were towns along the way, of course, although "town" was a rather grand description for most of them. The names, however, were always hopeful: Harmony, New Marseilles, Valhalla.

I'd alloted myself two and a half hours to cover the distance, setting off in the early morning darkness with an egg salad sandwhich and a thermos of coffee. Given no nasty surprises in the January weather, I anticipated reaching Pecking by eight.

For much of the way mine was the only car on the road. In and around Falls River there was the bustle of rush hour traffic, but otherwise, nothing disturbed the white emptiness of the plains for mile after mile. A faint breeze eddied powderlike snow across the highway, making the tracks of my tires disappear in a white sky. A litter of sundogs scampered in an arc around it. Passing through one small town, I peered down the main street. The time-and-temperature sign read –38°.

I was born and bred in the Montana Rockies, and my heart had remained in wide, wild places. Despite the enjoyable stimulation of city living, I found the confinement, the dirt, and especially the noise, oppressive. Consequently, what absorbed me most as I drove across the snow-covered prairie that January morning was not thoughts of the new life which lay ahead but rather a simple sense of unbridled freedom. I'd escaped from the city. I was alone with all that silent space around me, and the sense of deliverance it gave me verged on the ecstatic. I don't believe I actually thought about where I was going at all.

Fact was, it probably wasn't so much a case of not thinking as daring not to think. After nearly three years as a research coordinator and therapist at the Sandry Clinic, I'd thrown it all over in one wholly impulsive moment. Opening the Sunday newspaper one weekend before Christmas, I'd seen an advertisement for a special education teacher to fill a midyear vacancy in a class for the behaviorally disordered. A perfectly straightforward ad. Straightforward enough response, too. I saw it and I *wanted* it.

The strange part was that I hadn't been looking for a new job at the time. I hadn't even been thinking of looking. My time at the Sandry had been thoroughly enjoyable and professionally fulfilling. Staffed by seven psychiatrists and a handful of specialized psychologists like myself, the clinic was small, private, and pleasantly situated. I'd been taken on mainly for research expertise and for my experience in treating children with language-related psychological problems. In the years that followed, I'd often worked very hard and certainly there'd been a fair share of ups and downs, but the challenges had been worth it. I really did think I was happy there. Nothing available on a conscious level had clued me in to any desire to chuck the large, airy therapy room full of toys, the genial group of colleagues, and the stimulating research for another chance to gird my loins in denim and crawl around on some dusty classroom floor for the kind of money that would have paid traveling expenses at the clinic. But the Siren called and without a backward glance, I responded.

Like so many other little communities I'd passed through on my drive from the city, Pecking was in a state of sleepy decay. The wide, tree-lined streets testified to a time before the railroad had pulled out, before the interstate had passed it by, but now it stood, a wan ghost of small-town America, its A&W root beer stand still there but abandoned, its "Drink Coca-Cola" girl still gamely smiling from her faded mural on the side wall of the savings-and-loan building. The downtown district was virtually gone, all the big stores having moved to the shopping mall in Falls River. There was still a bank and a drugstore, a couple of cafés, a real estate agent, and a gas station on Main Street, and around the corner on First Street, a ranch store that sold saddles, boots, and hats, but there was no shopping district. What was available in Pecking had relocated far out on the southern fringe in an effort to tempt drivers from the interstate. A "shopping center" had been built there a few years before, and it consisted of a supermarket, another drugstore, and a parking lot so spacious it could no doubt have accommodated every car within five miles of Pecking and then some.

The school was on a side street two blocks over from Main. Built in 1898, it had once been the Pecking high school. The beautifully carved wooden plaque attesting to this status still hung above the door, although the word "High" had long since been puttied in. I didn't know how many schools there must have been in Pecking during its heyday, but this was all that was left now. An enormous monstrosity built from local sandstone, it housed grades K to six and the only special education classroom in the district.

"Good morning!" came a cheerful voice as I ascended the broad stone steps. One of the double doors swung open for me, and there stood Glen Tinbergen, the principal. "Getting settled in?"

"Just about," I replied and stamped snow from my feet. "But I don't get the keys to the apartment until Friday, so I've come down from the city this morning."

"Good gracious. All the way from the city this morning?" He was a tall man, and thin, wearing a gray suit. I guessed him to be in his midforties, although he had one of those soft, mild faces that could be any age. His smile was welcoming. "Well, I do hope you get settled in all right. Hope you find Pecking just what you want. We're so glad to have you." We started down the hallway. "I'll introduce you to the staff at lunchtime, but for now, I'm sure you're anxious to get to your room. It's all ready for you."

My new classroom was on the second floor, last room on the left. I hadn't seen it previously. They'd been in an understandable hurry to fill the vacancy, and I was too far away to manage anything more than the interviews and an afternoon's apartment hunting; so I was braced for the worst, knowing only too well the penchant principals had for sticking their special classes into libraries, ex-closets, or other unaccommodating places. What a pleasant surprise when I discovered myself in a spacious corner room with large windows running along two adjacent walls to give a panoramic view of the snowy schoolyard and the ancient elms bordering it. The room had been laid out carefully in an orderly but welcoming fashion, and my heart warmed to my predecessor. I knew nothing about her nor why she had left so unexpectedly, just before the Christmas holidays, and I hadn't felt I should pry, since no one offered any information; however, judging from the friendly look of the room, I was sure I would have liked her.

Adjacent to the room was an old-fashioned cloakroom with lines of coat hooks running down opposite walls and long, narrow benches beneath for sitting on to remove boots and such. The teacher's desk had been pushed in at one end of the cloakroom, and this idea impressed me. I'd never known what to do with a desk I could rarely sit at, and this seemed a nice solution to keeping it out of the way, yet accessible. Pulling open one of the bottom drawers, I dropped my sack lunch into it.

"Of course, you can change things to suit your taste," Mr. Tinbergen said as I removed my jacket and hung it on one of the hooks. "We've kept everything the way Mrs. Harriman had it, just for the kids' sakes. And for the substitutes'. Three whole weeks of 'em. The kids. God bless 'em, have had a lot to put up with. Been hard on them. How many substitutes have there been? Eight? Nine? I've lost count—too many, that's for sure. So I've tried to keep things familiar. But it's your room now. If you want to change things around, feel free."

Mr. Tinbergen had migrated back into the main classroom and was pushing chairs in around the several small tables dotted around the room to make a tidier arrangement. "Do you want me to stay? To introduce you to the kids?"

I didn't, to be honest. What I really wanted was some time to myself to go through the files again, to look at what the children had been doing, to acquaint myself with the nooks and crannies of the classroom and generally suss out my little queendom. However, not knowing him, I didn't think I'd better say that, so I smiled, nodded, and said it would be very nice, if he wanted to stay.

There were only four children in this class, making it the smallest I'd ever had outside an institution. Given this, the beautifully appointed classroom, the friendly principal, and the chance to live away from the city, I congratulated myself. Impulsive as the decision had been, it was a good move.

At quarter of nine, the first child arrived, tugged into the classroom by his mother. Reuben was a beautiful kid. At nine he was tall and slim, with an exquisitely well-formed body. His hair was dark and glossy, cut in a Dutch-boy style, which gave him a quaint, not-quite-real appearance, rather as if he were an actor preparing for a period part. His eyes, large and dark, looked everywhere but at me.

The diagnosis in the file said autism, and it took only a few minutes with him to realize it was accurate. Reuben functioned well, however, within the confines of his handicap. He could speak, use the toilet, and perform a number of academic feats with considerable skill.

Only child of a middle-aged professional couple, Reuben had had many advantages and a great deal of time spent in an effort to assuage the effects of the autism. He'd been to California, Pennsylvania, and South Carolina to participate in programs designed to modify the more difficult behaviors. At home he had two "nannies" employed specifically to see that Reuben got through his daily exercises and programming, had his vitamins, and was otherwise encouraged to follow various professional recommendations to ameliorate his handicap. And he had swimming lessons and piano lessons, not only for the experiences they provided but also to give Reuben a chance to mix with ordinary children. Despite both working in Falls River, his parents had specifically chosen to build their new home on a twenty-acre tract outside Pecking in the belief that a rural environment with its more varied seasons, clear-cut cycles, and numerous hands-on experiences would be better for Reuben than life in town. And it was they, Mr. Tinbergen pointed out, who had sought to have a special education program available locally for their son. Previously, all special education students had been bussed into Falls River, but Dr. and Mrs. Adams had been persistent and were influential enough in their own right to have seen the formation of this small class four years earlier. Unspoken but unmistakable was Mr. Tinbergen's intimation that we all had to kowtow a bit to the Adamses, as without them, none of this would have been.

After getting Reuben settled with a toy at one of the tables, I turned to see a small face peering through the window of the classroom door. "Hello," I said. "Is this your room?"

The door cracked open to reveal a small girl with thin, matchstick legs and pinched features dwarfed further by what could only be described as a Pre-Raphaelite hair style—a great wodge of dark, curly hair parted unevenly down the middle and descending over her back in a sheet. She was attractive in a pale, overwhelmed sort of way.

I knew immediately who this was—Jade Ekdahl—simply because she was the only girl in the class. What had caught my eye immediately in reading Jade's file was the fact that she was an elective mute. Although reportedly she talked at home, at school she had never uttered a word to anyone. Indeed, not only did she not talk, she also did not laugh, cry, cough, burp, hiccup or even sniffle, which, tales had it, left snot to drip inelegantly down from her nose into her lap. She had been retained an extra year in kindergarten in hopes that time might help her overcome her speaking difficulties, but nothing had changed. She'd been promoted on to first grade, where she seemed competent enough at her schoolwork, but she was dismally isolated. Still not speaking at the end of that year and by now almost eight, she was moved down the hall to this room.

The reason that Jade's case had caught my eye was that for the better part of the previous ten years, from college right through my work at the Sandry Clinic, my special research interest had been elective mutism. Fascinated by this disturbance, in which an individual is physically and intellectually capable of speaking normally but refuses to do so for psychological reasons, I had worked with these children extensively. Now I found it quirky that on finally deciding to end all that, who should turn up in my class but another elective mute. You're blessed with them, Mr. Tinbergen had remarked when I pointed out this coincidence. I'd replied something along the lines of not so much being blessed with them as haunted by them.

"Good morning, Jadie," Mr. Tinbergen said. "Come on in. This is your new teacher. Your real teacher, not just another substitute."

Jadie—as everyone called her—glanced up at me briefly and then scuttled by to hang up her coat in the cloakroom. What I noticed immediately was her posture, quite unlike anything I'd previously encountered while treating elective mutes. Hunched over almost double, she had her arms crossed and tucked up under her, as if she were clutching an unwieldy load of books. I made a mental note to inquire about scoliosis.

The two final pupils arrived by bus and so came into the classroom together. Six-year-old Philip was a small skinny black kid with a horsey-looking face. His hair was cut very short and his two front teeth stuck out, emphasizing the equine likeness. Born in Chicago to a mother addicted to hard drugs, Philip had had a very unpromising start to life. He'd been premature, addicted himself, and had failed to thrive throughout much of his first year of life. As he passed through a series of foster homes during the times his mother felt unable to cope with him, his development had been slow, erratic, and often unreported so that when, at age three, he was finally taken permanently from his mother's care, no one had any realistic idea what Philip was capable of. When he was five, he was placed in a long-term foster home with a local couple who had taken several other "hard-to-place" children and were raising them successfully. Without a doubt, the newfound warmth and stability were good for

Philip, but he had made dishearteningly little progress. Although he grunted and gestured, he still had virtually no speech. He urinated in the toilet but would only open his bowels when wearing a special diaper, which had resulted in horrific bouts of constipation and frequently soiled pants. And he had made almost no academic progress in two years at school. A class for mildly mentally handicapped children probably would have been a more appropriate placement for his educational needs; however, Philip's behavior made him unwelcome. Racked with fears, he was withdrawn and unwilling to approach new situations, and when frustrated, he responded with panicky violence.

The final student was Jeremiah, eight. A native American of Sioux descent, he was the oldest of five children in a family eking out a living doing God-knows-what on a five-acre tract of land littered with rusting car bodies and old stoves. Jeremiah was a fighter. His pugnacious behavior was so extreme, his mouth so foul that the parents in his previous school had banded together to keep him from returning, even with resource help. So he'd ended up here in a last-ditch attempt to save him from custodial detention. I had an irrational love for this sort of kid, for the loud, feisty, streetwise ones who never knew quite how to quit, and the moment I saw him with his black hair stuck straight up, as if it had never seen a comb, and his cocky little rooster strut, I knew I'd found another one.

"Well, children," Mr. Tinbergen said cheerfully, when everyone had arrived, "guess what? This is your new teacher. *Your* new teacher. Not just another substitute, but your own teacher. Miss Hayden. Miss Torey Hayden. And she says you may call her Torey. That's what her other boys and girls have called her. So let's say hello to Torey."

All four children stared at me. No one spoke.

"Well, come on, now. Let's make Torey feel welcome. Reuben? Can you say good morning?"

"Good morning," Reuben echoed in a singsong falsetto.

"Philip?"

Philip grunted and hid his head in his arms.

"Jeremiah?"

His grunt was not much more intelligible than Philip's.

"And Jadie says hello, too, don't you, Jadie?" Then Mr. Tinbergen turned to me. "Welcome to P.S. 168. Welcome to our school."

I smiled self-consciously.

"And now, I'll let you go. I'm sure you're anxious to get on with things." With that, Mr. Tinbergen finally went out the door.

Pressing it gently shut behind him, I turned back to the class, to the four of them sitting around the table. "Well," I said, "good morning. Good morning to you, Philip. And to you, Reuben. And to you, Jeremiah. And good morning to you. Jade—Jadie? Is that what you like people to call you?"

"She don't talk, so you might as well not make a point of it," Jeremiah said.

"I can still talk to her," I replied.

"Oh Jesus," Jeremiah replied and rolled his eyes. "You're not going to be one of *them* teachers, are you? Not one of them always wanting her own way."

"Is that what you're worried about?" I asked.

"Is that what you're worried about?" he mimicked perfectly. "Oh Jesus, you guys, listen to her. Listen to that boogy old broad."

I grinned. Back in the saddle again.

Chapter Two

That first morning was hell. No use pretending otherwise. Jeremiah was a nightmare. Every time my back was turned, he bolted out the door. He never went far, usually didn't even leave the building, but since he knew the building, whereas I didn't, he had no trouble eluding me. If I left him to his own devices and refused to chase him, he dashed up and down the corridors, banging on the other classroom doors. On one occasion, he got into the office and messed up all the internal mail. On another, he pulled off toilet paper and blocked all the toilets in both the boys' *and* the girls' rest rooms. And one time when I did chase after him, he got back into the classroom when I was out looking for him and locked me out. This was all before 11:30.

In contrast, Philip huddled in his chair and whimpered, cringing away from me every time I approached. When I tried to encourage him to join in the singing or listen to a story, he clamped his hands over his ears, squeezed his eyes shut, and rocked the chair frantically back and forth.

Reuben was in a frenzy most of the time. Up, out of his chair, he sailed around the room, deftly touching the wall with his fingertips as he moved and all the while making a soft, whirring sound. Then he'd stop, momentarily mesmerized by a dangling pull on the roller blind or some other odd object, but before I could corral him and try to reorient him, he would shoot off again. And toilet trained he may have been, but twice he whipped down his pants and peed into the trash can beside the bookshelf.

In the middle of all this was Jadie, carrying on as if she were in a completely normal classroom. Without being instructed to do so, she ferreted out her workbooks for math and reading, sat down and completed a few pages, returned them to be corrected, found a spelling sheet on the shelf, did that, handed it into the basket on the teacher's desk, then sought out a cassette, put it into the recorder, and slipped the earphones on. Occasionally, she would glance in my direction as I struggled with the boys, but otherwise she seemed impervious to my presence.

I felt immense relief when the lunch bell rang. Jeremiah, whom I'd just recaptured, heard it, too, and was out the door and down the hall before I could catch him. The second-grade teacher, whose room was next door to mine, was already out in the hallway lining up her children when I bolted by after Jeremiah. She smiled warmly and put her hand out. "I'll catch him on the way down," she said.

"Thanks," I replied in a heartfelt tone.

I must have looked as overwhelmed as I was feeling, because she smiled again in the same warm, sympathetic way. "Want me to take your others with mine? I'm going down to the lunchroom anyway."

"That'd be really great."

Going back into the classroom, I was dismayed to discover that now Jadie, too, had disappeared. I returned to the hall with Philip and Reuben.

"Oh, she goes home for lunch. She lives just across the street, so she doesn't eat here," the teacher replied when I explained that I'd lost another one. She abruptly extended her hand. "By the way, I'm Lucy McLaren. Welcome aboard."

I hung out my tongue in an expression of exhaustion. "I usually do better than this. Even on first days. But they've got the advantage at the moment. They know the ropes and I don't."

"Don't worry about it. You're doing all right. You've already lasted longer than a couple of the substitutes. There was one that left after about half an hour." And she laughed.

Back in the empty classroom, I threw myself down into one of the small chairs with the idea of catching my breath a moment before going down for the grand entrance into the teachers' lounge, an experience almost on a par with facing a new class. Five minutes' relaxation, I thought, and then I'd get my lunch and go down.

Abruptly, a scuffling rattle came from the cloakroom. Relaxed almost to a point of sleepiness in the silent classroom, I was badly startled by the noise. Jerking upright in the chair, I could feel my heart pounding in my throat.

Jadie appeared in the cloakroom doorway.

"You're still here? I thought you'd gone home for lunch."

Because of her hunched posture, Jadie had to tilt her head back at a difficult angle and peer through her eyebrows to see me, but look at me she did, her gaze steady and intent.

I, too, studied her. Her hair was very dark, almost black, as were her brows and lashes. Her eyes, in contrast, were a clear, pure blue. With her scruffy homemade clothes and tangled mass of hair, she wasn't exactly pretty, but there was a knowing, almost come-hither kind of expression in her eyes that lent her a certain beauty.

"You want to know something?" I asked.

No response. No step nearer, no blink, not even a breath that I could see.

"Come over here." I patted the chair next to mine at the table.

Laboriously, she hobbled across the classroom. Her eyes remained on me but her expression was unreadable. She didn't sit down.

"You know what I did before I came here?"

No response.

"I worked in a special clinic up in the city and you know what? I worked with boys and girls just like you, who had a hard time talking."

Jadie's eyes searched my face.

"Isn't that amazing, that first I was there and now I'm here with you? Boys and girls just like you. It was my own special job, helping them."

Her eyes narrowed.

"Did you know there were others like you? Who found it impossible to talk at school?"

A long pause and then very, very faintly, she shook her head.

I sat back and smiled. "There are. Not very many, which is why it's a bit of a coincidence, your being in this class, but I've known a lot of them. And it was my own special job, helping them be able to talk again."

The pupils of Jadie's eyes dilated, and for the first time she let slip the expressionless mask. A look of incredulity crossed her features.

Lowering my head like an ostrich in need of chiropractic help, I stuck my neck out and peered upward into her face to see her fully. I smiled. "You don't quite believe me, do you? Did you think you were all alone in feeling like you do? Did you think nobody knew about these things?"

No response.

"It's scary, isn't it, being all alone, not being able to tell anyone how you feel."

Again, the very faint nod.

Again, I smiled. "Aren't we lucky that you and I are going to be together? I've helped all those other children. Now I'm here to help you."

Her eyes grew watery, and for a brief moment, I thought she was going to cry, but she didn't.

Instead, she clutched her unbuttoned coat closed, turned tail, and ran, shutting the classroom door firmly behind her.

Over the lunch hour I set up the painting easel and mixed several pots of tempera paints. Within minutes of getting back into the classroom, Jeremiah discovered the paints and busied himself stirring the colors together. I separated him and the paints and then went off to catch Reuben, only to come back moments later and find Jeremiah painting lunchboxes. This distressed Philip immensely, as his Superman lunchbox was now a pale shade of mud brown; so I sent Jeremiah back to the sink with the lunchbox to wash it before the paint dried. The potential for mess created by combining Jeremiah, a sinkful of water, and a paint-covered lunchbox was not something I had fully appreciated until that moment, and by two o'clock I was making the acquaintance of Mr. O'Banyon, the janitor, and his mop bucket. Compared to the morning, however, this was an improvement.

After three weeks of substitutes, it was only fair to expect the children to be disrupted and disruptive. I knew it wasn't going to be easy coming in midyear and trying to recreate order. I'd appreciated that fact when I accepted the job. Jadie, Philip, and Jeremiah, however, seemed to take one more new face in their stride. Reuben couldn't. Nothing I did all day long managed to orient him to any meaningful activity. Most of the time he was up, dashing in broad circles around the classroom. When finally persuaded to sit down, he constantly rocked and flicked his eyelashes with his fingers.

Philip made an effort to join in during the afternoon. He liked the easel and paints and enthusiastically slopped bright blobs of color over piece after piece of paper. "Red?" I'd say encouragingly. "Orange?" This made him grunt something back in reply, although goodness knows what.

"That's baby painting," Jeremiah said, as he passed the easel. "Man, boog, that's not even a picture. Want me to show you how to paint something *real?*" He snatched the paintbrush out of Philip's hand. Picking up the container of black paint, he dipped the brush in and began to draw a long, black line over Philip's blodges of color. Indignant at this interference, Philip howled.

"Jeremiah," I cried, abandoning Reuben to halt what I feared would turn into real trouble. "That's Philip's painting. Now give him back his brush. You've already had your turn."

"Jesus, lady, I'm just going to help the little booger. Look at this, it ain't even a picture. And *you* sure ain't teaching him how to do it right."

Philip had begun to dance in frustration, trying to grasp the brush from Jeremiah's hand. Jeremiah, both bigger and more agile, kept it just out of reach. Black paint dripped everywhere.

"Give it back," I demanded.

"Want me to teach you how to make Mr. T?" Jeremiah offered suddenly. "You ought to like that. He's a black guy, just like you, only he's a big booger. You gonna be a big booger someday? Yeah? I bet you are." He put his free arm around Philip's shoulder in buddy-buddy fashion. "But you know something I can never figure out about you black people?" Jeremiah continued, as Philip, charmed by his attention, wrapped an arm around Jeremiah's waist. "I can never figure out how come the blackness just sort of wears off your hands. How come that happens? Look much better to me, man, if you was black all over." And with unexpected swiftness, he began painting Philip's palm black and then continued right on up his shirt sleeve.

Philip howled again. I separated the two boys, sending Jeremiah off to the "quiet chair" I'd placed just outside the cloakroom door and explaining he needed to sit there until he could keep his act together.

Jeremiah was not enthusiastic about this imposition on his freedom and got up immediately, shouting and swearing, I physically replaced him and was then obliged to stand over him for the fifteen minutes or so it took him to settle down. Even then, he muttered crossly under his breath, "Man, lady, you're gonna regret this."

Jadie might as well have been a ghost. No one spoke to her, looked at her, or even acknowledged her presence in the room. And this attitude was mutual. Jadie went about her business with absorption, but she gave no indication that there was anyone else in the room besides herself.

When it was Jadie's turn at the easel, she painted an elaborate picture of a white house with a blue roof. Beside it grew a lollipop-shaped tree and in front was a peculiarly shaped figure, rather like a bell with legs coming from it. It had yellow hair flowing down the sides, so I took it to be a person, probably a girl. The painting was small, covering only the bottom third of the paper. She made a strip of blue sky at the top and added a shining sun. This left the middle largely blank.

"I like that," I said, when she'd stepped back to view it. "You've used a lot of colors. Who's this?" I pointed to the figure.

"Man, lady, don't you take no hint?" Jeremiah shouted. "She don't talk. You been told that already. So don't go hassling folks about what's wrong with them. How'd you like it, if people kept getting at you for being so dumb? You can't help that, can you?"

"Thank you for your thoughts, Jeremiah, but I'm talking to Jadie just now."

At that moment the recess bell rang. Jeremiah shot out the door and Philip scampered after him, leaving me with Reuben and Jadie. I realized I should have been hustling out the door after them, either to catch Jeremiah and bring him back for a more appropriate exit or at least to supervise his departure, but I didn't. I stood a moment longer to see if anyone would reappear in the doorway or if any horrible noises would signal disaster. When nothing happened, I glanced over at Reuben, self-stimulating happily in the far corner, and then back to Jadie. Pointing directly to the figure on the painting, I asked again, "Who's this person?"

Silence.

"Who's this?"

Still silence.

I knew I had to work quickly now to keep the silence from growing potent. My research had yielded a highly successful method of treating the most salient symptom of the elective mutism syndrome—the refusal to speak—and it was both simple and efficient. All that was needed was for someone unknown to the child to come in, set up expectations immediately that the child would speak, and then provide an unavoidable opportunity to do so. Consequently, as a new teacher, I was in an ideal position to get Jadie to speak, but I had to do so right away before we'd established a relationship that included her silence. I also knew that to provide the "unavoidable opportunity," I had to be persistent, clinging like a terrier to my question, and not let the inevitable wall of silence deter me.

"Who's in this picture?" Silence. "Tell me what figure we have here." Silence. "What person is this?"

Still silence. I could see her muscles tense. Her hands began to tremble.

"Who's *this?*" I asked again, intensifying my voice abruptly, not making it sound angry, not even louder, just intense. And unavoidable. I tapped the picture smartly with the eraser end of the pencil I was holding.

"A girl," she whispered.

"Pardon?"

"A girl," she murmured in a hoarse half whisper.

"I see. What's her name?"

Silence.

"What do you call her?"

"Tashee." Still the hoarse whisper.

"Tashee? That's an interesting name. Is she a friend of yours?"

Jadie nodded.

"What's Tashee doing in this picture?"

"Standing in front of her grandma's house."

"Oh, so this is her grandma's house. It's pretty, all blue and white like that. Especially the door. You've made a beautiful door. And how old is Tashee?"

"Six."

"Same age as you, then?"

"No, I'm eight. I was seven, but I just had my birthday at Christmastime."

"I see. Do you and Tashee play together sometimes?"

"No."

"Have you been to her grandma's house with her?"

A pause. Jadie regarded the picture. "I don't know her grandma. She just talked about her sometimes."

"Oh."

Jadie touched the figure on the paper with one finger and some of the yellow paint smeared. Lifting her finger, she examined it. "I should have made her hair black."

"Tashee doesn't have yellow hair?"

Jadie shook her head. "No. Her hair was black, like Jeremiah's. Black and straight. I think maybe she was an Indian, but I don't know for sure."

"I see." Then I smiled at her. "I like this picture a lot. Maybe we can put it on the back counter to dry. Then I think maybe we'd better get outside to join the others, don't you?"

Jadie bent to put the lids back on the paints. I glanced over to see what Reuben was up to. Curled in a fetal position among the cushions, he lay, eyes closed, and gently stroked the skin alongside his temples. "Reuben? Reub, come on. Time to go outside."

Chapter Three

"You *didn't*? Holy cow. Holy Toledo. Glen? Glen, did you hear this? She's been here six hours and she's got Jadie Ekdahl talking. You hired Wonder Woman."

Mortally embarrassed, I ducked my head to hide my blazing cheeks. "Just coincidence, really ... This was my research specialty ..."

The speaker was Alice Havers, fiftyish maybe, small, trim, neatly turned out. She taught kindergarten and had coped with Jadie through two years of school. "So how'd you do it? What's the secret? What do we do now?"

Lifting my head, I glanced around at the others in the teachers' lounge. They were all there, from Mr. Tinbergen to Mr. O'Banyon, and they were all watching me. I smiled sheepishly and looked back at my hands. What would be best, I explained mostly to my fingernails, would be to treat Jadie as if she'd always spoken. No big fuss. No lavish praise. I explained how a lot of these children, in my experience, seemed to stay silent more from fear of the amount of attention they'd provoke when they started to talk again than anything else, and so it took a lot of work to gain the courage to try. And others seemed to feel they'd been defeated and somehow lost face by being persuaded to talk again. So it was very important to minimize the attention. After all, it wasn't the act of speaking that should get the attention, it's what people said that was important.

There, I thought, I'd said it. Given my lecture. Not even managed to make friends yet; in fact, I didn't even know everyone's name, and I'd already made a brilliant impression—Wonder Woman and wiseacre. It was too much for a first day. At the first available moment, I smiled politely, grabbed my coffee cup, and retreated to my room.

About twenty minutes later, Lucy McLaren appeared. "How're you settling in?"

I rolled my eyes. "I felt like a real dolt down there in the lounge. I wasn't trying to show off with Jadie, but that's what it came off sounding like."

"I wouldn't worry about it," Lucy said and smiled. "Alice is top class. She wasn't trying to make you feel uncomfortable. It's just that she's had Jadie for two years, so she knows what Jadie's like."

"The whole secret is in being an outsider—an unknown quantity to the child. That and not cosseting the child. You instinctively want to be gentle and supportive with these kids, and that's generally how the kid gets control. In most cases, you'll find the elective mute is a master of manipulation."

Lucy sat down on the tabletop across from my chair. "Yes, I can believe that. Poor June. She was the teacher here before. It was nothing but one big power struggle between her and Jadie. And June tried everything. In the beginning she was really nice, really warm, thinking Jadie was just needing confidence and once she felt secure, she'd speak. Of course she never did. So then June tried star charts, saying Jadie could earn all these privileges, if only she'd say answers to things. Then June got Jadie's parents to make a tape recording of Jadie at home and tried to prove to Jadie that she knew she could talk. She tried being underhanded, doing things like making Jadie run so that she'd make noise by panting. And this one time ..." Lucy paused. "Poor June, she was so thoroughly fed up. This one afternoon, she just said, no, Jadie couldn't go home until she'd said good-bye and that was that. So there they sat. And gosh, what an ordeal. Jadie did nothing. Just sat there. Picked her nose and that was about it. Poor June was right up the wall, trying to wait her out, but she couldn't manage it. Five-thirty came and she *had* to let Jadie go. June had to give in."

I nodded. "They're not kids to get into a power struggle with, because they've usually had a lot more practice at it than you have. That's why being a stranger helps, I think. The groundwork for the power struggle hasn't been laid yet, and if you're canny and a bit of an actor, you've got a chance of making them think the game's up ..." My words trailed off and we fell silent. I lifted my head and looked out across the room to the back window and from there to the playground beyond, white with snow.

Lucy, still on the tabletop, studied her fingernails. I cast a sidelong glance in her direction. She was younger than I was, no more than in her midtwenties, although considerably more formally dressed than was characteristic of our generation. She was pretty in a natural, lively sort of way, although carefully applied makeup gave her more sophistication than beauty. Her dark hair was in a well-cut pageboy. What really caught my eye, however, was the remarkable height of her high heels.

Then I glanced around the room again, surveying the neat organization. "Why did June leave midyear?" I asked. It sounded funny calling her by her first name, when I'd never even met her.

Lucy looked over and her eyes widened. "Didn't they tell you?"

"Well, I didn't think I should really ask. I felt it would be sort of nosy."

"Oh, golly. Did they *really* not say anything to you?"

"No."

A grimace. Briefly, she searched my face and then dropped her eyes again to her lap. "June committed suicide."

"Oh."

An appalled silence followed. What did one say in reply to something like that? Not having known her personally, I found myself filled with morbid curiosity and wasn't too pleased at having it.

"What on earth did they tell the children?" I ventured at last.

"We couldn't really beat around the bush. At least not about the fact she had died. But it was awful, believe me. It was right in the Christmas season, and we were in full swing with parties and plays and all the jingle-bell stuff." Another grimace. "Let me tell you, it was a downer."

"I can imagine."

"I don't know if anybody really knew what happened. She seemed okay. She'd been here about two years, and we all knew her. I'd always thought of her as a friend. She was older and stuff ... I mean, we weren't girlfriends, you know, like you are with people your own age, but ..."

Lucy paused and took in a deep breath. Holding it several seconds, she slowly released it. "I guess I did know things weren't going too well for her. The year had gotten her down. She'd said that a couple of times, but, golly, we all say things like that sometimes. I did feel sorry for her. She'd gotten divorced a few years ago and her kids were gone away to college and she hardly ever saw them. She complained about it sometimes, and I tried to be supportive, you know, listen and stuff, but I just thought it was ... well, you know. We all bitch a bit, don't we? I never thought ..." Silence. "I don't know. Something like this happens close to you and you spend gobs of time mulling it over. It's made me grow up a lot this year. It's made me face things I'd sort of ignored before."

"I'm just glad you've told me," I said. "I could have really put my foot in it."

"Yeah, we were all feeling sorry for you. They couldn't get anybody local to take the job. That's why they were advertising in the big-city newspapers. But you can understand how people around here feel. It's a small town and ..."

"Yes."

Lucy looked over. "If the kids get a bit wild, don't worry about it, okay? We all understand. It's a good school, this one. I mean, I know they look like a bunch of old fogeys down in the lounge." She chuckled. "Believe me, I was really glad when I met you and saw you were under fifty! But it doesn't matter. Everyone here's got good hearts. If the going gets rough, everybody'll help. Just tell us, okay?"

I smiled and nodded. "Okay."

Work followed me home that night. As I drove to Falls River, where I was staying in a motel until my apartment in Pecking was available, all I could think about was the school. The news about June Harriman had unsettled me more than I cared to admit, and I kept wondering what it must have been like to stand in that classroom, facing those children and feeling so desperate. When I'd arrived in the morning, all I'd been able to think about was how lucky I'd been to land this job. The small number of children, the beautifully appointed classroom, the bountiful supplies, the supportive principal, and friendly staff had made it seem as close to an ideal teaching position as I'd thus far encountered in my career. Now, abruptly, it felt tainted.

Appreciating more the turmoil the children had been through in the previous month, I decided it would be best to establish clear rules and a definite routine that would leave no doubt about my behavior. Normally, I liked a bit of spontaneity in my day and could tolerate a fair amount of chaos in the process; however, I knew now this was neither the time nor the place to be unpredictable.

I also decided it would be better to make the classroom mine immediately. My first inclination had been to leave things as they were until we'd had a chance to adjust to one another; however, after second thought, it seemed preferable to change everything at once and give more of a sense of starting anew. So on Tuesday afternoon after school, I turned the room upside down. I shifted the bookshelves around, moved all the tables together to form one huge one, pulled down the bulletin board displays. I brought in some large floor pillows and a red carpet remnant to form a specific area for morning discussion and reading. The movable shelves and cupboards I used to divide the room into several smaller areas, making one for art activities, one for construction materials and Lego, one for natural history and science activities, and one for dressing up and housekeeping. Last of all, on my way back to the motel in Falls River that night, I stopped and plundered a pet shop, buying us a flop-eared bunny, three green finches, and a pair of hamsters with a cage that resembled the Paris Métro system.

The weeks that followed were challenging, to say the least. I was very strict and very consistent about what I expected, pulling everyone—but most especially Jeremiah—up short every single time a rule was infringed. By the same token, I tried to make sure there was plenty of fun, too. We did a lot of singing, a lot of art projects, a lot of cooking, and a lot of building of fairly unrecognizable birdhouses and boats. Each morning, I tried to take the children outside for a period separate from recess. Usually, it went under the guise of science—studying seasonal changes or the weather or whatever—but it was mainly a chance for the children to let off steam, to run and scream a little without disturbing the other classes, a spell of good fun to charm the reluctant ones into behaving and reward the cooperative ones. No doubt it would come as a nasty surprise when the time arrived to spend more of the day reading and writing than we were doing at this point, but I didn't feel we were in any way wasting time or resources in those early weeks. The need to make us a group, to provide collective memories that included me rather than June Harriman, to resurrect the school year from the ashes of what had gone before, all seemed more necessary goals than the completion of a certain number of workbooks. And it was my good fortune to have a principal who agreed.

"Hey, how you doing?"

I didn't know the woman at the door. She was good-looking in a hearty, worldly sort of way, with big boobs and big hips but a waspish little waist, all appearing slightly disproportionate since she couldn't have been over five feet tall. Her thick brown hair was tied back with a red scarf into a ponytail.

"All right," I said and smiled uncertainly.

"Glen tells me you've settled in pretty good. Says you've cut Jeremiah down to size."

What was going through my mind as I studied her was that she would have made an archetypal country-western singer. She had about her that powerful aura of hardbitten wisdom, the kind evidenced by women named Lurleen or Loretta, whose men married them at fifteen and then ran off with the waitress from the diner.

"In fact," she said, "Glen tells me you've even managed to get Jadie Ekdahl talking." Pulling out one of the child-sized chairs, she sat down.

Intensely uncomfortable, I wondered if I should mention that I didn't know her. Did I? Had I forgotten her face? This was not an unknown happening for me, and I racked my brain to remember who was at my interview.

My predicament suddenly became clear to her, and she gave a broad smile. "Oh, I'm sorry. I'm

Arkie. Arkie Peterson. The school psychologist."

The name I recognized immediately, because it appeared as a signature on almost every paper in the children's files.

"So you've got to tell me all about it," she said, her tone zesty. "All about what you did with Jade. Did Glen tell you that I'd tried with her? Two blessed years, almost. I was coming in here every Thursday, trying to get that kid to talk. So, precisely now, what did you do?"

The affinity between us was instant. Talking with Arkie was like picking up a long-forgotten friendship, and before I realized it, we had whiled away the better part of an hour discussing our mutual interests in psychology, education, and disturbed children.

Arkie had been down all the usual routes with Jadie's mutism. She'd first encountered Jadie just past her fifth birthday, when it was picked up during a prekindergarten screening program. "I just wanted to gain her confidence," Arkie said. "Here was this little, wee mite of a thing under all that hair. She looked so scared and vulnerable when I came that first day. I took her down to the nurse's office, where I usually work when I'm here, and I said to her, 'Honey, we're going to be friends. We're going to come in here and do things together and have a real good time. And it doesn't matter if you can't manage talking right away, because we'll be friends anyhow.' And I just assumed once she got to know me, once she felt secure enough to trust me, she'd begin talking. I thought she'd *want* to talk to me. But she didn't. We played all these shitty little games Thursday after Thursday, 'til I wanted to brain the child."

From there, Arkie's relationship with Jadie had deteriorated into the same sort of power struggle June Harriman had experienced later. Indeed, it was Arkie's frustration that led to Jadie's placement in this class. "I still don't know if it was the right move," she said. "I mean, she's always done all right academically. She's a bright enough kid. I think her IQ scores have always been one twelve, one sixteen, somewhere in there, and she's functioning about there in her schoolwork. So was this the right move? If the mutism was not interfering with her learning, should she get stuck in a special class?"

I gave a faint shrug. "Good question. And hard to answer. Certainly she merited intervention, which lots of times these kids don't get simply because they don't cause adults much trouble. However, any kind of voluntary mutism, if it persists over months or years, shows a disturbing need to control." I looked over. "The sixty-four-thousand-dollar question, of course, is control what? Any ideas?"

"Not really."

"What's the family like?"

A shrug. "Pretty average. There's Mom, Dad, two younger girls. Traditional setup. Mom stays home with the kids. Dad has a job doing something with agricultural machinery. Socioeconomically, they're definitely in the lower bracket, but they're by no means poor."

"What about the psychological makeup of the family?"

A pause. Arkie considered her fingernails. "I don't think Mom's too bright. Sort of a go-alonger. You know the type. Anything you tell her, she goes along with. But she's easy to get on with. Dad's a bit quirky. Into health food in a big way. Got really het up because we served pork and beans in school lunches. I think he thinks Jadie's problems are coming from eating too much sugar or additives or something."

"Elective mutism as an allergy," I murmured and smiled. "That's a new one on me."

"Yeah, a bit silly. But basically, both of them are easy to get along with. I've had much worse parents to deal with in my time."

"Tell me something else," I said, changing the subject. "Has anyone investigated her posture? Does she have scoliosis?"

"No," Arkie replied bluntly. "I think it's just part of her emotional problems. We've had the school nurse look at her, and of course her own pediatrician has seen her, but no one's found anything to explain it. I think she's just a closed-up kid in all senses of the word."

The majority of the time, Jadie walked nearly doubled over. She kept her arms up under her, tucked against her chest, her hands dangling limply unless she carried something. While she kept her head up sufficiently to see, she would have to keep it at an awkward angle to see much, so most of the time she peered through her eyebrows and the tangled dark hair hanging over her forehead. This made looking Jadie in the eye an almost impossible task. The bent-over posture took its toll on her gait, too, and she moved about the classroom in a mincing hobble.

This physical behavior perplexed me. While it was not uncommon for the children in my elective mutism research to exhibit a tendency to keep their limbs close in and otherwise take on an inhibited posture, none had even faintly approached Jadie's florid display. Despite Arkie's assurance that Jadie had been properly examined by doctors and the problem seemed to be purely psychological, I remained skeptical, because, plain and simple, Jadie looked deformed.

One morning not long after Arkie and I had talked, I found myself watching Jadie as she went about her work. "Jadie?" I called. "Come over here, please."

Turning from the bookshelf, Jadie hobbled over.

I turned her around to face away from me and asked her to bend over and touch her ankles. This she cautiously did and, lifting her shirt, I studied the outline of her shoulders to reassure myself there was no evidence of scoliosis. Then I asked her to stand and turn around to face me. Doing so, she tilted her head to one side to see me better.

Very gently, I put one hand on her collar bone and the other in the middle of her back. "Let's see you stand up a little straighter." Carefully, I urged her upright.

I felt very unsure of myself in doing this and the uncertainty must have come through my hands, because I quickly met resistance. Reluctant to push harder in case I might do damage, I stopped and lowered my hands. "These muscles here," I said, indicating her lower back, "can you relax them?" Gently, I massaged along her spine with my fingertips, but it was like touching clothed stone. The more I touched her, the tenser she became. At last I dropped my hand.

"Does it hurt you when I push like that?"

"I don't want to."

"But does it hurt?"

"No."

"So, will you show me that you can stand up straight?"

She shook her head.

"If I take my hands right away and don't touch you, can you straighten up?"

"No."

"Why? Does it hurt?"

"No."

"Well, why then?"

"Because I need to bend over."

"Why?"

"Because I need to."

"But *why?*"

"To keep my insides from falling out."

Chapter Four

The following week, I made an appointment to see Jadie's parents, and since they lived so near the school, I offered to come over to their house to see them. They readily accepted, as their youngest daughter, Sapphire, was only a few months old.

The house was small and in the style of those built between the wars. Everything about it was ramshackle. Paint peeled from the window frames. The latticework around the front porch was broken. Large patches of grass in the front yard were worn away, leaving a battered tricycle mired in the mud. But when Mr. Ekdahl opened the door to greet me, I was led into a large room, warm and neat.

They were a wholly undistinguished-looking couple. Jadie's mother was small and drab, with mousy hair and badly chapped hands. She'd made a clear effort to appear attractive, apparent in the eye makeup and styled hair, but they had an aging effect. I knew she was probably near my age, but she had the aura of an older generation. Jadie's father had pale Scandinavian features. Thin almost to the point of gauntness, he looked worn out, like the winter-beaten buffalo grass slowly disintegrating in the prairie wind.

Jadie's five-year-old sister, Amber, was there, too, and I was struck by the fact that this was one of those odd cases where the children were much more attractive than one would have been led to believe, seeing the parents. Amber was quite unlike Jadie in some ways. Her hair was fair and much less curly than Jadie's, making her look more rumpled than ratty. Although her eyes were blue, they were a cloudy gray-blue, not the pure color Jadie's were, but Amber, too, had the long, dark lashes, giving her the same look of infant sensuality. She remained in the room with us, a naked doll in her arms, and watched me guardedly. Jadie, however, made herself scarce. I heard the familiar sound of her shuffle in an adjacent room, and Mrs. Ekdahl said something about her minding the baby. Whatever, Jadie never even appeared to say hi.

Jadie's parents were clearly ill at ease with me. They got me seated in a big chair, a cup of coffee in my hand, and then they just stared. I explained a bit about who I was and talked about my own background and my work with children like Jadie, in hopes this would break the ice some. I said how glad I was to have her in my class, how gentle and cooperative she was, and what good academic work she was doing. They sat together on a long brown vinyl couch, which had decorative stitching in the shape of a horse's head on the back, and said nothing.

After ten minutes of this, it occurred to me that whatever else might be contributing to Jadie's problems, a certain amount might simply be a familial trait. I endeavored to make conversation and ended up talking to myself, as no one else ever spoke. Mother, father, and daughter all sat motionless and mute, managing not even so much as a nod in my direction. Finally, I gave up and fell silent myself. Nothing happened. For three or four minutes, we all just sat.

"You can make that chair go back," Mrs. Ekdahl finally said.

"Pardon?" I asked.

"That chair, that one you're sitting in. It's a recliner. If you want to get yourself more comfortable, you just lean back some more and it lays out real nice."

"Oh. Thank you. I'm quite comfortable now, though."

"Do you want some more coffee?"

"No, thank you. I'm fine."

"You sure? No trouble. We got the pot on and it makes ten cups. We only just been drinking it, so there's plenty more."

There was pathos in all of this, and it left me feeling more uncomfortable and out of place than ever. "I'm fine," I said, "but thanks. What I want to talk about ... Jadie ..."

They looked at me.

"What do you think about Jadie's problems with speaking at school?"

"Nothing," the mother replied, her voice soft.

"Nothing?"

"Don't see it's a problem. Leastways, it isn't one for us. She talks fine at home. Sometimes she won't shut up."

"Oh? Can you tell me about such times?"

"She gets silly," the father offered.

"In what way?"

He shrugged. "Just silly. Jumping around. Her and Amber." He smiled at the younger girl, who ducked her head.

"Does Jadie talk then?"

"Yeah, all the time. Shouts. Says silly things."

"What do you do then?" I asked.

"Tell her to stop. Tell her you don't go jumping on the couch, 'cause she's going to rip it. She's already ripped it here, see?" He pointed to a place patched with what looked like duct tape.

"And tell her to stop talking dirty," Mrs. Ekdahl added. "She does, sometimes. Shouts these filthy words and then Amber hears them."

From my experience with Jadie in the classroom, I was finding all this very difficult to imagine.

"She picks them words up at school. From the big boys on the playground. And then, if she really wants to get you mad, she says 'em, 'cause she knows we don't talk like that in this house," Mrs. Ekdahl said.

"And does she usually stop when you tell her to?" I asked.

"Sometimes," Mr. Ekdahl said. "Sometimes not."

"What do you do then? Do you spank her?"

"*No,*" he replied indignantly. "I don't think it's right for a parent to hit their little children. We don't spank our girls. We just take away privileges. Mostly, when she does those things, I send her outside. Tell her to go yell out there."

"I see."

Silence followed. I regarded the parents; they regarded their hands. "So, you feel Jadie's problems with speech aren't anything serious?"

Mrs. Ekdahl looked over. "It's just shyness. Jadie don't get on real good with outsiders, that's all. She's always been that way. Both girls have. Just like their family best, that's all."

"Well, the other thing ... the way Jadie walks. What are your thoughts on her posture?"

"Oh, that, she can't help that. She was born that way," Mrs. Ekdahl said. "See, I had this real hard time getting her out when she was born. She was stuck in the wrong way, had her face like this." She gestured along the front of her abdomen. "So she came wrong. I had to have forty-two stitches in me afterwards, and the doctor said things might not be just right, because she didn't get enough air. That's because she was stuck in such a long time."

"Oh," I said in surprise. "I hadn't realized that. Nobody's mentioned birth trauma to me."

"We just got to be patient with Jadie," Mrs. Ekdahl said. "I don't think there's anything wrong with her. She's little and she's shy, but that don't mean there's anything really the matter with her. She's good at her work. She always has good report cards, so I think we just got to be patient."

I went home from the meeting in a state of confusion. This new bit of information fogged over my previous conclusions. Jadie did speak now. She had responded classically to the intervention method I'd developed to treat elective mutism, which lent weight to the evidence that hers was psychological, and surely someone, somewhere, would have noted the likelihood of brain damage in her files if it was felt to be contributory. On the other hand, while she spoke in class now, she still did not speak much spontaneously but rather only when spoken to. Also, there was her bizarre posture to consider. And goodness knows, I'd been victim before of critical information being omitted from files. On thinking the matter through, it seemed reasonable to keep an open mind to the possibility that Jadie was aphasic, unable to speak because of brain damage.

At the beginning of March, we had a two-day break. I used the time to go up to the city and visit all my old colleagues at the clinic. Of course, I was curious about how everyone had gotten on since I'd left, and I wanted to know about the children I'd been working with, who were all now in therapy with one of my partners; however, there was an ulterior motive as well. I wanted to borrow a video recorder.

I had long been accustomed to using video machines in my classroom. Back in the early seventies when I'd first started teaching, I'd been fortunate enough to be in a school with its own video equipment—a rarity in those days—and even more fortunate in the fact that most of the staff hadn't learned how to use it, so it sat idle much of the time. Subsequently, I appropriated it bit by bit and made it an integral part of my classroom routine. I found such a recording device invaluable. When I taught, I often became so absorbed in the process that I missed vital clues to a child's behavior. Now, for the cost of a few reels of videotape, I could go back at the end of the day and observe and evaluate both the children and myself in a way never possible before.

We didn't have a video camera or even a recorder in Pecking. Gracious and generous as Mr. Tinbergen was, he admitted that school finances did not stretch that far. He wished they did, he said, but it was rather too much of a luxury for a school that size. So back I went to the city over the two-day break to see if I could charm my old director, Dr. Rosenthal, into lending me one of the clinic's for a couple of weeks. And so I did, returning to Pecking with an elderly reel-to-reel machine and its accompanying camera rattling around on the back seat of my car.

"I know what that is," Jadie said, when she arrived in the classroom Monday morning.

"You do?" This surprised me, as cassette recorders were rapidly replacing these bulky older machines and even VCRs were still uncommon.

"Yeah. It makes TV pictures." She hobbled up to the recording deck. "Are you going to put us on TV?"

"Just on this little one here. It's called a monitor."

"Will my mom and dad see it?"

"No. It's just for us. When everybody is here, we'll turn it on so that everyone can see themselves. And maybe at the end of the week, we can act out a little play and record it. That'd be nice, wouldn't it? Maybe one of those plays from your reading book."

"Is that what you got it for? Us?"

"Well, mostly it's for me. So I can see what I'm doing when I'm teaching."

"What d'you mean?"

"See, what I do is turn it on and let it run and don't pay any attention to it. Then, at the end of the day, I can sit down and look at it and see what we're doing. I can look at each person carefully and decide if I'm doing the right things to help. This makes me a better teacher."

"Just you? You look at it all by yourself? Nobody else sees it?"

"Just me, usually."

Jadie peered into the camera lens and then went back to the deck. "This is how you turn it on, isn't it?"

"Yes."

"And here's how you stop it. You press this button, don't you?" She bent nearer to the machine. "Rec-ord," she read.

"*Re*-cord. That's the button you press when you want the picture to go onto the tape."

"Yeah, I know what it means."

I looked at her. "Have you seen one of these before?"

She nodded. "Bobby Ewing's got one."

"Is that a friend of yours?" I asked.

"Yeah. Him and J.R., when they come, they put you on TV."

"J.R.?" Confused, I searched her face for some explanation. "J.R.? Bobby? You mean like the Ewings on TV? On 'Dallas'?"

"No, I don't think he's on TV. He puts you on TV. So you can be a movie star and make lots of money when you're big."

Totally baffled, I said nothing more, but I filed the conversation away. It was the first truly spontaneous conversation I'd thus far had with Jadie, and it made no sense whatsoever to me. This lack of coherence lent credence to the aphasia theory.

Setting the camera up on the wide window ledge, I ran the machine for almost two hours in the morning. This allowed me to catch a good cross section of both tightly organized activities, such as reading, and freer periods, such as art. I switched it off just before lunch and intended to record a bit more after lunch; however, when I returned later and stopped to check the reels, I saw there wasn't actually enough tape left to make it worthwhile, so I decided to view what

I had first and then record in the afternoon another day.

I didn't get around to viewing the two hours of tape until after school the following day. The room was dark. We'd had a run of wet, heavily overcast days, and all I needed to do was turn off the overhead lights to plunge the schoolroom into gloom. Pulling up one of the small chairs, I flipped the monitor on and sat down, elbows on my knees, chin resting on my folded hands, and watched.

Much of the latter part of the tape was taken up with Jeremiah and me, just before lunch the previous day. We were at the table, and I was helping him with his reading, or at least trying to help. Jeremiah was fairly hopeless at most academic tasks and hid his troubles behind a constant barrage of defiant, distracting remarks.

Leaning forward, I studied the images. I listened carefully to my tone of voice. Did I sound as exasperated as I'd felt at the time? Was I inadvertently provoking him? Was I encouraging resistance? I looked at Jeremiah, slumped over the table, refusing to work. I heard myself saying that he seemed angry and unwilling to do his folder. Sometimes, I said, when people are afraid of being wrong, they get so worried about doing the work that they can't do it at all. Sometimes what comes out is anger, because it's frustrating, because something's got to come out, and because feeling angry isn't as scary as feeling afraid.

Studying the images of Jeremiah and myself, listening to myself as I posed these comments, I cringed. This was probably an appropriate place to make the connection between Jeremiah's constant anger and the fear I suspected it was covering, but the way I said it ... It made me sound as if I knew, when there was no way of *knowing* such things.

Then came the sound of the lunch bell ringing and Jeremiah shot off-screen. Then came the view of me rising to turn off the machine. The screen went blank.

I stood up to go turn the lights back on, but before I could move more than a pace or two from my chair, a picture came back on the screen. I halted midstep.

The picture was of very poor quality, gray and grainy from too little light. Studying the screen, I assumed it must simply have been something previously recorded on the tape. Wondering if it was done at the clinic, I tried to make out the features of the room. Then I startled. This was *our* room, at a slightly different angle. The camera must have been bumped. The machine must have been running when the overhead lights were off. But how? When? I distinctly remembered turning it off before going to lunch. In fact, my looming form approaching the camera was recorded.

"OOOOOOoooooooooooo," came a small, disembodied voice off-screen. Other noises—the shuffling of feet, the movement of chairs—accompanied it.

Confused and eerily discomforted, I sat back down in the chair and tried to make sense of it all.

"OOOOoooooooooo-oo-oooooooo." Jadie materialized only inches from the camera. "OOoooooooo," she continued to croon in a small, high-pitched voice. Weaving back and forth, first so close to the camera that only her mouth was visible and then swinging so far back as to almost disappear into the gray gloom, she kept at the noise for two or three minutes.

Jadie paused and for a second or two simply faced the camera. Then, turning, she took two pencils off an adjacent table. Pressing one length-ways against her upper lip and the other in the same fashion against the lower, she turned her lips outward to create a grotesquely exaggerated mouth. She was breathing out a sound toward the camera as she did so, sort of an "ucka ucka ucka" noise.

The weirdness of it overwhelmed me, pinning me to my seat. She was only barely visible, her voice almost disembodied. As she backed away from the camera, her mass of dark hair eventually merged into the gloom around her, leaving only her face palely discernible. She halted there and was momentarily silent. Then the image began to approach the camera again. A whispering started up and at first I couldn't make out the words. She was too far away from the microphone and speak-ing too softly. Then she came nearer.

"Help me," she was saying, almost sighing. "Help me, help me, help me, help me, help me ..." Coming nearer and nearer until all that was visible on the screen was a mouth forming the same words over and over again. "Help me, help me, help me, help me, help me ..." Then the monitor went blank.

Only then, when the screen turned to snow, and white noise buzzed in my ears, did I realize that throughout the whole eerie episode, Jadie had been standing upright.

Chapter Five

I must have watched that short segment of videotape a dozen times while trying to puzzle out its meaning. It was now obvious to me that Jadie must have slipped back into the classroom after I'd gone down for lunch with the others, and that was why the lights were not on; also why, when I'd returned from lunch, I'd found insufficient tape to record during the afternoon, although at the time I had never put two and two together.

But what was the point of it all? Had she wanted me to see this? Was it a direct message to me? Or had she simply been playing around with the recorder with no thoughts as to whether someone might view it? And what about her posture? There was no mistaking the fact that on the tape she was standing normally. Had she intended me to know she could stand upright, or had I fortuitously dropped onto secret information?

Unsure of these matters, I chose the patient approach. I didn't mention the tape, not the next day nor any of the days following, although we continued to use the recorder, and, as I had promised, I taped the children performing a little play from one of their reading books, which we all viewed "on TV." My hope was that if it had been a deliberate message, my silence would smoke her out. She'd either hint at it or else leave me another message. Neither happened.

As often does happen in this kind of environment, a more pressing crisis came along to scupper the subtle moment, however thought provoking. In this instance, Philip suffered a grand mal seizure in class. It was the first seizure he'd had in several years, but the whole following week was frantic, as one seizure followed another, until at last he was admitted to the hospital in Falls River. The experience proved deeply disturbing to the other children, particularly Jeremiah, who was convinced Philip would die with each seizure and often stirred the others into panic with his terror. All my time and energy was taken up trying to keep us on an even keel.

More than two weeks later, I was sitting alone after school at the table in the classroom, finishing my plans for the next day, when I was overcome with the sensation of being watched. I looked up, around, but saw nothing. Back I went to my work, but the sensation, powerful and unshakable, persisted. I glanced up at the clock. It was 4:15, so all the children were long gone and most of the other teachers would be down in the teachers' lounge. At last, I rose and went to the door to look out in the hallway.

There stood Jadie.

"Hello," I said.

She gazed up at me.

"This isn't really the right time for being inside. It's okay to come over and play on the swings after school, but I'm not at all sure Mr. Tinbergen would want children walking around inside the building. He might get cross."

She continued to gaze up.

"Do you need something?"

No response.

I glanced down the corridor. It was no joke about Mr. Tinbergen. I knew he didn't like children in the building outside school hours.

"This is my time to work on plans," I said. "I'm quite busy. If you need something, I'll try to help, but otherwise, I think you should go back outside."

Not a word out of her.

I regarded her. "Do you want to come in? Is that it?"

Still she gazed at me, her head cocked to overcome her hunched-over position.

"I am working hard," I murmured. "If you come in, you'll need to play very quietly."

Without so much as a nod, she slipped around me and into the classroom.

Scuttling over to the cabinet containing jigsaw puzzles, Jadie took one out and hobbled back across the room with it. Putting it down opposite me at the table, she slumped into a chair, then dumped the puzzle out and began assembling it. Furtively, I watched her. She'd changed from school and was now wearing a ratty-looking pink sweat-shirt and a worn pair of corduroy pants. Her long dark hair tumbled over her shoulders. Studying her hair, I wondered if it was possible to get a brush through it. Probably not.

Ten, fifteen, twenty minutes passed in complete silence while I finished my plans. Jadie worked diligently on the jigsaw. She was good at them and had done this one several times before, but it was a large one with nearly a hundred pieces, so it kept her busy. I found myself watching her more and more. Try as I did, I couldn't keep my mind on my work. What kept intruding were thoughts of that video.

"Sit up more, would you?" I murmured, my voice barely audible.

Jadie paused, her hand, holding a puzzle piece, halted midmotion.

"Show me how you do it."

Maybe it wasn't my voice that had made her pause. Maybe she had merely been trying to locate where the puzzle piece went. Anyway, she found it and fitted it in. Then she reached for another piece and continued on, as if I had never spoken.

"Show me how you straighten up. Like you did on the videotape."

There was still no indication that she was listening to me.

"I *know,* Jadie."

Very faintly, she nodded but she still didn't look up.

Silence.

"All right," I said and closed my plan book. "That's okay. The choice is yours."

Jadie lifted her head. She lifted it right up, so that she was looking at me squarely and not through her eyebrows as usual, but she didn't straighten up any farther. I saw her face fully so seldom that the blueness of her eyes caught me by surprise. They were so faultlessly blue, the intensity of the color heightened by the dark lashes.

She searched my face. "Who are you?" she asked, her voice oddly plaintive.

"Torey," I said, not quite sure what she meant.

"Torey?" It was said like a foreign word. "Torey? You're Torey?"

"Yes."

"Torey?" she repeated. "But who are you?"

Unable to understand what she wanted to know, I hesitated.

"Who are you?"

"A teacher," I said, uncertainly. "Someone who helps children."

For the first time, her eyes left my face. A deeply puzzled expression on her face, she turned and glanced around the room, then down at the jigsaw. "But who are you?" she asked a fourth time.

Bewildered, because I could tell I wasn't responding in a way that answered her question, I replied, "Who do you think I am?"

Jadie paused a moment, then shrugged. "Maybe you're God."

The following afternoon, I was in the cloakroom, sitting at the teacher's desk, when I heard the snick of the latch on the classroom door. While I could see into the classroom from the desk, the door was out of my line of vision, so I didn't know who it was.

"Yes? Lucy?" I queried, thinking perhaps she had come to drop off the dittos she'd promised earlier.

No answer.

Rising, I stuck my head around the cloakroom door. There was Jadie. "You like coming in for an after-school visit, don't you?" I said.

A faint nod.

"I don't think this can happen every night," I said. "Sometimes I have work to do outside the room, and I can't leave you in here alone. And if Mr. Tinbergen gets wind of it and doesn't like it, then there'll have to be a stop to it. Yes? You understand? Because he kind of has a rule about children in the building after hours."

She gave an almost imperceptible shrug of her shoulders and hobbled off to the corner where the animals were kept. Gently raising the top of the rabbit's cage, she lifted him out and cradled him in her arms. I returned to the cloakroom and went back to work.

Twenty minutes must have passed with Jadie playing quietly in the classroom, and I'd almost forgotten she was there. I couldn't see her from where I was and she made virtually no noise. Then she appeared in the doorway between the classroom and the cloakroom. In her hand she carried a sheet of paper.

Normally, the cloakroom wasn't lit. There were two doors in the long, narrow room, the one Jadie was standing in, and another at the far end, which opened into the hallway. Usually, these gave sufficient light for putting away coats and boots. Now, however, because I was working at the desk, I had the far door into the hallway shut and the overhead light on.

Jadie paused in the doorway, and her expression approached astonishment, as she scanned the high, old-fashioned walls, the ledges above the rows of hooks meant for storing lunchboxes and books, the hooks themselves, the benches beneath. Tentatively, she stepped inside.

"You haven't had a good look at it with the lights on?" I asked.

"Usually, it's dark in here."

"That's because I don't like to put the light on during the day. We always forget it and that wastes electricity. And there's no window in here to give natural light, but we usually get enough from the hallway and the classroom."

"There's no windows," Jadie murmured, looking up.

"No."

Once again she scrutinized the room carefully, then her attention went back to the paper in her hand. "Can I use this?" she asked. "Can I draw on it?"

"Yes, if you want."

She disappeared back into the classroom but within moments had returned, clutching the paper under her arm and carrying a margarine tub full of crayons. Laying the things down on the linoleum floor of the cloakroom, she knelt beside them and, without further comment to me, she began to draw.

The paper was a large 2 x 3-foot sheet, and Jadie colored virtually all of it black, except for a tiny area down in the right-hand corner. Here were two minute, faceless, bell-shaped figures.

"That looks interesting," I said, leaning forward across my desk.

Jadie lifted the drawing up and examined it. "It's me and Amber there," she said, touching the figures.

"I see."

Silence followed while both of us studied the picture. I then threw caution to the wind and said what was on my mind, although it probably wasn't ideal psychological technique. "You know, Jadie, to tell you the truth, those don't look much like little girls to me. They're a curious shape."

"That's because I just said it was me and Amber. I didn't say we were little girls. We're not there. We're ghosts."

"Oh. I see. This is you and your sister dressed up like ghosts. Is it at Halloween time?"

"No. We're not dressed up. We *are* ghosts."

"Oh."

Silence.

"Which one is you and which is Amber?"

Laboriously rising from where she had been working, Jadie brought the picture over and laid it on the desk in front of me. Taking a pencil from the holder, she wrote her name under one figure and her sister's under the other.

"What about your mom and dad? And Sapphire?"

"Don't got no mom or dad when me and Amber are ghosts. And Sapphire's too little. She don't know how to do it."

"I see." I leaned forward to examine the picture more carefully. "Just the two of you, then? It sounds like it might be lonely, just two little girls."

"But like I said, we aren't little girls. We're ghosts. Ghosts don't get lonely. It's nice being alone, when you're a ghost. We just float around, go way up high, and look down on people doing things. But they can't see us, 'cause we're invisible, so they don't know we're doing it."

I nodded. "That does sound interesting. What kinds of things do you see people doing?"

"Just things. Like going to bed or watching TV. We go and look in all the other people's houses."

"I see."

"I don't mind when it goes dark, then. Gotta be dark to be a ghost. But if it goes too dark before you get out, you can't do it. You can't get out of your body and you get shut in."

I looked over, perplexed. "What do you mean?"

An expression flickered across Jadie's face that I couldn't identify—alarm? concern?—I wasn't sure. She turned her head away sharply and didn't answer.

"What's the matter? Does it frighten you to talk about this?"

A pause. "Well, really I shouldn't be telling you."

"Why?"

"I'm not supposed to."

"Why?"

"'Cause what goes on inside your head is private." She looked over. "That's right, isn't it? You shouldn't know private things."

I shrugged faintly and gave a half smile. "Sometimes it doesn't hurt." I tried to keep the tone conversational. "Besides, I'm interested. How do you get to be a ghost? Could I do it? Would you be able to teach *me?*"

"I don't think so," she said, her voice dubious, then she hesitated, her gaze fixed on the drawing. "Well, you sort of make yourself go quiet. Real still. Like you're dead. Then, when you got all of you that way, you just sort of slip out of your body and go away." Another pause and she frowned at the picture. "But I don't know if a grown-up could do it."

"Is it easy for you?" I asked.

"Yeah, kind of."

"How do you come back into your body afterwards?"

Jadie didn't answer.

"You don't know?"

She shook her head. "I just wake up in the morning and I'm back."

"A dream?"

Jadie frowned. "No. I didn't say that. It's not just a dream. It's something I can really do. It's just that I try to stay out, but I always fall asleep."

"It sounds as if you don't really want to come back."

"Well, see, if you're a ghost when the sun comes up, then you stay a ghost forever. That's what Tashee says. You won't ever get back into your body after that, because if the sun comes up on it with no person in it, it dies."

"Oh."

"So I always try to stay awake. I drink Coke. There's always Coke to drink, but then I get sleepy. I fall asleep then and that makes me go back into my body. So when I wake up in the morning, I'm always still here."

"And you would rather have stayed a ghost?"

Jadie nodded.

The conversation seemed to peter out then. We both stared at the picture, as silence enveloped us.

"I like this drawing," I said at last. "Do you suppose I could have it?"

Jadie looked over. "What would you do with it?"

"Just keep it. Maybe put it up on the wall. It's a good picture. Maybe the others would like to see it."

"*No,*" Jadie replied, alarm in her voice. "I don't want anybody else to see it."

"No? Why not?"

"'Cause I told you. 'Cause it's private what goes on inside you. Besides, if you put it on the wall, spiders might walk on it. Spiders might see. Then the policemen would come."

She completely lost me on that one. "Policemen?" I said in bewilderment. "What do you mean?"

"They'd take me away for lying. They'd put me in jail. I might die. Sometimes policemen kill you with their guns, if they think you're trying to get away. And if they got you in the jail, sometimes they kill you in a chair."

Seeing that she was becoming agitated, I quickly changed tack. "So Tashee knows about being a ghost, too?"

Jadie nodded. "Yeah. Tashee's the one who taught me and Amber how to do it."

"That was clever of her."

Jadie nodded again. "Tashee knows lots and lots of stuff."

"Sounds like Tashee's very special to you."

For the first time, a slight hint of a smile touched Jadie's lips. "Yeah, she's my best friend. I like her better than anybody."

"Is she in school here? She's not in Mrs. McLaren's class, is she? Is she a third-grader?"

Jadie looked at me, her expression bemused. "Well, of course not," she said, her tone implying that I'd asked a very silly question indeed. "That's why me and Amber turn into ghosts."

"What do you mean?"

"So's we can go visit Tashee. Tashee can't come here. She's been dead more than a year now."

Chapter Six

I was disappointed when Jadie did not show up after school the next afternoon. Her appearance had been an intrusion initially, but after two visits, I was curious about her and looked forward to seeing her again in the undisturbed quiet of the late afternoon. Once the children were gone and I'd done what I needed to outside the classroom, I brought my work out to the table in the classroom, thinking this would make me more accessible than the cloakroom had done. However, Jadie went home at the end of the school day, as usual, and did not come back again. On two or three occasions, I thought I'd heard her outside in the hall, but whenever I went to the door, no one was there.

It wasn't until well into the next week that Jadie again appeared after hours. It was quite late in the day—after 4:30—and I'd finished all my work, had made a tour through the teachers' lounge, and was now back at my desk in the cloakroom, paging through a teaching magazine. Click went the latch on the classroom door, then no sound.

"Yes?" I called.

Jadie appeared in the doorway. She'd been home and changed and was now wearing a horrible home-made jog-suit with rickrack stitched unevenly around the neck and sleeves.

"Hello," I said, and smiled.

Jadie stepped just inside the cloakroom. Twisting her head, she surveyed the small room very thoroughly. Above the coat hooks were the shelves, and above the shelf on the right ran two heating pipes. They were about three inches each in diameter and entered the room through the far end wall to run parallel about two feet above the shelf for the entire length of the room before disappearing out through the wall behind the desk. In fact, the room was well supplied with pipes, because there was also a large plumbing pipe about eight inches in diameter that rose vertically through the floor in the corner near the far door and disappeared through the ceiling. All these things Jadie surveyed carefully. Then she turned her head and looked at the door, which was open between the cloakroom and the classroom. This was a heavy, old-fashioned door made of solid wood. Even without touching it, one could tell it was strong. There was a window in our classroom door, but there wasn't in this, nor in the one between the cloakroom and the hall. Jadie turned and put a hand out to feel the door.

Jadie examined the door minutely. She ran her hands over the wood, lingering to feel the grain. She pursued the ornamental molding with her fingers, then came to the knob and lock. These, like the door itself, were old-fashioned, and there was a proper keyhole. All of this, too, Jadie examined carefully, poking her little finger into the keyhole, turning the knob, watching the latch go in and out.

This whole procedure took a full ten minutes, and, throughout, I didn't say a word. Still at my desk, I simply watched. Jadie didn't seem particularly interested in my presence. All her attention was focused on the door. Gently, she eased it away from its stop and pushed it closed, shutting the two of us into the cloakroom. Then she turned the knob and opened it slightly. She fingered the latching mechanism.

"Here's the deadbolt," she murmured, more to herself than to me. She touched the bolt in its housing inside the latch. Then she shut the door again, tried the knob, opened it, felt the lock, closed it. This she did at least six or seven times before turning abruptly to me. "You got a key for this? Can you lock it?"

I nodded.

Her face brightened. "Give it to me, okay? Lemme lock it shut."

Fascinated by her behavior, I agreed and dug the key out of my desk drawer. Jadie deftly slipped it into the keyhole and turned it. The deadbolt slid into place with a satisfying thunk. "That's good," she murmured in a pleased tone. Removing the key, she tried to open the door but, of course, it didn't move. Then she unlocked the door, opened it, stuck her head into the classroom, pulled back, and slammed the door shut, relocking it. From there, she scuttled down to the other door, which opened into the hallway.

"Does the key work in this one, too?" she asked me. "Can we lock this one?" But before I could reply, she was already trying the key in the lock. It did fit both doors, and a satisfied smile crossed Jadie's face as she tugged at the newly locked door. Abruptly, she let go and scuttled back to the other door to try it again. This, still locked, too, refused to budge. "Got to cover this up," she muttered and came to the desk. Seizing a foil of masking tape, she tore a strip off and placed it carefully over the keyhole. "Key's in the other one. Can't see in, but got to cover this one up." Then, unexpectedly, she veered away from the door. Bent double, she began hurriedly moving around the circumference of the small room, her eyes on the floor.

"Are you looking for something?" I asked.

"Spiders. No spiders," she muttered. "There's no spiders in here."

"No. Mr. Tinbergen has a man who comes around and sprays. He was just here in February. So there're no spiders."

Jadie looked up. "No spiders. No windows. Nobody can get in."

"No."

She scuttled to the door that led into the classroom and tried it once more to see if it would open.

Being locked, it didn't budge, but she pulled and pulled and pulled, putting one foot against the door frame to give herself more leverage. When the door still failed to move, Jadie did something totally unexpected. She laughed.

I had never heard Jadie laugh. Indeed, I'd never seen more than the occasional faint smile, but now she laughed merrily, the sound filling the cloakroom.

"You certainly do like the fact that the door doesn't open," I said.

"It's locked. I've locked us in. No one else can be here. No windows they can see in at. No spiders gonna know. This is good."

"Yes," I agreed.

"This is good," she repeated. "I'm safe here."

"You feel safe."

What started as a pause grew. Jadie's eyes had wandered from the doors, the walls, the floor to rest on my face. "You wanna see me stand up?" she asked, her tone almost conspiratorial.

I nodded.

Slowly, a bit stiffly, she straightened her posture until she was upright. Steadying herself with one hand on the wall, she thrust her shoulders back and her stomach out. She smiled at me, an easy, knowing smile.

I smiled back. "Good."

Turning from me, she reached up and clasped a coat hook in each hand. Bracing her feet against the bench beneath the coat hooks, she arched her body outward, stretching what must have been very tight muscles. Repeatedly, she pulled herself up to the coat hook and then back in an odd kind of chin-up, until at last she audibly sighed with relief. All this time, neither of us spoke.

Jadie climbed down from the bench and, still standing upright, turned her attention to pulling down the cuffs of her cardigan and adjusting her clothes. "I know what that sign means now," she said quietly, not looking over.

"What sign is that?"

"Over by Ninth Street, there's a brown church, and it's got that sign out front. It says 'Safe with God.' I kept reading it when we went by, and I never knew what it meant." She smiled. "But I do now. I'm safe in here, aren't I? I'm safe with you."

The next afternoon Jadie appeared again after school. I'd ensconced myself early on in the cloakroom in readiness. The latch on the classroom door snicked and then came the quiet shuffling of Jadie's feet across the classroom, until she finally appeared in the doorway of the cloakroom. I smiled at her, and there was a hint of a smile in return in Jadie's eyes, although it never reached her lips. Opening my desk drawer, I took out the key.

"Do you want to lock the doors?" I asked.

This brought the broad, easy grin of a secret shared. She snatched the key from my hand and dashed for the far door to secure it, then back to the door beside my desk. She fastened the bit of masking tape over the keyhole, then pulled again at each of the doors to make sure they were fast. Already standing upright by the time she'd finished these tasks, she paused at the door into the classroom to gently caress the housing of the bolt.

"You like that lock," I said.

"I've locked us in," she replied.

"We're safe in here with the doors locked."

Again, Jadie went through the same calisthenics with the coat hooks to stretch her arm and back muscles. Then, in a totally unexpected flash of movement, she shot off around the cloakroom. Circling the room in a counter-clockwise direction, she ran her right hand along the wall as she went. I was surprised to see how rapidly she could move in the small space. Once, twice, three times she circled the room, all the while feeling the walls, the coat hooks, the benches. Then the large vertical pipe at the far end caught her attention. Putting her arms around it, Jadie hugged it, before wrapping her legs around it, too, as if to shinny up. She didn't, but she remained like that for three or four minutes.

Confounded, I sat in silence. Was this really the same child I'd had in class only a few hours earlier, the one who sat statuelike and never spoke unless spoken to? Was this *Jadie?*

These afternoon visits quickly became a routine. Almost every day around 4:15 or 4:30 Jadie would appear, lock herself in with me, stand upright, and begin the circular jaunt around the room. There was seldom any variation in what she did, and, indeed, I seemed fairly superfluous to things. All her attention appeared focused on physical movement, relentlessly going around and around in the tiny room. After some twenty minutes of this frantic action, she'd stop, say she needed to go home, unlock all the doors again, and in the process fold back into the hunched crab of a girl we were used to.

More than two weeks passed. Then there was a sudden variation in the theme. After arriving and locking the doors one afternoon, Jadie straightened up. I was expecting her coat hook calisthenics, when, abruptly, she screamed. It was a playful scream, a high-pitched, ear-splitting girlish squeal, and the small room resounded with it. Jadie spun around, a grin from ear to ear, and screamed again. And again. And again. I sat, deafened.

Jadie danced, head thrown back, arms out. Around and around in a circle she went and she continued screaming. This must have gone on for five minutes or more before a knock came on the cloakroom door that led out into the hallway.

"Torey?" It was Lucy's voice, sounding alarmed. "Is everything all right in there?" She turned the doorknob, but, of course, being locked, the door did not open. Jadie, who had frozen at the sound of Lucy's voice, let out an audible sigh when the door remained fast.

"Yes, we're okay," I replied.

"You sure? Do you need a hand with anything?"

"No, it's okay, Luce."

Muffled sounds came from beyond the door. "Well, all right," Lucy said uncertainly. "If you're sure." Then she departed.

Jadie remained stock-still until she was certain there was no one outside the door. Then she turned her head to look at me, and covering her mouth with her hand, she giggled. "She heard my voice," she whispered.

"Yes, she did, didn't she?"

"She heard me scream."

"And you're still safe, aren't you?" I said.

Jadie bolted off across the room. Making three or four circles of it within seconds, she ran her fingers lightly along the walls and jumped with nimble feet up onto the benches and down again. On the third time around, she veered off unexpectedly and approached the vertical pipe. As so many times before, Jadie wrapped her arms and legs around it in a tight hug, but after clinging to it a few moments, this time she actually did shinny up. Before I realized what was happening, Jadie had reached the two smaller pipes traversing the room along one side and was out onto them, like a gymnast kneeling on parallel bars. Alarmed because she was a good six feet off the floor, I rose from my chair.

"Jade, those pipes weren't made for climbing on."

She laughed heartily.

"I'm not sure they can take your weight, and I don't want you to hurt yourself, so come down now."

She made no effort to get down off the pipes.

Grabbing the desk chair, I maneuvered it over and prepared to climb up to get her. This prompted a swift response. Jadie scurried out of range, still laughing, then, clutching one pipe, she let herself down off it backward, swung a moment or two in midair, and then finally dropped the last couple of feet to the floor.

In the classroom it was as if none of this had ever happened. Jadie's days continued to be spent in nearly total silence, her body hunched over, her head down, her arms pulled up. I had to repeatedly quash the feeling that somehow I was making up those after-school visits, that *I* was the one with hallucinations. Indeed, during one bleak moment, I wondered if perhaps this hadn't been June Harriman's experience with Jadie, too. For the most part, I disciplined myself away from contemplating June Harriman too much. Not knowing her personal circumstances, but sharing her class, it was too easy to extrapolate from what we had in common to form opinions that might be wildly inaccurate and equally destructive. However, as I glanced across the classroom at Jadie, contorted in her chair, it struck me that perhaps this was why June Harriman had committed suicide—driven to believe that somehow *she* was the crazy one. It was just a one-off thought, but it was dagger sharp. An ideal script for a horror film.

* * *

On Friday of that week, I decided to attempt collage making with the children. Coming in with a large collection of old magazines and a box containing a huge assortment of riffraff—everything from feathers and chunks of sponge to bottle caps and uncooked pasta—I tried to explain the elusive nature of a work of art. We had been studying a loosely constructed unit on emotions, and I hoped to relate their collages to this, saying that when everyone was finished, we'd talk as a group about their work, about what feelings the collages generated in the people looking at them, and what feelings had gone into making them.

The boys dived into the box with lively abandon and set to work immediately.

Reuben loved the pieces of fabric, particularly the bits of silk and velvet. Picking each one up tenderly from the box, he stroked them against his upper lip and flapped his hands in excitement.

Philip, in the chair next to Reuben's, had a Montgomery Ward catalogue out and was enthusiastically cutting out pictures of toys and pasting them down.

"What have we here?" I asked, pulling a chair up and sitting down beside him.

"Haaahhh," Philip breathed. His whole vocabulary consisted of heavily breathed syllables, most of which were unintelligible to me.

"Toys?" I inquired.

He gestured wildly.

"That's his Christmas stocking," Jeremiah said from across the table. "That's what he's trying to tell you. Ain't it, Phil? Him and me are making up pictures of what we want in our Christmas stockings."

I thought it best not to point out to Jeremiah that this was the twenty-ninth of March.

"And Jadie, too," Jeremiah said, expansively gesturing to include them all. "Jadie and me and Philip are doing that for our collage. What Santa's gonna bring us." Jeremiah was pasting down pictures of Jaguars and gold bullion bars.

Fact was, Jadie was doing nothing. She sat humped over in her chair, her chin almost on the tabletop. She stared morosely at the blank piece of paper in front of her.

"Having a hard time getting started?" I asked.

No response.

"You know, of course, you don't have to do a Christmas stocking. That was Jeremiah's idea. If he'd like to fill his paper with a collage of things he'd like to find in his Christmas stocking, that's lovely, but you can choose to do something else. You can make your collage any way you want it."

Silence.

"An important thing with art is not to spend too much time thinking about it. Just look in the box and see what catches your attention."

A pause. I regarded her. "You know how we've been talking about emotions lately? About that place way down inside you where your feelings are? Look down there and find out what you're feeling. Right now. See if you can make a collage of what you find."

I went back to the boys and left Jadie alone with her blank piece of paper. She usually did very well with tasks that were rigidly laid out, such as her academic work, but she always seemed to have trouble with ambiguous projects. Consequently, I didn't want to be tempted into structuring the activity too much for her.

When I looked over a while later, Jadie had begun to work. Taking up one of the magazines, she started cutting out pictures. I watched a moment, trying to discern a relationship among the pictures, but I couldn't.

Jeremiah had nearly finished his collage and was beginning to grow restless. He leaned over Jadie's shoulder. "What you doing?"

Jadie didn't respond. She just kept cutting out. Then, after acquiring about two dozen pictures, she shoved the magazines away. Laying the pictures in front of her, she took up her scissors again and started carefully snipping the pictures into small bits.

"Man, lady, look at her. She's crazy, all right. Look what that girlie's doing," Jeremiah shouted.

I shot him a black look.

"You're crazy," he said to Jadie, then flopped into his chair and sighed dramatically. "I suppose we got to sit here waiting 'til she gets done now. She fucks around all the first part, when she shoulda been working, and now *we* got to wait. Hey, girlie, how come you're always so slow? How come you never do stuff when the rest of us do? You just sit around like a retard."

Ignoring him totally, Jadie continued with her cutting.

I realized my initial plan to talk about the collages as a group was going to have to be jettisoned, as, if we waited much longer, the boys' behavior would deteriorate to a point of no return. Indeed, in the moment it took me to contemplate this, Jeremiah scooped up Reuben's collage and sent it sailing through the air. "Hey, boog!" he shouted at Reuben, "Say 'fuck.'"

"Say fuck," Reuben echoed.

"Say 'fuck,' Reuben. Fuck, fuck, fuck, fuck. Fuck it to you."

I jammed a record onto the record player and began a rousing chorus of "She'll Be Coming 'Round the Mountain" to drown Jeremiah out. Catching Philip, I pulled him comically through the motions. We sang several verses in quick succession, all with lively, exaggerated actions to expend a bit of energy. Then, when the song came to an end, I picked up the book I'd been reading aloud to them and sat down on the carpet in the reading corner to start a new chapter. I read until the recess bell sounded.

Throughout all this, Jadie remained working at the table. When the bell rang, Jeremiah bolted past her on his way to the cloakroom.

"Hey, lady, look what she's doing," he cried and whipped up her paper before Jadie could stop him. He turned it for me to see.

The relationship among the disparate pictures became obvious now—they all contained a lot of red. Snipping them into small pieces, she'd stuck the pieces on, mosaic-style, to form a large circle around a black cross made out of yarn. That's all the picture was: a quartered circle.

"Hey, this is good, man!" Jeremiah cried. "You ain't so stupid, if you don't want to be."

"It is interesting, Jadie," I said.

"Interesting? Man, it's grrrrr-eat!" Jeremiah shouted with Tony-the-Tiger ferocity. "You know what this is, lady? A bull's-eye! Raa-aa-aaaTTT!" He tossed the paper into the air and machine gunned it with his finger.

Jadie just sat.

Bending down, I retrieved the collage from the floor and laid it back on the table, while Jeremiah pounced on Reuben and rode piggyback into the cloakroom. "You'll have to tell us about it," I said cheerfully. "The mosaic was a very clever idea."

Cupping her hands over her mouth, Jadie muttered something.

"Pardon?"

She hunched farther over and muttered again.

"I'm afraid I can't hear you, lovey." I bent down very close to her. "What did you say?"

"Throw it away."

"You want me to throw your collage away? After you've done so much work on it?"

She nodded tensely, all her muscles rigid.

"Is there a reason?"

No response.

"Something Jeremiah said? Did his taking it and playing with it upset you?"

Faintly, she shook her head.

"I think it's interesting. I'd like to keep it. We don't have to put it up, if you don't want, but let's not throw it away just yet. Okay?"

Tears came to her eyes. "Throw it *away.*"

"Why?"

"X marks the spot."

Chapter Seven

Over the years, I had acquired a large box of dolls and doll clothes. The dolls were of a type known as "Sasha" dolls, boy and girl dolls, appearing to be of middle-childhood age, with beige, nonethnic-colored skin, thick, combable hair, and wistful, rather enigmatic faces. I had six of them, two boys and four girls, plus two Sasha baby dolls. One year when I'd had a particularly boring summer job, I had filled the extra hours making doll clothes, and there was now an extensive wardrobe of shirts, pants, dresses, overalls, jackets, pajamas, underclothes, and anything else they could want for. A friend had caught the spirit and knitted small sweaters, hats, and mittens for them and even bootees for the babies. In addition, I'd collected small bits and pieces over the years to enhance play, such as appropriately sized dishes, bedclothing, stuffed animals, and a few tiny toys and books. These had always been particularly successful toys, both in former classrooms and in therapeutic settings; so when all my things finally arrived at my apartment in Pecking and I came across the dolls while unpacking, I looked forward to bringing them into school. Unfortunately, cultural influences had arrived considerably ahead of me.

"*Dolls?*" Jeremiah cried out in an utterly appalled voice. "You don't expect me to play with a bunch of *dolls*, do you? Those are *girls'* toys!" He jerked his hands back from the box, as if he'd contaminated them.

"See here? Look. There are boy dolls in here, too. And good things to do with them. See here? See this little football? These boys could be getting ready for a football game. Maybe we could look in the scrap box and see if there is something to make a football helmet out of."

"Man, lady, if you think I'm going to play with dolls, you got another think coming. Come on, Phil. Come on, Reub, get away from them boogy dolls."

"You don't *have* to play with them. Nobody has to play with anything in here, do they, Jeremiah? By the same token, there's no need to make people feel bad for enjoying something interesting. One doesn't need to think of them as dolls. They're just ... representations of people."

"They're *dolls.*"

It would have been easier at the beginning of the year. In all my previous classes, the dolls had simply been there from the start, and, like any other item in the room, they could be picked up, played with, and put down again without anyone paying too much attention; as a consequence, many of my boys had enjoyed them. Bringing them in like this, however, called too much attention to what they intrinsically were. Enticingly as I had set the dolls out on the back bookshelf, no one went near them.

After school that day, Jadie arrived, as she now commonly did. She hobbled into the cloakroom, slammed the door, took the key from me, locked it, then pressed the little tab of masking tape over the keyhole. Afterward, she went and locked the other door. Immediately becoming upright, she gave a little scream. This over, she darted off around the room, circling it quickly, lithely. This done, she stopped. She scanned the room, then came to stand beside my desk.

Silence followed. I always had my plan book out during this time, not only because it was my planning time but also because it allowed me to focus on something other than Jadie, and this gave these little get-togethers a less intense timbre.

"You know what?" she said softly.

"What's that?"

"There's nothing for me to do in here."

"You're feeling a bit bored?"

She nodded.

"What do you suppose we might do about it?" I asked, hoping this might lead to expansion beyond the locked doors of the cloakroom.

"It'd be nice if those dolls were in here."

"If you want to play with those dolls, that's okay," I replied.

"But they're out there."

"You could go get them. The box with the clothes in it is on the bookshelf. You could put the dolls you wanted into that and bring them in here."

Jadie studied me. I could tell she wanted me to go get the dolls for her, but when she didn't speak, I went back to my work. Jadie continued to stand, her expression morose.

"If you open the door, you'll be able to get the dolls," I said, not looking up. "It isn't very far from the door to the bookshelf. You can bring them back in here and close the door again."

Jadie turned her head and looked at the door. Not only would she have to leave the safety of the cloakroom to do this, but to carry the box of dolls back, she needed to remain upright. Unlike her speech, which had generalized quickly to include the others in the classroom, her posture seemed unchanged outside the privacy of the cloakroom. Sighing sadly, she slumped down on one of the benches.

"Do you want some help?" I asked.

She nodded.

"You know, if you explain to me what you want, then I am much more likely to help. I can't read your mind. You need to tell me when you want help."

Still silence.

I rose from my chair. "I'll open the door." Getting the key from the other door, I peeled back the masking tape and unlocked it. Jadie shrank back. "Come on," I said, extending my hand. "We'll go together. You get which dolls you want, and I'll carry the box of clothes."

Jadie accepted this. Taking my hand, she crept behind me into the classroom, where I gathered up most of the big dolls and put them into her arms. Jadie, not quite bent double by this time but definitely slumped, scurried back into the cloakroom ahead of me. As I closed the door and relocked it, she relaxed visibly, but not quite trusting me, she had to get up and check that the door was well and truly locked and then return the key to block the other keyhole.

The trauma of having had to go out into the classroom to get the dolls clearly overwhelmed Jadie. Still hunched over, she sank down onto the bench adjacent to the doll box and peered in at the collection of hard-won dolls, but she seemed unable to summon up enough strength to take them out and play with them. For five minutes or more, she just sat, all the usual liveliness she brought with her into the cloakroom momentarily gone. Then, at last, she reached in and started to take the dolls out. One by one, she lined them up on the bench. When she had finished, she sat back a little and observed them.

"These dolls are pretty," she said softly.

"Yes, they are nice. I think so, too."

"Where'd you get them at?"

"I bought them. Not all of them at once, but one at a time, over the years."

"How come? You're too big to play with dolls."

"I bought them for the children I work with."

Jadie paused, reaching a finger out to gingerly touch the hair on one of the dolls. "Are them the boys and girls you were telling me about that one time? The ones like me that don't talk?"

"Yes."

"Did you *really* work with those kids?"

"Yes."

She looked over. "*Really?* You're not just making that up?"

"Yes, I really did work with girls and boys like you before. I worked at helping them start talking again and at getting over the kinds of problems that made them stop in the first place. That was my special interest, you see. It's called 'research.' That's when you want to learn more about something people don't know much about already. And I was very interested in children who found it hard to talk in certain places. I wanted to know what was wrong, and I wanted to find ways to make things better for them, so that was my research."

"And did you find out about them?" Jadie asked, her attention going back to the dolls.

"I think so, yes."

A pause came and it lingered. Jadie was still not playing with the dolls, not even touching them. She just sat, gazing at them. "Them other kids," she started slowly, "they really didn't talk? Like me?"

"Yes, just like you."

"But then you made it better for them? Did you? And then did they talk? They talked to you then? They told you things?"

"Yes."

She looked up at me. "They told you things?"

I nodded.

"And you believed them?"

"Well, I always try to listen to what people tell me."

"And then you tried to make it better for them?"

"Well, I did try."

Silence then. Jadie reached over and picked up one of the Sasha dolls. It had thick, waist-length black hair, which she gently smoothed down. "Can I change this doll's clothes?"

"Yes, of course. You may dress any of them any way you want. They're meant for playing."

Again she caressed its long hair and gazed into its face. Then, bending over the box, Jadie sorted through the clothes, taking out a complete outfit consisting of undershirt and underpants, shirt, overalls, sweater, mittens, coat, shoes, socks, and woolly hat. I went back to work on my plans but stole occasional glimpses of her. She remained tenser than usual. Her shoulders remained hunched, her limbs drawn in close. Even with the doors locked, she didn't seem much more relaxed than she generally was in the classroom, but she was very intent on what she was doing. So intent, in fact, that it didn't have the aura of play about it.

With immense care, Jadie removed the clothes that had been on the doll. When it was totally undressed, she gazed at it, running her fingers lightly over the smooth contours of its body. She examined the joints, now rather loosely strung after years of play, and poked her finger into the sockets. She felt the faintly indented belly button. She looked for genitals. Then, with the same tenderness she'd shown undressing the doll, she began to gently ease on the new clothes, starting with the socks and underwear. She worked very slowly, however, and inevitably I had to acknowledge the time.

"We've got only a few minutes left, Jadie. It's almost five o'clock."

"Don't say that," she replied, not looking up.

"There'll be enough time to finish putting the clothes on, but then we need to go. Mr. O'Banyon will want to lock up."

"Don't *say* that." A bit tetchier in tone.

"You're not quite ready to go yet, are you?"

"I got no time to play today."

"Yes, well, perhaps tomorrow. We can leave the things as they are. I don't think the boys'll mind if we keep the dolls in here. Then you can pick up where you left off, if you come in tomorrow afternoon."

Unexpectedly, I saw her lower lip tremble. She clutched the doll tightly between her hands.

"You're really feeling bad about having to leave. I can see that."

"I need to finish what I'm doing. I need more *time!*" Then, abruptly, Jadie burst into tears. Leaping up from the bench, she clutched the doll to her chest. "I need to make a place for her! I can't go now. I need a place for her to be safe!" And with that, Jadie bolted off to the far side of the cloakroom and pressed herself face first into the corner.

Startled by the tears, as I'd never seen Jadie cry before, I rose from my chair.

Still clutching the doll tightly, she darted away from me when I approached. "There's no place for her to hide," she wailed, frantically turning her head from side to side in search of concealment. "This is a dumb room. A dumb, stupid room. Where's she going to hide in a dumb, stupid place like this? There's no place, and I gotta find a place now, before I go!"

"Jadie, sweetheart—"

"You don't *understand!*"

"Maybe I do," I said, keeping my voice soft and reassuring. "And there are still a few minutes left. If you need to do something with the doll and it'll only take a few minutes, I'm sure there's time."

A moment or two longer she watched me through teary eyes, then slowly she began to relax.

I smiled. "Come on, lovey. Finish what you want to do."

Jadie slowly approached me. "I need to make a place for her," she said softly, her cheeks still wet. "I want her to be warm and cozy." Jadie glanced up at me, her expression almost one of embarrassment. "See, that's why I put these clothes on her. 'Cause she's always cold. And I was always telling her I'd get some warm clothes for her."

"Yes."

"But now I need a place for her."

"How can I help?" I asked. "What kind of place do you have in mind?"

Jadie scanned the room. "That's just it. There isn't any place in here. It's bare. And I don't have time to make one for her before I got to go home." The tremor of tears was in her voice again.

"You want some place to put the doll?"

"A warm place. But it's got to be safe. She's got to hide."

I cast around the room. Jadie was right about there not being many hiding places in here. Then I glanced at the box of doll clothes. "What about in there?" I pointed. "Maybe you could make a good place down in the midst of the doll clothes for her."

Standing silently beside me, Jadie considered the box a moment and then bent over it and felt into the thickness of clothes. She nodded.

I collected the other dolls and put them into the lid of the box, which was separate, while Jadie knelt and made a hole among the doll clothes. Tenderly, she laid the black-haired doll in and covered her all up, except for her face. "There you are," she whispered. "All nice and warm."

Rising, she contemplated the doll in the box; then, with great care, she began picking up the other dolls and placing them gently over the top, leaving the dark-haired doll's face hardly visible. "She can breathe like that," Jadie explained, as she arranged the other dolls. "I've left an air hole for her. But when anybody comes in here and sees this, they're not going to know she's there. They'll think it's just an old box of toys." An anxious glance in my direction. "Won't they?"

"I'm sure they will."

"They won't know she's in there. She'll be safe." Jadie looked up. "And you'll lock the door, okay?"

I began pulling on my jacket. "Yes, I'll lock the door. I always do."

This seemed to satisfy Jadie, and she went to get her own things.

Then, as we prepared to leave, I paused and picked up the lid to the doll clothes box. Gently, I placed it on the box.

"No!" cried Jadie.

"I'll just put it on lightly, so that it doesn't get separated from the box and get stepped on or something."

"No. No, don't put it on the box. She'd think she was being buried alive, if you put the lid on, and Tashee's so afraid of that."

Chapter Eight

For the next few days, Jadie didn't come after school. One afternoon I was busy with a meeting; another was Reuben's birthday and she'd been invited to his party; a couple more slipped by and she simply didn't turn up. Then, on Friday, there she was.

As always, the first thing she did was lock the doors and test their security. The second was to run to the box of dolls, which was still sitting on the bench. "Where are you? Where are you?" she called anxiously, flinging off the dolls that lay on top. However, any anticipation I might have had about a continuation of the tender scenes from Monday was rudely dispelled when she jerked the dark-haired doll up from the box.

"Poopy pants!" she shrieked, then gathered all the dolls up in her arms and flung them down across the floor. "All these dolls got poopy pants. And you know what I'm going to do? I got to change them and get all this poop out. Shit. That's what it is. Shit. Gonna get a big pile of shit right here." She indicated a place on the bench. Sitting down on the floor, she began tugging the overalls off the dark-haired doll.

There was an unmistakably manic quality to her play. She yanked, jerked, shouted, and threw. The doll so tenderly put away on Monday was screamed at and flung around with the others.

"Did you poop your pants, too?" she inquired of one doll. "You did, did you? Well, let's get the dish then." Putting down the doll, Jadie glanced around quickly. "Where's something I can use?" she asked absently, then jumped up. "There. That Play-Doh. Gimme that. I need it." She pointed to a canister sitting on the far edge of my desk. I handed it to her. Prizing off the lid, Jadie returned to the dolls. "This is going to be the dolly's shit." She pinched off bits of dough and stuffed it into the doll's underpants.

Her play did not include me. She wasn't making any special effort to shut me out, but her comments were all to herself. I just happened to be in the same room.

The entire scenario revolved around dirty pants. Carefully, Jadie laid out all the boy and girl dolls and inserted Play-Doh feces into their underwear; then there was a big to-do about standing each doll up, peering down the back of the underpants, and discovering the contents.

"Oh, look! Have you done something shitty in your pants? Is there something there? Has everyone shat in their pants?" Over and over she went through this, with ever-increasing volume, until she was virtually shouting at the last doll. Then she took one of the small bowls from the doll-sized tea set in the box and began collecting the bits of dough from the underpants. "There. There. There," she muttered each time she extracted some Play-Doh. "There's plenty now. Look how much poop."

Sitting silently at my desk, pen still in my hand, I watched with fascinated horror. There was an urgent, compulsive quality to her play which would have made any interjection from me an interruption, so I did nothing but watch.

Once she had all the Play-Doh out of the dolls' underwear, she completely undressed them all and laid them out side by side on the bench. "Here. Here's what's going to happen now," Jadie muttered to herself as she picked up the small bowl of Play-Doh feces. "Now you're going to eat it." Taking a piece of dough, she pushed it onto the doll's mouth. When that didn't satisfy her, she smeared it all over the eyes, nose, and face. "*Eat* it," she demanded. "*Eat* it."

"Why should they do that?" I inquired, enable to stay silent any longer.

Jadie must have forgotten about me entirely because, at the sound of my voice, she started violently, spilling most of the rest of the contents of the little bowl. Leaping up from where she'd been kneeling, she flung the bowl at me.

"Shit!" she cried. "Shit on you! That's what it means. Shit on you!" And she tore off around the room in a frenzy, hitting against the benches, stumbling, leaping up again. "I'm going to get you now! I'm going to get you! I'm going to kill you now!" she shouted, but her words seemed directed more at thin air than at me.

On about her fourth circle around the room, she careered by my desk. Reaching out, she snatched the felt-tip pen from my hand. "Shit! Shit! Shit!" she continued to shriek. Bumping into the far wall, since the room really was far too small to run in, she whipped up the pen, and before I realized what she was doing, she had drawn several encircled crosses on the wall.

"Hey ho," I said, jumping up. "I can't let you do that, Jadie."

"You can't stop me!" And she continued to draw more.

"I *can,*" and I did, catching her by the arm and pulling her up close against me.

"You can't. I can kill you," she retorted and attempted to draw the cross with the circle around it on my skin, until at last I pinned her arm down and removed the pen. Jadie struggled violently for several moments, kicking and jerking to get free, but I held on, eventually enveloping her in a massive bear hug to the point where she could no longer move. Her hysterical screaming degenerated into sobs and we both sank wearily to the floor. Jadie wept, first from frustration at being unable to get free, then finally the desperate note disappeared and she just cried, pushing her face into the fabric of my blouse.

"I'm sorry," she began to say through her tears. "I'm sorry. I'm sorry."

"That's all right. Don't worry about it."

She reached to rub away the marks she'd made on my skin with the pen. When she couldn't remove them, she brushed her fingers across her cheek and then tried to rub them out with her tears. The poignancy of this gesture affected me, and I pulled her closer.

"Don't be upset. They're just marks. They won't hurt me."

"I don't want you to die. Don't die."

"It's just felt-tip pen, Jadie. I can wash it off. Don't cry about it."

"Just don't die. Please don't die."

I came away from school that night deeply unsettled. I don't know if it was the intensity of what had happened or simply the unexpectedness of it, but I couldn't leave the incident behind me at school the way I usually did with things that happened during the day. Under normal circumstances, I enjoyed living alone. The silent serenity of my apartment and the total lack of demands was a healthy contrast to my work; however, with its lack of distractions, my apartment was not a good place to take problems I couldn't shake. So instead of going home that evening, I drove out to the supermarket-cum-drugstore on the edge of town to do some shopping. Even then, as I wandered up and down the brightly lit aisles, reading labels on the breakfast cereal and contemplating what flavor of cat food might tempt my confirmed mouse-eater away from things that required regurgitation on the carpet, I still couldn't keep my mind from wandering back to Jadie.

On the way home, I impulsively stopped by Lucy's house. We'd become quite good friends at school. She was a likable, easy-to-talk-to person, and youth was our common ground in a workplace where most were members of the AARP; however, we'd never made the transition to friendship outside school.

Even within the confines of a homogenizing environment like school, the contrast in our lives was obvious. Lucy was a local girl, married at twenty-one to the boy literally next door, in a storybook wedding with carriages and white horses and most of the community present. She'd gone to the state university to get her teaching degree and she and Ben, her husband, had done a three-week tour of Europe for their honeymoon; otherwise, Lucy's entire world was Pecking. I envied her her connectedness and her certainty about her place in the universe. When we talked about it, she said she envied me my freedom, but I'm not sure she really did.

"Hi!" she cried in delighted surprise when she saw me at the door.

"Sorry for bothering you on a Friday evening, but I was coming by and I still have that material on the teaching centers in my car. Thought I'd drop it off." Which was true enough, although not the whole reason I'd stopped.

"Oh, how nice of you," she remarked cheerfully. "Want to come in?"

I entered a small, neat-as-a-pin living room with green shag carpeting and an electric organ against the far wall.

"Ben's out for the evening. He and his dad. They're pricing a job in Falls River, and so he's not going to be back 'til late." Lucy smiled. "So it's nice you stopped by." She disappeared into the kitchen. "You want some soup? Have you eaten? I was just heating some up." She returned, carrying a can. "It's this kind. Vegetable-beef. Do you like that? Or I could open something else."

"No, that's fine." I followed her into the kitchen. "What's Ben do? He's a builder, isn't he?"

Lucy nodded. "Yes, he and his dad did this house." She gestured widely. "Afterwards, after we eat, I'll show you around. It's got three bedrooms. That's for when we get around to starting a family. At the moment we've got Jilly in the second bedroom, and she's doing the family bit. Wait 'til you meet Jilly."

Jilly turned out to be a toy poodle, proud mother of three-week-old pups. Lucy also showed me her needlepoint and then her wedding photographs. That put us on to the honeymoon pictures of Europe. I needed the distraction, and Lucy was providing an ample amount.

When we came to the last of the honeymoon photographs, Lucy lingered over the album.

"I probably don't need to be showing you these," she said quietly. "You've been to Europe, too, haven't you?"

"Yes. But not as many places as you and Ben have seen."

"You've been all over, though. You've been to New York."

I nodded.

"How come you came here?"

"It looked like an interesting job, and I was fed up with the city. My own hometown isn't much bigger than Pecking. I'm perfectly happy in small places."

"Do you like it here?" she asked.

"Yes."

"We haven't got the kinds of problems they have in the cities. That's what I like about it. You hear about all this junk, like drugs and child abuse, and I'm just really glad I don't have to deal with it. But I bet you came across it a lot up in the city, didn't you?"

I looked over. "It's probably here, too. Those sorts of things don't really respect boundaries."

"Well, yeah, probably out on the reservation."

"Probably right here in Pecking. Odds are, at least with child abuse, right in your classroom."

Lucy was silent.

"It's hard to think that these kinds of things happen to people we know, but, unfortunately, that's often the case."

Lucy looked down at the album with its soft, pale gray leather-effect cover, trimmed in gold.

"I've probably lived a pretty sheltered life." A pause. "But I can't say I'm not thankful for that. It's easier to believe in the good in people if you don't know all the bad."

I studied Lucy's face. What I wanted more than anything was to share the eerie experience of being locked in the cloakroom with Jadie. I was so confused, not knowing what to think about her behavior. Was she aphasic? Brain damaged? Was there an organic basis for what she did? Or could it all be psychological? Mutism had ceased to be a problem from the first day, as Jadie now responded to anyone who spoke to her, but only with me did she speak spontaneously. Why? What for? How come? I did enjoy my new life in Pecking, but it had brought with it unaccustomed isolation. My network of professional colleagues and friends remained in the city, and I had found making new contacts here slow going. But did I tell Lucy about life in my classroom? Was it the right thing to do? Was it fair, either to Lucy or to my children?

In the end, I said nothing. Instead, Lucy took me into the kitchen, where she showed me how to make brownies in the microwave in only ten minutes. Then we sat down in front of the television, scoffed brownies, and drank tall glasses of milk, all the while laughing like a couple of schoolgirls.

After school on Monday, Jadie joined me in the cloakroom. She was late, arriving at twenty to five.

The first thing she did was to take the key and lock the two doors and then secure the masking tape over both keyholes. She didn't really test the doors this time, however, just locked them and handed back the key. Nor did her posture improve. Still hunched over, she shuffled to one of the benches and sat down.

"You don't look very happy."

No response.

"You've been quiet all day. Do you feel okay?"

"Yeah."

"How was your weekend?"

She shrugged.

A moment's silence passed between us. She was bent almost double, her dark hair tumbling down over her shoulders.

"You look like you want to cry," I commented.

At that, her mouth dragged down in a grimace of tears and she bent forward on the bench, burying her face in the jacket on her knees.

Rising from my chair at the desk, I came over and sat down beside her. Gently, I put my arm around her shoulder. "What's the matter, lovey?"

"I don't got my cat no more," she wailed.

"Oh dear, how awful. What happened?"

"She isn't there no more. She's gone."

I hugged her to me.

"She was just little," Jadie sobbed, pulling back to look up at me. "She wasn't even grown up yet."

"Poor puss. Poor Jadie."

"She was skinny. I always saved some of my supper in my napkin and then I'd take it out for her to eat. 'Cause she was always hungry. She was a girl cat. I named her Jenny."

"And now something's happened to her? What was it? Did she get hit by a car?"

Rubbing the tears from her cheeks with the backs of her hands, Jadie shook her head. "No, she was in the shed, but she's not anymore."

"Was this just a little kitty you'd found? A stray?"

Too choked up to say anything, Jadie didn't respond.

"Well, she's probably all right. Most likely she's just moved on. Sometimes wild kitties do that. They aren't very used to being with people, and even when you're good and kind to them, they don't know they're supposed to stay in one place."

"She *didn't* run away," Jadie replied. "She couldn't. She was in a box."

"In a box? Where?"

"In our shed, like I was just telling you. Out in back of my house. That's where I was taking the food to her and I was putting it in the box. But now it's gone."

"How'd she get in a box? Who does the box belong to?"

"They've taken her away and they're going to kill her," Jadie cried, her voice trailing off into a whine.

"Who's going to kill her?"

"Them."

"Them who, Jadie? I don't really know what you're talking about."

The tears evaporated and Jadie's eyes grew wide and dark. She sat very still, as if holding her breath. Then she inched closer to me on the bench.

"Who's taken your cat?" I asked.

"Miss Ellie," she whispered.

"Pardon?"

"Miss Ellie," she said a little louder.

"Miss Ellie who?"

"Miss Ellie. Who's with Bobby and J.R."

"Miss *Ellie?" I* echoed in disbelief. "The lady who's on TV?"

"Sometimes she's on TV, but sometimes she comes to my house."

"Miss *Ellie*?"

Jadie looked up, a pained expression on her face, and I realized she knew I didn't believe what she was saying. Anxious not to destroy the trust growing between us, I backed off quickly.

"So, Miss Ellie has your little kitty."

Jadie nodded, tears filling her eyes again.

"And she comes to your house? What does she do there?"

"She comes," Jadie said, her voice small and apologetic. "She comes to be on TV sometimes, but mostly she just comes. To get me and Amber. To have us go with the others."

"The others? Who else is there?"

"Bobby and Sue Ellen and J.R. Pam's there sometimes and Clayton and some of the others, but I don't know everybody's names."

Absolutely baffled, I tried my best to make sense of all this without seeming to disbelieve her. Jadie's earnestness gave me no reason to suspect she was knowingly making this up. "These are the Ewings you're talking about? From 'Dallas'?"

Jadie nodded slightly. "It's the Ewings, but I'm not sure where they come from."

I sat back and a small silence ensued.

"Is Jenny Miss Ellie's cat?" I asked finally.

"No. They just caught her, I think. I don't know whose cat she is. Don't belong to nobody, I think. Just a little cat."

"But who caught her? How did she end up in a box in your shed?"

Jadie shrugged. "She was just there."

"Maybe she got into the box accidentally. Kitties do get into very strange places sometimes. That's just the way cats are, especially young ones. Maybe nobody really caught her after all. Is that possible?"

Jadie's shoulders sagged, and she shook her head.

"Well, Miss Ellie wouldn't hurt her, would she? Maybe she's just going to give her a new home."

Shaking her head, Jadie began to cry. "No, it isn't like that."

I looked at her.

"She'll kill Jenny. Miss Ellie'll eat her."

Chapter Nine

The hardest adjustment I had to make in returning to teaching after three years at the Sandry Clinic was the sudden and total loss of professional peers. Teaching was a natural activity for me, and I found I fit back into the routine of a school very quickly indeed. And I unashamedly loved it. I got on well with Mr. Tinbergen and the other teachers, enjoyed the camaraderie of the lounge, joined in the gossip, and took up my position in the pecking order. However, I soon realized that, while I'd always find a sympathetic ear when I wanted one, I wasn't necessarily going to find good advice. In the Pecking school district, I was state-of-the-art where special education was concerned.

This came as a disheartening insight, because if I'd learned anything over the years, it was how much I didn't know. Access to a wide range of professional colleagues—psychiatrists, psychologists, medical doctors, social workers, speech therapists, other special education teachers—had always been an important part of my method of operation. If I couldn't come up with a solution of my own to try, I'd find someone who could, or, at the very least, someone to shoot ideas around with. Suddenly, however, I was isolated. Twenty-three miles separated me from even the nearest special education teachers, who were in Falls River. And while Falls River undoubtedly had a full complement of mental health services and related resource personnel, I knew none of them personally and was too shy in my reduced status as teacher to phone them and ask for complimentary advice out of the blue.

My single professional contact was Arkie Peterson. I'd only seen her a handful of times since January, usually at meetings, and as a consequence, we'd had very little opportunity to talk. A brief look at district statistics told me why I didn't see her more often. Arkie was responsible not only for the Pecking school district but for more than twelve hundred other students spread over a wide, sparsely populated rural area. Although based in an office in the administration building in Falls River, she spent most of her time on the road and was scheduled to be at her desk only on Thursday afternoons. Hence, the biggest trick of all with Arkie was catching her.

Increasingly, I felt the need to discuss Jadie's case in depth with another professional. In the classroom, Jadie was making slow but steady social progress. While still disinclined to speak spontaneously, she did now join in with the boys and participate in group activities, and just occasionally Jeremiah could provoke her into arguing. However, it wasn't the classroom that concerned me most. Rather, it was our little after-school sessions, and I honestly did not know what to make of those.

As time went by, I was beginning to doubt the likelihood of any significant brain damage. When Jadie did speak, she was generally forthright and articulate. There was none of the hesitance or slight spaciness that I had come to associate with aphasics; instead, she maintained the aura of intense control that so characterized elective mutism. Thus, I was satisfied that Jadie's problems were psychological, without physical underpinnings. The question that remained unanswered was to what extent she was disturbed. In class she gave every indication of being well grounded in reality and functioning on a fairly high level, certainly much higher than any of the boys. On the other hand, after school, when she was alone with me, Jadie's conversations were often weird and unreal.

Arkie was the only person I felt I could turn to in regard to Jadie. My affinity for Arkie, based mostly on that first meeting in January, had been instant. Despite her Dolly Parton appearance, she struck me as an intelligent, articulate woman with sufficient experience to give the kind of feedback I was feeling so in need of.

"Hey!" Arkie cried cheerfully down the phone, when I finally managed to track her down. "How are you surviving?"

I explained that things weren't going too badly in general but that I felt I needed a chance to discuss Jadie's case more completely, especially now that we were coming up to the end of the school year and needed to make decisions for the next year's placement.

There was a pause and through the phone I could hear the shuffling of paper. "Listen, Tor, I'll tell you what," Arkie said. "My schedule's pure hell at the moment, and if I waited for a decent amount of time to get out to Pecking, it'd be next fall already. So what are you doing next Friday night? You want to come up here? What about dinner? Shall we have dinner somewhere and talk about everything then?"

That sounded divine.

Arkie and I met for dinner in a small, extremely popular restaurant in Falls River called Tottie's. By the time we arrived, the place was congested and noisy, and we were escorted to a table the size of an average serving tray and located at the junction between the kitchen and the public toilets.

"Hi there! I'm Keith," a young man cried enthusiastically when he saw us. "I'm your waiter for the evening, and our chef tonight is David."

"Great. I'm Arkie and I'm your customer, and, listen, Keith, haven't you got anything better than this?" Arkie gestured widely to indicate the table's location.

"Now, let's see, Arkie, what have you booked? Party of two? Yup? That's what I've got."

"Well, that's what I've got, too, but I wasn't planning on spending my evening conferring with David and I pretty much can from here, so what do you say we give him some peace? Suppose you find us somewhere else."

Thunderstruck by Arkie's calm audacity, I shrank meekly behind. Keith, too, seemed a bit stunned. He checked his list again, then glanced around, as if seeking help. "Well, I suppose there is a table over there by the fireplace. They haven't arrived yet ... I suppose you could probably have that one and then ..."

"Good," said Arkie. "I suppose we could."

"Now," said Keith as we sat down, "can I bring you girls some wine? We have three choices of house wine, sold by the glass, the half carafe, or the carafe. Or perhaps you'd like Debbie to bring you the wine list."

Arkie, covering her eyes with one hand in mock exasperation, lifted a finger and looked over at me. "Makes you sorry for our generation, doesn't it?" she whispered.

Arkie and I spent a pleasant twenty minutes or so in choosing our meals, ordering, and then, just small talk. As with our first meeting, I was greatly impressed with Arkie, her calm assertiveness, her relaxed friendliness. Talking with her was like being back with my colleagues at the clinic: a nice mix of wit, personal topics, and shoptalk.

The conversation eventually came around to Jadie. I told Arkie how Jadie had been coming in to see me after school, how she locked the door and seemed to need the safety of the cloakroom before she could be wholly open. I mentioned the doll play with its faintly sexual overtones, and finally, I spoke of Tashee, Miss Ellie, and the others.

"Whee," Arkie muttered when I'd finished. "You've got yourself a live one there, don't you?"

"Let's just say that I don't think we have to make any immediate plans for moving her back to the regular classroom."

"Well, no, there's a point. But where do you think all this is coming from?" Arkie asked. "When I was working with her, I got no wind of this. What do you make of it? Is it just fantasy?"

"I don't know. This is the problem for me. At this point, I honestly don't know what to think about her behavior. In the classroom, I get an extremely withdrawn, hunched-over, shuffling mouse. She's cooperative, concentrates well, performs academically, and yet hardly makes a spontaneous movement. In the cloakroom, I get this brash, noisy, provocative creature who swings from the pipes and flings the toys around. Never in all my career have I come across such extremes."

"Dual personality?"

I wrinkled my nose. "Can't really imagine it."

"Do you think she could be hallucinating? Particularly when she's talking about all these 'Dallas' characters?" Arkie asked.

"I'd hate to think that," I replied, and I would. My worst fear was that Jadie was genuinely losing occasional contact with reality, since this would indicate a much more severe emotional problem than elective mutism. The prognosis for a child suffering from any kind of hallucinatory psychosis is very poor, and I dreaded being the one who might have to officially identify such a problem and thus pass the life sentence that would probably result.

"But do you think it's a possibility? Or is she just making them up?"

"But why?" I asked. "Why have all these secret relationships? Especially as she doesn't seem to actually *like* any of these people, other than Tashee?"

Arkie forked through the remainder of her food, shifting the leftovers to the sides of the plate.

"Is there any history of abuse in the family?" I asked.

Arkie looked up sharply. "What do you mean? Being beaten? Is there evidence of that?"

"I was thinking sexual ..."

"No, there hasn't been anything," Arkie replied, her eyes wide. "How come? Are you suspecting something?"

"Well, I don't know. It's just that ..." I paused. "In the past, I've found quite a high correlation between certain types of abuse—among them, sexual abuse—and some kinds of elective mutism, so it's something I always need to consider. And in Jadie's case ... there is a sexual quality to some of what she does. Nothing more, really, but I do get that certain feeling, if you know what I mean. That sense that there's more to it than what's on the surface."

Arkie frowned and took up her wine glass. Slowly, she shook her head. "No. Nothing I've heard of. They seem sort of an inadequate couple to me, especially him. He strikes me as a real wimp. I always get the feeling that he's bowled over, having to cope with a house full of females. The mother doesn't seem like a particularly forceful personality either, but I don't think she's bright enough for it to matter. But there's been nothing to make me think any of the children have been abused. We've been involved with the family since Jadie was about three, and the girls have always seemed reasonably well cared for. It's just Jadie. The other two have been fine, but she's always been the odd one out."

Turning my attention back to my meal, I fell silent. I didn't know what else to say. Perplexed, confused, and more than a little disconcerted by Jadie, I had no idea how to interpret what I was encountering. I didn't really know even how to put it into words.

Three weeks remained until the end of the school year, and final arrangements were getting under way. All four children were due to return to the class in the autumn, so my job was greatly simplified in comparison with other years. All I needed to concern myself with was arrangements for the summer vacation.

Reuben was spending the summer in Los Angeles, where he would be part of a program for autistic children that emphasized a strong behavioral approach. One of his nannies was going along to stay with him, and his mother had arranged to go down herself for one week a month. Both parents were very excited about this newest venture and had come into the last parent conference clutching brochures and booklets outlining the program's goals. While we had made steady, albeit very slow, progress with Reuben through the five months I'd been at the school, mine had not been a heavily behavioral approach, although I was well trained in the technique. I wasn't fully convinced this summer program was going to make much difference in Reuben's situation, but it sounded more beneficial than not, and his parents were so keen that I wished them well and promised to follow through in the fall if they found behaviorism the answer to Reuben's problems.

Philip was going off to a camp for handicapped children. It was a local camp, run by one of the men's benevolent organizations in Falls River and lasted for only two weeks. I liked the idea very much, however. Most of the children involved were severely handicapped, and all were assigned their own individual counselor, most of whom were college-aged boys. Philip would be one of the less seriously afflicted children, and this, I hoped, in combination with his engaging personality, would give him a chance to be popular and competent, experiences Philip richly deserved to enjoy.

Jeremiah had been difficult to plan for. I wanted to make sure he wasn't left to his own devices the entire summer, because he was reaching the age where he could get up to serious mischief. We'd made a lot of progress, he and I, but it all depended on tight structure and a firm hand—things Jeremiah didn't regularly experience at home. All I could come up with was a six-week summer school program for low achievers in Falls River. This meant a long bus journey back and forth, and Jeremiah was not an ideal bus passenger. In addition, the program was not precisely geared to his needs, but it was the best we could manage. I also arranged for him to be taken into the Boys' Club on the nearby reservation for one day a week to provide additional structure.

This left Jadie. As with Jeremiah, I felt a strong need to see Jadie in some kind of structured setting for part of the summer, but I had a much harder time finding something. There were no school programs in Pecking whatsoever, and Jadie wasn't behind in her schoolwork anyway. Thus, there was no justification for putting her into the same summer school class as Jeremiah. The only options left were a once-a-week arts-and-crafts program in the local park and two weeks at the Methodist Church camp.

"We're not Methodists," Jadie's father said to me when I brought up the possibility of sending Jadie to camp.

"No, I realize that, but I've had a talk with the minister down at the church on Sixth Street, and he says their program is very ecumenical. Since it's the only camp in this part of the state, they're quite accustomed to taking children from other churches. A lot of the local children go."

Mr. Ekdahl frowned. "We're not what you'd call atheists, but we're not believers. I just don't believe in chucking all that Jesus crap down a little kid's throat. We're trying to raise Jade and Amber to have open minds, to have respect for all living things, not just the white-Anglo-Saxon-Protestant garbage. I want them to grow up able to decide for themselves what they believe."

"I was thinking less about the religious side and more about the benefits of Jadie's being able to spend time with other children and have fun in a natural environment."

"Jade'll have plenty of fun at home with her sisters," Mr. Ekdahl replied.

Mrs. Ekdahl spoke up then. Previously, she had been sitting silently beside her husband. Sapphire in her arms, but now she leaned forward. "Jadie's too young for something like that."

"She's eight and a half. While that does mean she'll be in the younger group, there'll be plenty of other girls that age at the camp."

"But how would she cope?" Mrs. Ekdahl's voice sounded plaintive. "She's never done anything like that before."

"Would this be her first time away alone?" I asked. "Has she ever stayed overnight with friends or with relatives?"

"Oh, no. We've never left the girls."

I looked at her.

"They're *our* girls," Mrs. Ekdahl said. "I wouldn't trust them with strangers. What if something happened? What if they needed their mama? We never even leave them with a babysitter."

Incredulously, I looked at her. "*Never?*"

"No. Why would we want to? I think it's plain terrible the way some folks go off and leave their children. Why bother having them, if you're going to dump them on somebody else?"

"But you've *never* left any of your children with *anybody*? For *any* length of time?"

"No," she replied straightforwardly, and I could sense this pleased her. "Why should I want to get rid of them?"

"So you see, don't you," Mr. Ekdahl put in, "that this is why we couldn't possibly send Jadie to camp."

During most of my years of teaching, I had celebrated the final day of school with a picnic. When the day approached, I suggested this to Mr. Tinbergen. There was only one park in Pecking, and it was quite a way from the school, but I thought that as a special treat, perhaps we could go there. Mr. Tinbergen and the other teachers discussed the idea, and in the end, we all decided to have the picnic right on the school grounds. While there was a sizable asphalt playground, a much larger field of grass extended away from the back of the school, and we could move folding tables out, Mr. Tinbergen said, bring in a couple of barbecues, and have a proper picnic right here where there'd be no need to haul things around nor to rush back for buses.

My class's contribution to this festive occasion was to make a cake; so on the penultimate day, I took the children down to the teachers' lounge, where we mixed up the batter. This proved to be a challenging, somewhat raucous experience, as none of the children had experienced cooking firsthand, other than the few attempts we'd made over the past few months, and we'd never tackled anything on the order of a cake. Making matters more difficult was the fact that we needed to make a very large sheet cake, and the oven wasn't large enough to take it all in one go. Consequently, we spent the afternoon with a bowl of icing and four smaller cakes, "cutting and pasting" them into one grand one.

Jeremiah put the record player on to give us music while we worked. Reuben and Philip had to be constantly distracted from eating the cake and icing there and then, and even as it was, we needed to make up a second batch of icing, since we'd "tasted" the first so often there was insufficient left to cover the cake. Then, with an unexpected burst of creativity, Jeremiah, who could normally not keep his mind on anything for more than a few minutes, sorted a bag of jelly beans out into separate colors and carefully laid them across the white icing on the cake in the shape of a rainbow. It proved a marvelously effective design in its simplicity, and we all paused upon seeing it, momentarily overcome by its beauty.

Even Jeremiah was surprised by his success. Stepping back, he regarded the cake in stunned silence. "I done good, huh?" he murmured incredulously.

"It's gorgeous," I replied.

"I wish my mom could see this. I wish she could know I done good."

"I've brought my camera in to use at the picnic," I said. "Shall we take a picture of the cake now?"

This idea was greeted cheerfully by the boys, and I went to get my camera. When I returned, they were all jockeying for a position behind the cake.

"Come on, you too, Jadie," I said. "We'll make it a class picture."

She stood apart.

"Come on."

She shook her head.

"You can stand beside Jeremiah. You helped mix the batter, so it's your cake too."

"No," she replied.

"No?"

"I don't want my picture taken."

"Come on. We've never had a class picture. The school photographer came before I was in the class, so I don't have anything to remember this year by. Let's take one now. To commemorate our cake and the good times we've had this spring."

"I don't want my picture taken," she said again. The boys were losing patience. Coming around from behind the table, Jeremiah grabbed hold of Jadie and yanked her into place. "Don't be such a boog, girlie-wurlie."

"Okay, smile, you guys." I focused the camera. All three boys produced wide, toothy grins. Jadie scowled.

I paused a moment to see if Jadie was going to get in the mood, but nothing materialized. "Jade, can you find a smile?"

"You can't see her anyway, the way she always bends over like that," Jeremiah said. "If she smiled, it'd just be at the ground, so you might as well take the picture. Jadie's here and that's good enough. Her smile don't count."

Chapter Ten

The last day of school. Mr. O'Banyon and Mr. Tinbergen set up long folding tables on the grass at the far end of the playing field. The smell of the barbecues came wafting in through our wide-open windows as we finished the last few details of the old year. There was still a poignancy for me in inventorying the supplies and taping shut the cupboards. The last day of school had always proved a more significant year's end to me than December thirty-first, and I was always filled with the same type of reflective thought. However, this year wasn't quite so sad, as all of us would be returning in the fall, so it was easy, too, to catch the festive spirit of the day.

When everything was finally done and we spilled out onto the playground at lunchtime, we found all the picnic things laid out and Mr. Tinbergen throwing wieners onto the grill. Lucy and I wrestled ice cream cartons from the cooler while the other teachers distributed paper plates and napkins.

It was a gorgeous June day, sunny, almost hot, the ideal sort for a picnic. When the hot dogs were ready, I rounded my four up and passed them plates. Lining up behind Lucy's children, we helped ourselves to potato chips, baked beans, and cans of pop before retiring to a far corner under the shade of a giant sycamore tree.

"Hey, look at me!"

I looked up to see Jeremiah swarming along one of the low, spreading branches of the tree.

"I'm going to eat my lunch up here. Gimme my plate."

"Magic word?" I inquired, as I handed Jeremiah's food up to him.

"Look! See what Reuben's doing!" he shrieked in response.

My back had been turned just long enough for Reuben to grab one of the squeezable catsup bottles and begin decorating the grass. Twirling around and swooping, I snatched up the catsup bottle too tightly and it spurted out in a crimson stream. Everyone laughed, even Jadie.

After lunch, we joined in the games. Jeremiah refused to play Drop the Hanky or Simple Simon, since those were "baby games," and demanded to be let off to go play kick ball with the bigger boys. This lasted only a few minutes, as he couldn't bear not being chosen first. In the end, Jeremiah swarmed up the monkey bars and played noisily at being He-Man all by himself. Reuben and Philip entertained themselves in the sandbox, and Jadie drifted aimlessly about.

"You want to help me?" I called to Jadie as she wandered by. "It won't be long before going-home time, and we need to carry all these things back inside again."

Jadie nodded and came over. I stacked dirty paper plates and cups together and shoved them into a garbage bag.

Just in the midst of all this, Reuben came running up, clutching the crotch of his pants. "Wee-wee!" he cried urgently.

"All right. Inside. Quickly," I said and shoved him toward the door. Jadie knotted the garbage bag. "Can you carry that over and put it just inside the door? Mr. O'Banyon will get rid of it in the incinerator after school."

Jadie nodded and staggered off with the bag.

Jeremiah had managed to persuade Philip to be Battle Cat to his He-Man and was thus leaping lustily on and off Philip's back, as Philip, on all fours, plowed around in the sandbox. Checking to make sure they were well occupied, I carried the other things we'd brought out back to the classroom.

As I went up the stairs, I could hear Reuben sobbing. Bolting the last few steps, I dumped what was in my arms just inside the room and went in search of him.

"Reub? Reuben, where are you?"

Normally, the children used the boys' and girls' rest rooms in the basement; however, there was a toilet for the disabled much nearer our room. The others were not usually allowed to use it, but I let Reuben, as he was inclined to get lost if left to go downstairs on his own. It was just a small, closet-sized room with a toilet and small sink, and because it was for the disabled, it latched for privacy but did not lock.

I quickly traced the sound of Reuben's sobs to this toilet. Judging he was in distress, I didn't bother to try to get him to open the door himself. Instead, I stopped by Mr. O'Banyon's cleaning closet to pick up a screwdriver and flipped the latch on the door.

When I opened the door, my jaw dropped. There was Jadie, sitting on the toilet, her dress hiked up around her waist, her underpants around her ankles. Reuben, standing in front of her, his overalls down, was howling pathetically as Jadie clutched his penis.

"Let go of him *now!*"

Jadie had frozen stock-still at the opening of the door, but she didn't let go. Surprisingly, she didn't look particularly embarrassed at being caught, either. Instead, there was an odd, challenging expression on her face.

"I said, let *go*." This time she did. "Now, get your clothes on and go wait for me in the classroom." This, too, she did.

Alone with Reuben, I did my best to comfort him as he stood, clutching his penis and sobbing.

The room was a mess. There was urine on the floor and toilet paper strewn everywhere. Taking paper towels from the dispenser, I attempted to wipe the floor as best I could and then disposed of the unraveled toilet paper. Concern about the other children, about the impending buses, and about what Reuben's parents were undoubtedly going to say, was filling me with a nasty, rushed sort of feeling.

"Oh, poor, poor Reubs," I said and cuddled him against me. "That frightened you awfully, didn't it?"

"Wee-wee," he sobbed.

"Yes, you went for a wee-wee and what happened? Can you tell me what Jadie did?"

"Wee-wee," he wailed.

Frustrated, because I knew I would probably never get the straight story, I continued to comfort him. "Did Jadie come in while you were using the toilet? What did she do?"

"Wee-wee!"

"Yes, you wanted to go wee-wee and Jadie frightened you."

He tugged impatiently at me. "Reuben's wee-wee," he cried and then took his hand away from his penis for the first time. With dismay, I saw it, red and swollen, the human teethmarks all too apparent.

Jadie was gone by the time I got back to the classroom. The clock hadn't quite reached 3:30, but the buses were out front and chaos was reigning generally. Suspecting that something had held me up, Lucy had taken charge of Jeremiah and Philip, but Jadie was nowhere to be found.

Turning a whimpering Reuben over to his nanny, I explained briefly what had happened and apologized profusely. His parents could phone me, I said, if they wished to discuss the matter further, and I gave my home telephone number. And again, I said how sorry I was that it had happened. And I was. I hated these sorts of incidents, which were inevitably traumatic, and for which, in my own mind, I could never absolve myself completely of responsibility.

Back upstairs after the children had left, I dropped into Lucy's desk chair while she finished some last-minute putting away.

"She *what?*" Lucy asked in disbelief, when I explained what had been happening.

"You heard me, I'm afraid," I replied.

Lucy wrinkled her nose. "Yeuccch. What are you going to do?"

"What can I do? If she's gone, she's gone. It's probably not worth going over to her house, especially as this is the last day. I mean, what would I do anyway? I can't make it unhappen." I sighed. "But what an awful way to end the year."

Lucy paused at what she was doing and looked over. "She hasn't done this sort of thing before, has she?"

"Not that I know of."

"Well ..." There was another pause, more contemplative, and Lucy looked down before looking back to me. "Where would a little girl learn something like that? I mean, that's sick, Torey. She wouldn't think of doing that kind of thing herself. Would she?"

I shrugged. "I dunno. With the kinds of things kids can see these days—on videos, on TV, for that matter—who knows? I suppose it's possible she has seen such a thing done before, but …"

"But it's sick," Lucy filled in. "Maybe I don't know a lot about what's going on in other places. I know you think I'm kind of inexperienced sometimes, and you're probably right, but I don't care what anybody says about something like that. Little girls doing that is sick."

Back in the classroom, I finished up my own end-of-year details. There wasn't much to do and I hoped to get home early. Putting the few things of my own that I didn't want to leave in the room over the summer into an apple box, I carried it downstairs and around the building to the teachers' parking lot. Bending down, I set the carton on the ground and then unlocked the trunk of my car and opened it. When I closed the trunk after putting the box in, Jadie had materialized between my car and the next one.

"Well, hello," I said.

She'd obviously been home, because she was now wearing a sunsuit, one of the cheap cotton kind bought at discount stores. It was orange, a bright contrast to her dark, tousled hair that ruffled across her face in the gentle breeze. She wore no shoes. I looked at her. She was a sensuous-looking child with her pure blue eyes and dark lashes, her wide, rather pouty lips, and her long, tangled hair. This fact was not lost on me.

"I'm glad you came back," I said. "I wouldn't have wanted us to end the school year on an unhappy note."

Jadie regarded me.

"Do you want to go back up to the room with me so that we can talk?"

She was like an apparition, standing there between the two cars. I could easily have believed I'd simply imagined her there. The fact that she didn't speak enhanced this sense. The breeze blew a rather large lock of hair across her face, and Jadie put a hand up to push it away, the first substantive movement she'd made since soundlessly appearing between the cars.

"I'd like to understand what happened between you and Reuben," I said. "I'd like you to tell your side of it."

I could sense she wasn't going to come up to the room with me and that if I wanted to straighten the matter out, I was going to have to do it here and now in the parking lot.

"I'm going to think that what you did to Reuben was a mistake," I said softly. "I'm going to assume that you didn't know any better, that if you'd realized how unhappy it was going to make Reuben, you wouldn't have done it."

Jadie sucked her lips between her teeth.

"There are parts of a person's body that are private. That means they belong to that person and that person alone, and nobody else has the right to touch them or do anything to them the person doesn't want. On a boy or a man, the private areas are his penis, his testicles, and his bottom. On a girl, it's her vagina and her bottom, and as she gets bigger, it also includes her breasts. These are all special, sensitive areas that feel different when they're touched, and because of that, we keep them private and we have the right to decide who touches them. *No one* has the right to touch them without permission."

Jadie's eyes, wide and unreadable, remained on my face.

"Do you understand that?" I asked.

A faint, terse nod.

"That's why I can't ever let you touch anyone again the way you touched Reuben this afternoon. If Reuben doesn't want to be touched on his penis, he has the right to tell you no and expect you not to do it. And it's my job to make sure you don't."

Tears filled Jadie's eyes.

"Like I said before, I assume you just didn't know this. Now that I've told you, we won't have to worry about it happening again, will we? So we'll just put this incident behind us." I extended my arm to bring her in for a hug. When I reached out, however, she stepped back and eluded me.

"You said you could help me," she murmured.

"How do you mean?"

"When you first came." The tears thickened her voice. "You said you knew about kids like me. You said you were going to help make it better."

I regarded her.

"I believed you that day, that day when you came. That's why I talked to you. I thought you were going to help me. I thought you said you could."

Chapter Eleven

The first few weeks after school let out, I remained in Pecking to do the hundred and one small jobs I'd never quite gotten around to while I was working. Mostly, I spent time on the apartment, which had remained in a rummage-sale state since I'd moved in. Having had to locate a place to live on such short notice, I'd never had a chance to do more than sweep the apartment out before moving in. Consequently, I'd never really moved in at all, having told myself that the place needed a good cleaning and a lick or two of new paint first, and it was easier to move boxes than bits and pieces. Of course, I'd never envisaged the boxes still being there in June, but they were. So at long last I got around to buying the paint, stripping the walls down, painting, and finally, emptying all the boxes out.

There was an odd finality in doing all this. Despite having lived in Pecking for almost six months by that point, I don't think I'd ever considered myself a resident. I remained a willing outsider, a transient putting foot temporarily to earth, and with everything still in boxes, it was possible to conceive of flitting elsewhere as easily as I'd flitted here. With the boxes gone and everything put away, I could only conclude that I was genuinely living in this place.

The summer warmed, and I idled away the first few weeks after settling in. The only person from school whom I saw with any regularity was Lucy. She and Ben had a small powerboat, which they kept at a nearby reservoir for waterskiing on weekends. I was pleased the first time she and Ben invited me to go along. Having always been athletic, I looked forward to the opportunity to learn to waterski and fancied I'd cut quite a figure when I did. Fact was, I was awful at it and hated the sensation of being dragged through the water, which was what always happened. All that could be said for my efforts in the end was that I didn't drown. However, I did continue going with them most weekends, because I discovered I enjoyed driving the boat and I could barbecue a mean hamburger.

The last six weeks of the summer were spent back in the city, where I'd agreed to participate in a training course at the clinic. Initially, I was going to stay in temporary accommodations rented from a nearby university, but in the end, I accepted the offer to stay with my former boyfriend, Hugh.

Since moving to Pecking, my private life had been a shambles. Indeed, it probably had been for some considerable time before that. Hugh and I had had a fairly serious relationship for the better part of the three years I'd been at the clinic. We'd never considered marriage during this time. With a blossoming career and a fickle, footloose side to my nature, I knew I wasn't ready for a long-term commitment, and neither was Hugh. He already had one failed marriage under his belt, and he was not impressed with the institution. We did share an increasingly close relationship, however, and finally decided to move in together.

We didn't. In the time it took me to notify my landlord I was moving and get my things together, the relationship disintegrated. This was no great surprise, I suppose, as we were two very different people. I was cast as the intellectual, the professional, the goody-two-shoes to Hugh's hard-drinking, salt-of-the-earth good old boy, and most of our humor, banter, and spirited times together revolved around this disparity. So did most of our arguments. Hugh was a college dropout who'd set himself up in business as a pest exterminator, and, having a keen business mind, he'd parlayed it into one of the largest independent exterminating businesses in the city. Indeed, it was this occupation that had initially attracted me to him, because he drove around downtown in a van with dead bugs painted all over it, and I admired the humor and devil-may-care confidence that allowed it. Unfortunately, however, it wasn't a line of work that lent itself naturally to small talk at clinic cocktail parties, and inevitably, after any evening spent with my friends, Hugh's taunts about my being an "uptown girl" were guaranteed to get a rise. He saw my work as well meaning but unreal, and, as he was very fond of pointing out, for all my education and expertise, I made much less money than he did.

What had kept me going for so long in the relationship was the laughs, because Hugh was a genuinely good-humored man. This was where the disparity between us worked well, because no matter how difficult my day had been, I could always fall back on Hugh to put things in perspective and cheer me up. Also, I enjoyed the slightly schizophrenic experience of being as comfortable in Hugh's world of country-western bars and pancake houses as I was in the theaters and restaurants I frequented with clinic colleagues. However, reality hit us with the decision to live together. We both seemed to realize simultaneously that we needed something more than our differences to survive sixteen hours a day of each other. The parting was mutual, and, like the rest of the relationship, it was good natured.

That had been in August. In January I'd come to Pecking, and in the interim there hadn't been any special relationships. I'd been out occasionally, but for the most part, Pecking was a social desert. When I'd agreed to go back to the clinic for this six-week period in the summer, it hadn't been for social reasons, and certainly it hadn't been with the intention of starting up with Hugh again; however, we'd never lost touch in the intervening months, and when he suggested I stay with him, it sounded more friendly than staying on my own, so I said yes.

Those were a strange six weeks. At the clinic, I'd always shared an office, and latterly my office mate had been Jules, a quiet, serious man who had taken on child psychiatry as a second career after several years as a urologist. When I returned, I found the office belonged solely to Jules; they'd never filled the second desk, which remained in the corner as it was when I'd left. Consequently, it was as if things had never changed. I moved back in, strewed my things around the office the way they'd always been, returned my coffee mug to the tray in the staffroom, and put my name back on the same mail slot in the office. Yet, it was different. Knowing my tenure there was short, I was like a person with a terminal illness, unable to take anything for granted. I spent much of my time noticing all the little, familiar things I had missed so much without realizing it. I was treated differently too—with much warmth and cheer, rather in the manner of the prodigal son. Even with Hugh, things altered. We returned to doing all the things we'd loved doing most together, as if the separation had never occurred, yet there were none of the usual arguments and irritations that had marred the relationship previously. A sense of fragility lingered now. We could never shake entirely the knowledge that time was passing and I'd soon be gone.

I'd brought Jadie's file with me when I returned to the clinic. Of all my children, she remained the most perplexing. I couldn't always help Reuben, Philip, or Jeremiah, but had still felt I had a fairly good grasp on their problems and what caused them. With Jadie, I felt as if I understood nothing. So I brought along the videotape where she had asked for help, several examples of her schoolwork, and the extensive notes I'd made about the content of her after-school visits, all in hopes that Jules or one of my other colleagues might be able to shed some light on her disturbance.

The videotape proved of great interest and everyone took time out to view it, including Dr. Rosenthal, the clinic director. They were fascinated by her change in posture and her direct appeal to the camera for help. She clearly knew what the camera was for, everyone maintained. They felt she was genuinely asking me.

I had also brought along quite a lot of the artwork Jadie had done in the cloakroom with me. I pointed out her bizarre bell-shaped figures and her persistent references to herself as a ghost. I also brought out some of the more symbolic work, particularly the cross in the circle—"X marks the spot," as she always referred to it—as it was certainly the most frequently made symbol, done mainly when she was angry. And I talked quite a lot about the content of those after-school sessions, about the locked doors, the fear of spiders, the doll play and its occasionally sexual nature. And, of course, I mentioned the incident on the last day with Reuben.

Everyone at the clinic seemed to have an opinion, but to my dismay, I found their ideas heavily couched in the psychoanalytic framework, which, while interesting and possibly accurate, were of little practical use to me in trying to help Jadie in the classroom. In the end I could accept this, as I don't suppose I had really come expecting any answers. I'd been in the business long enough to know it was never that simple, but I had hoped that sharing the material, talking it over with my old colleagues, and hearing their ideas would cause something, somewhere, somehow, to drop into place.

At home with Hugh, I usually didn't discuss my work. When we'd been together in the past, I had occasionally mentioned a case in passing, if I was having a hard time with it, but I seldom told him anything in depth, just as he seldom discussed his rats and spiders with me. However, one evening, as was my way when I came home from the clinic, I threw my things down on the dining room table first thing after coming through the door. Jadie's materials were in a large, brown pocket folder.

"What's this?" Hugh asked, as he was clearing the table to set it for dinner.

I turned to see him picking up the folder, which, in the course of being flung energetically onto the table, had disgorged part of its contents.

"One of my kids in Pecking. I brought some of the stuff up to see what Jules and the others might make of it."

"Jesus," Hugh muttered, looking through Jadie's drawings. "Weird. What's wrong with the kid?"

"Don't know for sure."

"Look at this one," he said. It was the encircled-cross mosaic that Jadie had done when we were making the collages.

"Yes, she's pretty heavily into symbols. Makes a lot of different kinds of marks, sort of like writing, but this one's her favorite. She's always doing that one on things. Jules says it's symbolic of sexual intercourse. He says the circle represents the vagina, the cross, the point of penetration." I paused, leaning over Hugh's shoulder to regard the picture. "I don't know if I necessarily agree with his reasoning. Jules sees vaginas and phallic symbols in everything. On the other hand, I think he might be right in this case. I'm beginning to suspect she's sexually abused."

Hugh pursed his lips and regarded the picture thoughtfully. "I think I know something else this might represent."

"What's that?"

"There's an occult bookstore down on East Marl Street, just across from where Barry and I get those nice sandwiches at lunchtime that I was telling you about. I've stopped in there a couple of times when Barry was late and I had to wait for him. And I've seen something that looks like this in one of those books. I mean, I'm not saying your guy's wrong. I suppose it could be anything. It is, after all, just a cross with a circle around it. But I do remember seeing something like this. It was what satanists carved on trees and stuff to call a Black Mass."

Silently, I regarded Jadie's mosaic.

"It's a bit of a hoot, this place," Hugh said. "All full of crystals and candles and these weird books.

Very weird, in some cases. And this girl who works in there is a witch. Wicca, she calls it. A white witch."

"You were talking to her?" I asked.

"Yeah, why not? Told her if she ever needed any spiders' legs or bats' wings, I was her man. Told her I could probably get her a discount on a bulk order."

"Oh, honestly," I said and swiped at him playfully, because no doubt that was exactly what he did tell her. Leaning over, I let Jadie's picture drop onto the pile with her other things. "Satanists?" I muttered. "I don't know. Maybe the fairies got her. Maybe she's a changeling and the fairies made off with the real child, maybe that explains it. Maybe she's gotten zapped by a flying saucer. I suppose that isn't any farther out than Jules's concern about what thoughts she was thinking during toilet training."

And then the six weeks came to an end. My last night in the city, Jules and his wife took me out to the theater and then to a late dinner at a downtown restaurant. The conversation through the meal was pleasantly animated and mostly over the play we'd seen. Then came after-dinner coffee.

"Don't you miss this?" Jules asked, looking across the table at me.

I was uncertain what "this" referred to, whether he meant the theater, life at the clinic, or perhaps simply the cup of well-brewed, good-quality coffee taken in civilized circumstances.

I had to answer yes to all three counts, because I realized there was much I did miss from my old life. On the other hand, I also had to answer no. In the six weeks I'd been back, I was surprised to find myself increasingly uncomfortable at the clinic. I became aware of feeling a quiet resentment toward the patients for the way they could afford to pay for such good treatment, could capture such high-quality professionals with their pocketbooks, and thus, automatically have a better chance of getting over their problems than those less financially fortunate. It brought back to me memories of my early teaching experiences, the only time I'd taught in a regular classroom. I'd had a room full of first-graders, nice, clean kids from a quiet suburb in a midwestern town, and I remembered looking at them and thinking how they never knew they had it so good, and I'd resented them for that ignorance. Realizing such an attitude did no one any good, I left regular education permanently after that year and went on to the special classroom. Now, as this summer had passed, I'd become cognizant of feeling the same sense of resentment and realized it was this, more than anything else, that had driven me from the clinic.

Consequently, when I returned to Pecking at the end of August, it was with positive feelings toward the new year. The move from the Sandry Clinic had been so sudden and impulsive that I'd remained uneasy about it. Why would anyone choose to abandon the city and the clinic for the likes of life in Pecking? Not sure of the answer, I don't think

I had wholeheartedly abandoned it. Five months of living out of packing boxes had reassured me it was just temporary, that I could go as easily as I had come. However, I returned to Pecking more at peace. Impulsive and atypical as the decision may have seemed, for me it was right.

Chapter Twelve

Reuben was the first to arrive. From the window I saw his mother's car pull up and Reuben hopped out, clutching his lunchbox and something else I couldn't make out from that distance. He slammed the car door and made a bee-line for the school doors, ignoring the other children on the playground, who were waiting for the bell to ring. I could hear him thundering up the stairs.

"Good morning, Reuben," I said as he burst into the classroom.

"Good morning, Reuben," he muttered and searched for his old place at the table.

"Let's put your sweater on your hook in the cloakroom. You can put your lunchbox on the shelf. And what's that you're carrying?"

He appeared to be clutching the top half of a

cookie jar. It was in the shape of a Dutch girl, but all we had was her head, her bust, and her arms placed firmly on her hips, which then flared into nothingness.

Reuben clasped the Dutch girl to him as if I might snatch her away.

"Is this a new friend of yours?" I inquired.

"A friend of yours?" he echoed and turned away, still tightly holding the cookie jar girl.

"It's pottery, Reuben. That's a type of glass. That means it'll break if you drop it. Perhaps we'd better leave it with your lunchbox. To be safe."

But off he went, carrying the lid into the classroom.

Philip arrived next, bursting into the classroom and running toward me at breakneck speed. A huge grin spread over his face, and he leaped up into my arms with such gusto that I staggered backward.

"Hey ho, Phil, good to see you. How was your summer? Good?"

He nodded enthusiastically. "Nhhaaaahhh, haaahh," he breathed into my face.

"Did you enjoy camp?"

Another nod and another breathy "Haah."

Then came Jeremiah, looking a little shoddier than in the spring, with his T-shirt dirty and his jeans clearly outgrown. Jeremiah had shot up. He'd been squat and muscular previously, but over the summer he had gone lean and leggy.

"Hi, Jeremiah. Welcome back."

Finding his old seat at the table, he dropped into it moodily. "Man, lady, what makes you think

I want to be in this fucking place, looking at your fucking face?"

Next through the door was my new boy, Brucie. Brucie was six and a half, a short, round boy with a thick thatch of white-blond hair and a cherubic face.

"Oh, look, Brucie!" his mother cried cheerfully, as they came in. "Look at this nice classroom! Oh, you *are* going to be happy here. And look! Here is your nice teacher."

I knelt down. "Hello, Brucie. My name is Torey."

"Will you say hello, Brucie? Come now, do try for Mommy. Say hello to your nice teacher. Isn't she nice? See her pretty hair? See her nice blue eyes? Just like Brucie has. And Brucie does like nice blue eyes, doesn't he?" She chucked him under the chin, then turned to me and smiled warmly. "Brucie just loves blond, blue-eyed people." Brucie, still smiling cherubically, eyed me with the savvy of Dennis the Menace.

"Brucie must have sieved food. Did Dr. Larson tell you that? Have you spoken with Mrs. Peterson about Brucie's diet? He can't tolerate lumps in his food. It makes him choke."

"Yes, I've heard."

"To make things easier here at the beginning, I've brought in a few jars of baby food. I don't want this to be a regular practice, of course; he should have fresh food and here's his grinder, but until you get used to it, you can use these." She handed over a carrier bag filled with baby food. "There's a week's supply. Two jars at a time. He may also have applesauce or yogurt, if it's being served, but *no* lumps. It makes him gag."

She passed another parcel over. "And here are his diapers. Now, he needs to be changed at least four times a day. He suffers a terrible rash if he isn't changed often enough, and where he was last year ... well, the number of times he had that rash. And it can be completely prevented."

Smiling politely, I took the baggage.

"Good-bye now, little love," she said, turning to Brucie. "Say good-bye to Mommy."

Brucie never turned his head in her direction. He was too busy taking my measure.

Then the bell rang. Jadie, still hadn't arrived, so I stood waiting a few minutes longer, but when it became obvious she wasn't coming, I turned to the others.

"Does this kid piss in his pants?" Jeremiah inquired, coming over to where Brucie was. "Has he really got diapers on?" Then Jeremiah peered curiously into Brucie's face. "Hey, boog, how old are you? Don't you think you're a bit big for this kind of shit?"

I stifled a laugh at Jeremiah's unintended pun and then propelled Brucie in the direction of the table.

"Don't he talk?" Jeremiah persisted. "What is it with this class? How come I'm the only one who can talk?"

"Because you're the only one lucky enough."

"I ain't lucky. Shit, man, luck don't got nothing to do with it. You're *supposed to* be able to talk. There shouldn't have to be no luck about it."

"There shouldn't have to be luck about a lot of things, Jeremiah, but, in fact, that's the way it is."

Brucie's grin grew less cherubic and more dumb and vacant. Once seated at the table, he started to pound on it rhythmically, as if presented with a set of bongo drums.

"Hey ho," I said and reached over to quiet his hands. "Too much noise."

"He don't half know how to bug a person," Jeremiah commented. "You didn't do us no favors letting him in here. I don't think he's going to do the class a lot of good."

We set about reestablishing ourselves in the room. Philip, Reuben, and Jeremiah located their old cubbies and examined the things left in them from the previous school year. They reclaimed favorite coat hooks, bounced again on the floor cushions, visited the animals, and then looked for old friends among the books, toys, and games. Meanwhile, I sat down with Brucie to see what sense I could make out of him.

Just after 9:45, Mr. Tinbergen appeared at the door. He beckoned me out into the hallway. "Will you go down to Alice's room?" he asked, when I came out.

I raised an eyebrow.

"Your Jadie is down there. Her sister is in kindergarten this year, and, well ... We don't seem to be having much success in separating them. Would you go down and see if you could get her to come up here?"

My Jadie, indeed!

Downstairs, I found the class seated on the floor around Alice and singing a lively version of "The Wheels on the Bus Go 'Round and 'Round." In a far corner of the room beyond the sand table was Jadie and, behind her. Amber.

Without interrupting Alice's activity, I went over to Jadie and her sister. "Time to come upstairs now," I said, matter-of-factly.

The summer hadn't changed Jadie much. Her thick, tangled mass of hair was perhaps a little longer and a little more matted, but that was all. Hunched deeply over, arms drawn up, hair spilling down, she reminded me briefly of some fairy-tale witch. Amber, cowering pale-faced and wide-eyed behind her, enhanced this image.

"I'm sure you're ready to join the others with their song," I said to Amber, reaching my hand across Jadie's back.

Jadie sprang up to prevent my touching Amber and crowded her sister farther back into the corner. The music momentarily paused, and I could sense the breath-held attention of the rest of the class.

"No, Amber belongs here. This is her room and her teacher."

The other kindergarteners watched in horrified silence as I firmly pulled Amber up over the top of Jadie and carried her across the room to Alice. Jadie scrabbled along swiftly, grasping, grabbing, finally managing to get hold of one of Amber's feet before I could transfer her to Alice. Amber began to cry, breaking the appalled silence that surrounded us, although whether her tears were from fear of

Alice or from pain at having her foot pulled, I did not know.

Then the moment Alice had hold of Amber, I spun around and grabbed Jadie. Physically lifting her off the ground, I carried her out of the room.

Once I had picked her up, Jadie didn't struggle any further. In fact, once we were outside the kindergarten classroom, the fight seemed to go out of her entirely, and she wavered uncertainly on her feet when I set her down. The sound of music once again filtered through the door.

"She'll be all right," I said quietly. "I know you were just concerned. You were being a good sister. But you don't need to worry. Mrs. Havers will take good care of Amber. And now it's time for you to come upstairs to our room. Everyone else is already there."

We walked up the stairs together, hand in hand, Jadie hobbling laboriously from one step to the next. As we passed the door between the hall and the cloakroom, Jadie paused.

"I used to go in there," she said.

"Yes."

We'd reached the classroom door, and beyond I could hear the rise and fall of Mr. Tinbergen's voice, as he tried to get Jeremiah to stop doing something. I was momentarily distracted by it, worrying what Jeremiah might be up to, but Jadie gently tugged my hand to keep me from opening the door.

"Do you remember that?" she asked, her voice soft but insistent. "Last year? When I used to go in there?"

I nodded.

"You used to let me lock it."

"You liked to lock it," I replied.

"Do you remember what I used to be like then? Do you remember what I used to do?"

"You mean when we locked the doors?"

She nodded.

"Yes, I remember."

She gazed up at me, not an easy thing to do from her doubled-over position. It meant wrenching her head to the side and peering sidelong upward, which gave her a broken, deformed appearance. "You're not afraid of me, are you?" she asked.

"No," I said and smiled. "You don't frighten me."

"*I* made you go away."

I raised an eyebrow quizzically. "What do you mean?"

"That last day. I made you go away. Like I done with the other teacher. And I didn't think you were going to come back."

"You didn't make me go away, Jadie. It was the end of the school year and time for summer vacation, and that's why I went away. Now summer vacation is over, so I've come back again."

"You're strong," Jadie murmured.

I smiled faintly, for want of a better expression.

"I knew you were strong," she said, as she prepared to go on into the classroom. "I knew you'd come back."

In a new school year I always reckoned on needing about eight weeks to establish control and bring the children together into a cohesive, well-functioning group. The time in the interim was one of limit setting and limit testing, of taking one another's measure. With this group, I'd hoped the period of adjustment would be shorter, since all but Brucie were old-timers. This wasn't the case, however. Chaos was the byword for those early weeks.

Brucie threw a real monkey wrench into the works. Previously, the old four had paired off well. Reuben and Philip functioned on much the same level, while Jadie and Jeremiah functioned on another. But God alone knew where Brucie was. Most of the time he was like a great big baby, willing to lie on the floor until physically repositioned, never making any effort to do things for himself. This made him appear both much younger and much less capable than either Reuben or Philip. It also made him a great deal of work. On the other hand, he had some truly inspired moments of activity. All that time flopped about in a heap had not been wasted; Brucie had unusual savvy about what made others tick, no doubt acquired from so much observation, and his sole joy appeared to come from disrupting relationships. In fact, my gut feeling about Brucie was that he had devoted so much effort to manipulating those around him that he'd had no time left over for normal development.

As a consequence, Brucie wreaked havoc in the classroom during those early weeks, in many respects, simply because of the amount of time he required from me, which was enormous. Feeding him, changing his diapers, dragging him physically from one place to another would have been time consuming enough on their own; encouraging him to do any of these things for himself could easily absorb the entire day. Worse was what he did to the other children. In nasty, small ways he pitted Philip against Reuben, Jadie against Philip, and Jeremiah against everybody. Indeed, Jeremiah suffered most. Impulsive, distractible, and quick to temper, Jeremiah fell and fell again for Brucie's subtle manipulations, and no amount of forewarning got through to him in time. The quiet corner did a roaring trade. The classroom was seldom quiet and never peaceful.

During this period, I didn't have much chance to see Jadie alone. Most of her afternoons after school were spent on the playground with Amber. I knew, because I often saw them from the classroom window as they played on the swings. For me, the afternoons in those early weeks seemed to be one long round of staff meetings, in-service training, and individual conferences, making me not very accessible anyway; and the afternoons I did have free, I spent trying desperately to plan for a more successful day than the one I'd just survived. In any case, Jadie gave little indication of wanting to see me. Like the other pupils, she simply came and went with the bells.

Summer left us behind, and the first breath of winter could be felt in the air. Even in the best of years, autumn was a short season across this broad expanse of plains, a brilliant pause between the dry, brown heat of August and the all-too-soon winter whiteness; but this particular year, we had virtually no fall whatsoever. September withered us with eighty-degree heat well into the middle of the month, then came a wet and windy weekend, a frost, and the leaves died on the trees, turning brown and falling within the space of ten days. The wind backed to the north, and the first arctic air mass moved southward. We were dusted with snow by the beginning of October.

It was a gray, overcast afternoon, and I was at the table in the classroom, putting the next day's work into the children's folders, when I heard a noise in the hallway. Looking up, I saw Jadie peering in through the window in the classroom door. The unlit hallway had been plunged into premature darkness by the weather, making Jadie, who was standing a bit back from the window, indistinct.

I beckoned to her, but she didn't respond. Finally, I rose and went to the door. "Do you want to come in?"

She was heavily dressed against the weather, her features disappearing under hat and muffler.

"Do you want to come in?" I asked again.

Nodding slightly, she entered the classroom.

"I'm just getting things ready for tomorrow," I said and reseated myself at the table.

Slowly, laboriously, she began removing her outer clothing. Piece by piece she laid it on the chair next to her. Finally down to her cardigan and ratty little cotton dress, she stopped. Then she stood.

A minute, two minutes passed in complete and motionless silence.

"Would you like to sit down?" I asked.

Slowly, she drew out the chair opposite and then sat. Again, complete silence.

"How are things going?" I asked, trying to keep my tone pleasant and conversational.

There was no answer.

"Are things going all right for you?"

Nothing.

"Amber? How's Amber liking school?"

Still nothing.

"And Sapphire? I'll bet Sapphire's getting big. How old is she now? Can she walk yet?"

I looked over to see Jadie shrunk down and hunched over almost to a point of having her face on the tabletop. Silence thumped down around us like a wet blanket.

"You know what? I've still got that key. If we went into the cloakroom, we could lock the door," I suggested.

Although she didn't look up, I saw Jadie's shoulders relax slightly.

"Let's go in there. It's cozier. Besides, I think I've got things to do at my desk that I'd forgotten about."

Even after we'd gone into the cloakroom and I'd locked both doors, Jadie remained tense. Sitting down on the right-hand bench, she slumped forward until she was nearly doubled over, her arms clutched around her middle like someone with a bad stomachache. Not wanting to focus too directly on her, I sought something to occupy myself with at the desk.

Several minutes passed without a break in the silence. Jadie, still bent double, shifted her hands to support her head, first covering her face with them, and then eventually turning her head to allow her to see around the room.

"You're finding it hard to talk?" I asked quietly.

Her eyes searched my face.

"That's okay. I don't mind."

Back to the silence.

"Has that man come?" she asked at last.

"Which man?"

She raised her head slightly to see me better. "That spider-killer man you told me about last year."

"You mean the fumigator? From the pest-control company?"

She nodded.

"Well, Mr. Tinbergen has them come twice a year, so, yes, I expect he's just been. Probably right before school started last month."

A pause.

"You're not very fond of spiders, are you?" I said.

"I *hate* spiders."

"How come?"

"They get everywhere. They see what you do." A great weariness seemed to overtake Jadie at this point, and she dropped her head to rest it right on her knees. For a brief moment she closed her eyes, then reopened them. "What do *you* do with spiders?" she asked. "Do you kill them?"

"Not usually. I'm not frightened by them, so if they don't put their webs in my way, I leave them be."

"But they watch what you do."

"I'm sure what I do is not of great interest to spiders," I replied.

A small pause ensued.

"It sounds as if perhaps you're worried that they're watching you," I said.

Slowly, Jadie nodded.

"What makes you think that?"

No reply.

I looked back at the papers before me on the desk. Jadie, with almost aching slowness, brought herself up into an upright position. She rotated her shoulders, as if they were stiff, and then rotated her head. Folding her hands in her lap, she regarded them. "I gotta ask you something," she murmured.

"What's that?"

Jadie continued to look at her hands for several moments. Finally, she looked over. "Do you believe me?"

"About what?"

"Like when I tell you stuff. Do you believe me?"

"I try to. Do you worry that I don't?"

A small pause. She frowned down at her hands. "Sometimes things don't sound like they're true, and then people don't believe you. Even if it is true, people think you're making it up."

"And you're concerned this might be the case with me?"

Faintly, she nodded.

I smiled and leaned forward on the desk. "Well, I'll tell you what. What if I always try to believe you? What if I promise I'll always listen, and if you tell me something's true, I'll try to believe."

Jadie's brow puckered. She lowered her head. "What I gotta tell you is that you need to be careful about spiders."

"I see."

"They *are* watching you. The spiders are seeing what you're doing, so you got to never talk to me, except when there's no spiders."

"Oh."

"You're going to die otherwise. That's the truth. The spiders want you to die. And if they ever see I'm telling you this, I'm going to die too."

Chapter Thirteen

It was only the first full week of October and already we were being attacked by Halloween hysteria. Jeremiah, by far the most vocal child in my group, was also the most smitten by the opportunities Halloween presented.

"Me and my brother, when we go out trick-or-treating, we're gonna take pillowcases. We're going to go all the way around town, to every house, to every *single* house, and we're going to get a hundred candy."

"A hundred pieces of candy," I corrected.

"Well, probably two hundred. Or even a thousand. Probably a thousand candy."

"A thousand *pieces* of candy."

"Yeah, well, that's what I said."

We were all sitting around the table working on a jack-o'-lantern decoration for the bulletin board.

This was one of my more demented projects. I'd read about it in a teaching magazine, about how the design was drawn on a large sheet of paper and then the children took tiny squares of tissue paper, wrapped them individually around the eraser end of a pencil to form small flowerlike shapes, and glued them closely together onto the design to make a lovely, three-dimensional wall hanging. As it was listed as suitable for kindergarteners on up, I'd thought it was just the thing for us to work on as a group. What I hadn't counted on was just how many pencil-twisted squares were needed to fill in a design the size of the one I'd drawn, nor how intrinsically boring twisting the squares and gluing them on was.

"What house do you live in?" Jeremiah asked me. "I'm probably going to come there. And you know what I'm going to be wearing as my costume? I'm going to be He-Man, Mightiest Man in the Universe." This caused Jeremiah to leap to his feet and thrust his pencil into the air, shrieking, "By the power of Greyskull! I GOT THE POWER!" Jadie, beside him, covered her ears.

"I think that's a bit loud, Jeremiah," I said.

"No, I'm not going to be He-Man. I've changed my mind. Maybe I'm going to be Batman." He swooped his arms out to the side.

"Jeremiah, please sit down."

"What you gonna be, Philip?" Jeremiah asked.

Philip, across the table, was earnestly trying to twist his bit of tissue paper around a contrary pencil. Ten minutes of concentrated effort and

Philip had managed to make two of the twisted shapes.

"What 'bout you, boogy Reub? What you gonna be?" Having paused to flick a bit of tissue paper against his eyelashes, Reuben was momentarily lost in a reverie of self-stimulation.

"What's Reuben going to be?" Jeremiah asked me.

"I think he's going to be a pirate, aren't you, Reuben?" I said and gently lowered his hands from his face. "And Brucie's going to be a hobo. We're going to make your hobo's stick and bundle right here in class next week, aren't we, Brucie?" I smiled at Brucie, whose main contribution thus far had been to stay upright on his chair.

"He ain't gonna be as good as me. I'm gonna be best. I'm going to have the best costume of anybody, and I'm going to win the prize. Mr. Tinbergen *always* gives out prizes, and this year, *I'm* gonna win it." Jeremiah looked over at Philip again. "So, what's your costume gonna be?"

"Huh-huhh," Philip intoned.

I reached over to press his lips together. "Try again, Phil. Buh-uh-uh."

"Buh-huhh."

"Bunny. That's right. Very good, Philip."

"Bunny?" Jeremiah shrieked. *"Bunny?* Whose asshole idea was that, man? What kind of boog are you, gonna be a *bunny?"*

"It sounds like a very nice costume, Jeremiah. Philip's foster mom was telling me all about it. He's going to have long ears and even whiskers."

"Does it got a tail?" Jeremiah shrieked again, thinking this was a tremendously funny joke. Leaping from his chair, he hopped around the room, waggling his hands behind him. "Got a tail! Got a tail!"

Trying to ignore him, I looked over at Jadie, solemnly forming her tissue paper shapes and sticking them onto the jack-o'-lantern. Although she interacted considerably more with the boys now than she used to, she still tended often to carry on as if none of the rest of us were there. "Have you started thinking about your costume?" I asked.

Jadie didn't answer.

Jeremiah leaped up on the back of Jadie's chair and wrapped his arms around her neck. "What you gonna wear, girlie-wurlie? What you gonna be? A witch? A witch-bitch? Hinx minx, the old witch stinks. That fat begins to fry—"

"Jeremiah, *please,*" I moaned. He climbed down. Jadie dusted off her shoulder as if he'd left fleas.

"Know what I'm gonna be, girlie-wurlie?" This time he threw himself down in front of her, knocking her pieces of tissue paper all across the table. "I'm going to be Dracula and eat your throat! Arrrghhhhhh!" At this he grabbed Jadie's neck again, not an easy maneuver to execute from his position on the table.

"*Jeremiah!*" I said. "Settle down. Now get off that table and back to your place immediately. You're supposed to be helping us make this. We've still got a long way to go, so please *help.*"

"I'm gonna get teeth," he said, sliding himself over the tabletop and pushing his face close to mine. "Get some of them Dracula teeth that glow in the dark, and I'm going to have a whole mouthful of catsup. Then, when I open my mouth, it's gonna all drip down just like blood. Grrrrawwwwww!" He went for my jugular.

Grabbing him firmly by the shoulders, I pulled him off the table and sat him down in his chair.

"I *am* going to make blood drip down. 'Cause me and Micah been stealing them little catsup things from McDonald's every time we go. So I'm gonna put all them little catsup things together in my mouth, and then I'm going to open it and *eeuuhhhhhh!* It's gonna be real pukey," he said enthusiastically. "I'm gonna have the best costume of anyone. Probably, Mr. Tinbergen's going to give me first prize. Probably, he's gonna even give me some money or something, because it'll be so good he can't believe it."

"Your plans do sound interesting," I said. Turning to Jadie, I asked, "So, do you have any ideas for your costume?"

She shrugged slightly. "Don't got a costume."

"Don't *got* a costume?" Jeremiah shrieked out in surprise.

"Shush," I said and pushed him back into his chair. "There's still plenty of time."

"You don't got to have a costume," Jadie said. "I didn't have one last year."

"But don't you *got* one?" Jeremiah asked in disbelief.

"I don't want one."

For once, Jeremiah was stunned into silence. Admittedly, I was surprised myself. Knowing that all the children had the financial means for a costume and none came from homes holding fundamentalist beliefs, I'd just assumed everyone would be participating.

"Well, what you gonna do for the costume parade?" Jeremiah asked. "How you gonna go from room to room showing them other boogs your costume, when you ain't got no costume on?"

"I don't want to be in the parade."

"But how you gonna win a prize then?"

"I don't want a prize."

"What you come to school for, then, if you don't want nothing good? How come you don't just stay home?"

Jadie raised her head and tilted it to one side, eyeing Jeremiah across the table. "I come here for the same reason you do. 'Cause if you don't go to school, you get tooken away to the police by the truant officer. I come here 'cause I have to." There was an unexpected vehemence in her voice. "But they can't make me do stupid things I don't want. They can't make me look like something I'm not."

"Whew," Jeremiah said, sitting back, "that girl there knows her mind. Whew! You hear her, lady? Better watch out, your job's gonna be on the line, if that there girl gets her way. Kick all the teachers out! Take all their money." Then a pause. Jeremiah gazed at Jadie a moment longer. "You can probably hate me for saying this, but it's a good thing they stuck you in this here class. No doubt about it, your mind's not right."

The house next door to the playground had a golden retriever bitch, a beautiful, good-tempered animal, who often played out in the backyard, which abutted the schoolyard. My children frequently gravitated to the fence to talk to the dog and reach through to stroke it; and so they were delighted to discover in September that she had had a litter of puppies. By October the puppies were lively and playful, romping around in the backyard and yapping joyfully at the children during recess. More than once, we had had to repossess a puppy that one of the children had managed to haul over the fence. Consequently, it was no major surprise when, during one after-lunch playtime, one of the older children stopped by the teachers' lounge to tell me that Jeremiah had made off with a puppy.

Jeremiah adored dogs, and despite his total lack of respect for anything on two legs, he was quite trustworthy with animals. Consequently, I wasn't too alarmed by the news; however, I felt it would be better if I went in search of him and let the lunch aides on playground duty keep on watching the other kids.

It took a few minutes to discover where he'd hied off to, but at last I heard his voice coming from a blind stairwell, which led down to a long since bricked-up basement entrance. Shielded from view, he was chattering away, and I realized there must be someone else with him. Pausing just out of sight, I recognized the other voice as Jadie's.

"Lookit, that's his thing," Jadie was saying. "He's got a boy's pisser," Jeremiah replied. "Those other puppies, they've got girls' pissers, but this one's a boy. That's why I like him best."

"I know another name for that," Jadie said.

"Yeah, me too."

"What word you know?" Jadie asked.

"Penis," Jeremiah replied, his tone serious.

"I know a better one. Pecker," Jadie said.

"My cousin calls it a weenie," Jeremiah added.

"Yeah, weenie. I know that one, too. And ding-ding."

"That's a girl's word for it," Jeremiah replied, his tone derisive. "And it's silly."

"D'you know any more?" Jadie asked. When Jeremiah didn't immediately respond, she said, "I know one. Dick."

"And prick." The first licentious giggle followed.

"Worm," said Jadie. "'Cause that's what it looks like."

"Don't either," Jeremiah answered in an offended tone. Then a pause. "What else words you know?"

There was no immediate response from Jadie, and I was about to go on down the stairs to retrieve the puppy when I heard Jeremiah say enthusiastically, "Lookit, you can pretend it's a cow. I'm going to milk it. Pull! Pull! See, pretend this is gonna be one of them long sucky-bit things cows got hanging down."

"Pull his dicky and get milk," Jadie replied.

"You don't get milk out of a cow's pisser. You get it out of its boobs. He's got to be a girl."

"No sir. I know a way to get milk out of a pisser. Out of a dicky," Jadie said. There was a boastful tone to her voice, making it clear that she relished this moment of one-upsmanship with Jeremiah.

"You can't," Jeremiah retorted.

"You can too. But you don't squeeze it like that. You got to suck on it, like this."

"Jadie," I said, hurrying down the steps.

She startled violently and dropped the puppy to the ground. Beside her stood Jeremiah, looking absolutely appalled. "Did you see what she was gonna *do,* lady? She was gonna put her mouth on that dog's pisser."

"There's still time left before the bell rings, Jeremiah. If you hurry, I'm sure you can still have a turn at kick ball."

"But—" Still the shocked expression on his face.

I eyed him. "But you'll need to go right *now.*"

Getting the message, Jeremiah zoomed off.

Jadie attempted to zoom off, too, but I caught her by the shoulder. "I think we need a few words."

Leaning down, I scooped up the puppy and cuddled it a moment. Jadie's eyes were wide and wary, their pupils dilated.

"Last spring you put your mouth on Reuben's penis. I explained then that that was a private place on Reuben and we don't do those sorts of things because of it. At the time I wanted to think a bit of silliness had come over you, because I know boys and girls can get pretty silly sometimes about things like this. Now I'm beginning to get concerned that maybe there's more to it."

"I was just playing," Jadie muttered and lowered her head.

"I'm not angry. And I'm not going to get angry, so you don't have to worry about that. I am concerned, though, Jadie. When little girls do something like you were just doing, it's usually because they've seen it done before. Sometimes, someone older shows them or does it to them, and so they know."

Jadie sighed wearily.

"It's not your fault, Jadie. I'm *not* angry. But if someone is making you touch the private places on his or her body or is touching you like that, it's important to tell me. Or, if not me, then some other adult you can trust."

Jadie shifted restlessly from foot to foot. I studied her, small and slight, her long dark hair rumpled over her shoulders. Even in her bent, deformed state, there was a brooding attractiveness about her.

"If something like this is going on," I said, "chances are, someone has told you not to tell. Chances are, they've said something like, if you do tell, you'll get in trouble. Or that people will think it's your fault it happened. Or that no one will believe you. Or that you'll get taken away from your parents or some other equally horrible thing. When a grown-up is doing something wrong, that is the sort of thing they will say to you, because they want you to stay quiet and not tell, because they know they shouldn't be doing what they're doing. They're lying to keep you from getting help. But if someone is touching you or making you touch them, you need help. You're just a little girl, and these are grown-up matters. You need a grown-up to help you sort it out."

"But I wasn't doing anything," she said. "I was just fooling around. Nothing else. I was just playing."

I fell into frustrated silence.

Jadie shrugged in what seemed an annoyed, put-upon way. "I'm sorry," she muttered. "I won't do it again."

"That's not the point. Jadie, I want to *help* you."

She shifted her feet again, kicked a dead leaf aside with the toe of her shoe, and then sighed very heavily. When I didn't say anything further, she finally looked up. "Can I go now?" she asked.

Disgruntled, I stared at her, willing her to talk to me.

"Please? I'm missing my playtime. I said I'm sorry, so can I go?"

At last I flapped a hand at her. "Yes, go ahead."

Chapter Fourteen

Thursday afternoon, Arkie Peterson dropped by. Like so many of her visits, this one was completely unexpected. She was wearing an unusual combination of calfskin vest and long, dangly rhinestone earrings that gave her the sort of tarty cowgirl appearance only Arkie seemed to be able to carry off and still not hurt her professional image.

"How's it going?" she asked, sitting down on the edge of the table where I was working.

I rolled my eyes. "You found me a corker in Brucie."

She grinned gleefully. "I told you last spring I'd picked a winner."

"Ever notice how the really weird ones get their names reduced to silly diminutives?" I remarked, rising to get a pen from the canister on top of the bookshelf. "Like Brucie instead of Bruce? I've had a load of them. Dirkie. Cliffie. Jamesie."

"Jadie," Arkie added.

"Yes, *Jadie.*"

"Hoo-hoo," said Arkie knowingly. "Enough corks for a winery there, eh?"

"I'm going to need to have a long talk with you about her."

"Ah, wrangling for another expense account dinner at Tottie's?"

"Wrangling for a chance to have you sitting still in one place for twenty minutes. I've *got* to talk to you. I mean really talk. Seriously. And privately."

Arkie sobered. "Why? What's the matter?"

"I think she's being sexually abused."

"Really? Has she said something?"

"Not in so many words, no, but one can put two and two together. Something very strange is up with this girl."

"Is this all from that incident with Reuben in the spring?"

"Well, I found that unsettling, but I think I could have accepted it as a one-off incident. Kids are sexual, whether we like to think it or not, and disturbed kids can get pretty creative in that realm. But it's adding things up." I then told Arkie about the incident with the puppy.

Arkie frowned in revulsion.

"She was talking about sucking milk out of a penis, definitely a penis and not a teat, and it doesn't take a lot of imagination to substitute 'milk' for 'semen.' Your average eight-year-old wouldn't come up with that on her own. Most kids that age are appalled by the idea of sexual intercourse, much less fellatio."

Folding her hands together in front of her, Arkie rested her thumbs against her lips in a pensive pose. "All it takes, though, is one blue flick. Who's to say her daddy doesn't have a whole porn library sitting at home on the shelf? Who says she's not sitting up at eleven-thirty at night watching the wrong TV station? Kids know more these days, Torey. They have access to a lot more information than we had."

"I don't dispute that, but there's a big difference between seeing it and doing it. Even Jeremiah was horrified by what she intended, and God alone knows what he sees at home. And that's the point. It's even more than doing it, it's *wanting* to do it."

Arkie fell silent.

"I realize there's nothing much I can do at this point. If she doesn't make a specific accusation, I know I can't push. I'm all too aware of the danger of 'leading questions' and 'eliciting information' and all that crap, if something does come out and it does go to court, but I'm starting to get very worried about this kid. To use a hoary old hippy phrase, I really do get bad vibes."

"Yeah," said Arkie, "I can appreciate that now. I'll make a note in her file, and I'll have a browse through all the old notes to see if there's anything mentioned that might contribute. Otherwise, I think you're following the best path. If she is being abused, either we need concrete evidence or she has to say something outright; so it's eyes and ears open and let's see if we can ask the right questions."

"Yes," I replied, but, in fact, what I'd been hoping for were the right answers.

During the following week, just after afternoon recess, all of us were seated around the table in the classroom. Reuben, Jadie, and Jeremiah were doing written work from their folders; Philip was cutting and pasting pictures from a magazine as part of his project on foods; I was working with Brucie on color identification. Indeed, we were just reaching the stage where, as a class, we could all sit down and work together and genuinely accomplish something in the process, so I was finding the peace blissful. Then, Jeremiah started making a quiet scrabbling noise with his fingers on the underside of the table.

"Jeremiah, please finish your work," I said. A pause ensued and then the scrabbling again. "I'm going to get you," he whispered playfully to Philip, sitting across from him.

"Jeremiah," I said, a little more firmly.

He brought his hand back up onto the table and feigned work.

This time he laid a sheet of paper over the top of his hand and then wiggled his fingers. "It's one of them tarantula spiders," he whispered with mock malevolence and made the paper edge toward Philip. "One of them great, big, hairy boogers and he's coming to get you."

Jadie's eyes went wide and dark as she watched Jeremiah's obscured hand. Reaching over quickly, I snatched the paper off, exposing his creeping fingers. "Silly boy," I said to her. "Just pretending."

Showing Jeremiah up didn't stop him. His fingers scrambled the rest of the way across the table to Philip. "Coming to getcha!" he shrieked and then, with the lightning swiftness Jeremiah was renowned for, he leaped over the table and had Philip playfully by the throat.

"*Jeremiah!* I mean it. Settle down. This is your last warning."

Rolling his eyes, Jeremiah settled back into his seat. "Probably just say that 'cause I'm an Indian kid. Wouldn't always be getting so mad at some kid with white skin."

"White, brown, black, or purple with pink polka dots, I'll get after you, if you keep disrupting everything. It's not your skin I'm worried about, it's your actions."

"Whew, listen to this lady, man," he muttered. "Not even worried about our skins."

We returned to our activities for perhaps three or four minutes before Jeremiah's fingers began to wiggle yet again. With exaggerated effort, he tried to control them, falling off his chair and pinning them to the floor.

"I'm *trying* to, man," he said to my unvoiced disapproval and got back up on his seat, "but these fingers, they got a life of their own." And with this comment, he wriggled them again, running them up his other arm and leaping them over onto Jadie's shoulder.

Jadie jumped with a scream from her chair. "Get him *away* from me!" she cried. "Make him *stop!*" Before I could react, however, she had bolted from her chair. Scuttling across the room and into the cloakroom, she slammed the door behind her. I struggled to catch up with her, but before I could, I heard the key turn in the lock.

"Jadie? Jadie, let me in."

No answer.

Gently, I tried the doorknob to make sure it was actually locked, but I didn't rattle it, in case I frightened her further. "Would you please let me in?"

No reply.

"It's only me, Jadie. Let me in, please."

Nothing.

At last I turned and went back to the table, where the boys sat, wide-eyed, watching.

"How come she did that?" Jeremiah asked.

"How come do you think?" I replied irritably.

He looked at the door a moment, then wearily shook his head. "You know, you can probably hate me for saying this, but you're really not such a hotshot teacher. You're supposed to be making it so they don't keep thinking there's crazies in here. Now she's gone and locked herself in the closet."

"She just wants to be alone for a bit."

Jeremiah frowned and ran a hand through his dark hair, making it stand straight up. "Just that last year she didn't talk, but there really wasn't nothing wrong with her otherwise. Now she talks and you find out she's fucking crazy. And I hate to say it, but that's probably your fault."

Throughout the remainder of the afternoon, Jadie stayed in the cloakroom. The occasional muted thunk of movement passed through the wall to us, but otherwise, there was no indication she was in there. Certainly, there was no indication she was coming out. At last, the going-home bell rang.

"What the fuck we gonna do now, lady?" Jeremiah asked. "We don't got no coats or nothing."

Rising, I approached the door. "Jadie? It's time to open up. That was the bell, and the boys need their things so they can go home."

Beyond the door there was no sound whatsoever.

"Gonna have to break the door down, lady."

"Open up, Jadie. The buses are waiting. The boys need their things."

Reuben, distressed by this change in the usual routine, began to cry.

"AHHHHHHH!" shrieked Jeremiah with ear-splitting loudness. He gave the air a martial arts-style kick. "Gonna bust that door right down!"

"No, you are not. Now cool it," I said and grabbed him. *"Jadie!"* I called through the door.

Nothing.

I knew I could get in there if I had to, as Mr. O'Banyon had a master key for all the doors, but I was reluctant to call him up. A major part of Jadie's and my relationship revolved around the security of these doors, and I didn't want to damage her faith in them. On the other hand, I was growing desperate.

"Now, if I have to, I *will* open that door, Jadie," I said in my sternest, most definite teacher's voice. "Or else you can. And I think it'd be a much better idea if you opened it."

At last came the soft sound of the key turning in the lock. The latch snicked and the door came open. Jadie, her eyes red and puffy, stood forlornly inside the cloakroom.

"Jeremiah," I said, "pop out and see if Mrs. McLaren is still in the hallway with her boys and girls. Ask her if she'd be kind enough to see that you and the others get down to your rides." Going into the cloakroom, I quickly snatched up the boys' wraps and lunchboxes and Reuben's ever-present Dutch girl cookie jar top.

Lucy appeared.

"Do me an enormous favor, okay?" I asked and smiled as winningly as I could, then I disappeared back into the cloakroom.

Head down, long hair falling forward to obscure most of her face, Jadie just stood. Beyond her on the bench were the Sasha dolls, removed from their box and all carefully laid out, side by side.

"Looks like there's a family there," I said, approaching the dolls. "This one could be the mama and this one the daddy. And these look like they could be the children."

Jadie didn't move as much as a muscle.

I sat down on the bench beside the dolls. "What's this one doing?" I asked, picking up the doll with the long dark hair, the one Jadie favored. "I wonder how she's feeling."

Jadie remained motionless.

Gently, I caressed the doll, pushing back its unbrushed hair. "Shall we play at dolls?" I asked Jadie. "This can be your doll. You pretend to be her and tell my doll what yours is thinking about. Okay?" I held the doll out to her.

Jadie turned away to avoid my giving it to her.

Pulling the doll back in, I stood it on my knee. "Oh, I'm feeling unhappy," I whimpered in a high-pitched falsetto on the part of the doll. "I've got terrible feelings inside me, all scared and miserable."

"Oh dear," I replied solicitously in my own voice. "Why's that?"

"I'm frightened. I'm so, so scared," the doll whined.

"Oh? Why's that? Can you tell me about it?"

"Terrible things are happening to me and I don't know how to stop them," the doll cried.

"How awful for you," I murmured sympathetically and enveloped the doll in a tender hug. "Oh, poor you. I feel bad for you when I hear you're unhappy. Come here and let me hold you. Let me help."

Jadie took a step closer. Watching her furtively with my peripheral vision, I continued my conversation with the doll.

"I'm frightened! I'm frightened!" the doll cried in a piteous voice. "It's hard for me to tell you. I'm afraid you won't understand. I think you won't believe me. I'm scared you'll think it's my fault."

"Oh dear," I said, turning to look at Jadie, "she's so unhappy. What can we say to her? Come here.

Can you think of something to tell her to make her feel better?"

Staring at the doll, Jadie hesitated, a perplexed expression on her face. Then, very cautiously, she took a step nearer. A pause, then she extended her hand in an uncertain manner. "Don't be afraid," she whispered and lightly caressed the doll's hair.

"I wonder why she's so frightened," I said.

"It's her birthday."

"Ohhh," I said in a wise and knowing tone, although I hadn't any idea why Jadie should consider a birthday frightening. "Poor dear," I said to the doll. "You're so, so scared, aren't you? But I'll hold you tight." I cuddled the doll against my body. "Words are a good thing, because they help me understand. I'll keep you close and you can tell me all about what's wrong. Then I can help."

Jadie began to weep.

"Come here, lovey," I said, extending my arm toward her. "You can tell me, too."

"I can't."

"You can."

"I can't. You won't understand."

"You can. And I will."

"I *can't* and you *won't.*"

"Give me a chance, all right?" I smiled gently at her. "Right here, nice and safe. I'll keep my arms around you."

"I *can't,*" she cried passionately. "You just don't understand." And with that, she broke out of my grip and turned on her heel. Running to the door, she unlocked it and bolted out before I could get to her. I was left with the sound of her footsteps echoing away into the silence of the empty corridor.

School began at 8:45, so most mornings I came about eight. I used the forty-five minutes to lay out last-minute materials, make sure I was organized, and then, on most mornings, to socialize. Getting a cup of coffee from the lounge, I would wend my way back via the front office, Alice's room, and a few others, just to say hello and see how things were getting on, before ending up in Lucy's room, where I often stayed until the bell rang.

So my rounds started the following morning, but before stopping in to see Lucy, I went back to my own room to put my now empty coffee mug on the desk. Opening the door, I was surprised to find Jadie sitting in her chair at the table.

"How did you get in here?"

Jadie didn't respond. She was still dressed in all her outer clothes, right down to her mittens.

"Mr. Tinbergen's going to be mad, if he sees you. He's been pretty tolerant about letting you come in after school, but I don't think it's a good idea to try to push him too far. And he's always been very strict about children staying outside until the bell goes."

"My sister's got a birthday," Jadie replied. Her eyes were on me. Such beautiful eyes she had, such a sheer, clear blue, their intensity heightened by the thick black lashes. Her forehead wrinkled in concern.

"Your sister's got a birthday?" I echoed, bewildered.

Jadie's eyes grew wide and dark, the pupils dilating as she searched my face. I could sense her imploring me to understand, and I was briefly overcome with a feeling of utter helplessness, because I knew I didn't in the least. "Which sister?" I murmured.

"Amber."

"Oh."

Jadie hunched forward. "She's going to be six on her birthday." Her voice was so soft as to be barely above a whisper. "On the twenty-seventh."

"And that upsets you?"

Clearly, it did. Head down, shoulders bent, Jadie twiddled a tassel on one mitten. A thick snuffle betrayed her nearness to tears.

Pulling out the chair opposite, I sat down at the table. "Could you tell me a little more?"

No answer.

I reached my hands across the table to touch hers. "Lovey, I want to help you. I can tell that you've been very worried lately; I know you're unhappy. I know you want to help, but you *have* to talk to me. Otherwise, I can't tell what to do."

"Amber might die."

"Why do you think that?"

Jadie looked up, her expression one of anguished exasperation. "I just *told* you! She's going to be six on her birthday."

I paused in puzzlement.

"And I don't *want* her to die."

"Actually, sweetheart, people don't usually die just because they've turned six."

"Tashee did. And Amber might, just like Tashee. Maybe it's going to be the same. I think it's Amber's turn now."

"Tashee died?"

Jadie's brow furrowed in an expression of suspicion. "You knew that. I already told you."

"Sometimes, lovey, I get a little bit confused. This isn't because I'm not listening or because I don't believe what you're saying. I don't mean to. It's just that ..."

Jadie's chair had begun to slide backward, and I realized she was about to run away again. *Oh please,* I was praying, *let me know what to say next.*

"When Tashee died," I said softly, "how did it happen?"

Jadie regarded me warily. Then she glanced around the classroom, her eyes scanning the mopboards and crevices for cobwebs. At last she leaned toward me and said in a whisper, "Miss Ellie took the knife, the one shaped like this," she paused to trace a design on the tabletop with her finger, "and she put it right there on Tashee's throat."

Jadie paused again, swallowed, leaned even closer, until our heads were almost meeting. "When she done it, the blood came out. Sort of like in a hose. It didn't run down, like when you cut yourself, but it sort of came up, like when you turn the hose on, and Miss Ellie caught it in the cup."

Placing a hand under my chin, I laid my fingertips against my lips to keep from betraying my feelings. A moment, two moments passed before I could trust my voice. "Miss Ellie killed her? Miss Ellie? The lady from TV?"

Cocking her head, Jadie met my eyes. "Yeah," she said hesitantly. "You know about it?" There was a note of relief in her voice. "You know? You saw it on your TV, too?"

Chapter Fifteen

On Wednesday afternoons, I allowed the children an hour of "free time" after recess to pursue whatever activities they might choose. For Brucie, this usually meant lying on the floor on his beloved blanket and mouthing objects. For Philip and Reuben, it was a chance to play at the sand table or with water in the sink, two activities both boys enjoyed tremendously and got spiritedly messy with. Jeremiah and Jadie, however, tended to have wider-ranging tastes. Sometimes they played, sometimes they drew or colored or read, sometimes they continued on with an interesting project brought over from another lesson. And Jeremiah, who had an unaccountable tidy streak, occasionally spent the time cleaning out my cupboards for me.

This particular afternoon, Jadie couldn't settle at any activity. Up and down from her chair, she wandered around the classroom, absently touching the books on the shelf, the fish tank, the stacked work folders. In front of the bulletin board, she paused and studied the schoolwork pinned there. She gazed at the posters on the wall. At last she came to the shelves where I kept the art materials. She passed them by initially, then pulled herself back. There were several squeeze bottles of premixed tempera paints standing in a row. These she considered, then fingered. "Do you mind if I paint?" she asked at last, lifting up one of the bottles.

"No. The big sheets of painting paper are up there on top of the cabinet." And I returned to what I was doing at the table.

Jadie busied herself setting up the easel, tacking on a sheet of paper, slipping on a paint shirt, and then filling one of the foam egg cartons we used as palettes with an assortment of colors. Picking up a paintbrush, she paused in front of the paper. When I next glanced up several minutes later, she was still standing in front of the blank paper.

A few moments later, Jadie, still clutching the paintbrush, came over to me. "Can I take my stuff in the cloakroom?" she asked softly.

"All of it? The easel and everything?"

She nodded.

"I suppose so. But could you manage without locking the door?"

"Can I lock the other one? Not this one into here, but the one into the hallway?"

I nodded.

Arduously, Jadie dragged the easel into the cloakroom, then came back to carry the paints, brushes, palette, and newspapers for the floor.

Needing to get a correcting pen from my desk, I went into the cloakroom just as Jadie was preparing to put her first strokes on the paper, and what I noticed immediately was that she was standing nearly erect. Startled by my noise, however, she jerked and hunched over.

"It's only me," I said and picked up my pen.

"Close the door when you go out, okay?" she asked. "And make everybody knock before they come in. Okay? If I don't lock it, make everybody knock."

We left Jadie on her own for perhaps fifteen or twenty minutes, during which time it was obvious that she was enjoying what she was doing. Several times she'd come out for additional materials, more paint, bigger brushes.

At last I went into the cloakroom to warn her about the impending bell. The small area was in artistic chaos. Bottles of paint were strewn about on the benches. Mucky, disintegrating paper cups were on the floor and an assortment of brushes, all covered in paint, lay everywhere.

"May I have a look?" I asked.

She nodded, so I came around in back of her.

It was a painting of a huge, black-striped cat, so enormous that it nearly filled the paper. Its head, outsized for the rest of its body, was turned outward, its eyes wide and white-rimmed with round, yellow pupils. Its ears were tall ovals, and a dense brush of whiskers stuck out from either side of the two dots representing its nose. The mouth, however, was its most prominent feature. Gigantic, it took up fully half of the cat's face in a red, rather malevolent grin, which bared six broad, rectangular teeth. Indeed, given the size of the cat's head in the picture, the red grin covered almost a quarter of the entire paper. There was no mistaking the amount of sheer aggression in the cat, so tightly confined on its page.

"That's Jenny," Jadie said. "Do you remember Jenny? She was my cat for a little time."

"It's beautiful. I really like this painting."

"She looks like a tiger, don't she?" Jadie said.

"Yes."

Then Jadie picked up a cup containing orange paint. Without warning, she began to paint heavy bars downward across the whole picture.

Stunned by the sudden action, I couldn't help expressing my dismay. "What did you do that for?"

"It wasn't safe, leaving it like that. Tigers are dangerous. She might have gotten out and killed somebody."

In an odd way, the bars looked more fierce than the cat had. What, I wondered, did they represent? Had the cat been symbolic of the frightening world around her and the suddenly applied bars an effort at safety? Or was the cat representative of her own internal aggressive feelings and the bars her struggle to keep them in?

"Did you mean to put those bars on when you started?" I asked.

Jadie burst unexpectedly into tears. "It's ruined," she wailed and reached to tear it from the easel.

"Hey ho, don't do that. It's still good." I caught her hand.

"It's *ruined.* I wanted just the tiger! I didn't mean to do that and now it's ruined."

"No, it's not. The tiger's still there, underneath. We'll get rid of the bars." Reaching forward, I scraped much of the orange paint of one bar off with my finger. "We'll need to let it dry some. If we try to do too much now, while it's wet, it'll just smear; but when it's dry, I'll show you how we can take the other colors and go right over that orange. We'll just paint the bars out."

Jadie calmed slightly.

"If you want a tiger, we can make it a tiger again. We're in charge here, not the paint."

"It's not a tiger, really," she murmured softly. "It's Jenny."

I hugged her gently against me.

"It's Jenny's ghost. She's a tiger ghost. When she was alive, she looked like a cat on the outside, but really, she was a tiger. Most people didn't know that, but I did. I could see in her and I could see she was strong. And so, when she died and became a ghost, it was a tiger ghost."

"I see."

Jadie remained cuddled against me. "That's the real Jenny. Because, see, your body don't count. It dies. Don't matter what happens to it, 'cause in the end, it falls off your bones, but the ghost part of you stays alive. The only time you're real's when you're a ghost."

When Thursday arrived, Philip came roaring in, full of excitement. His natural mother, now living in Chicago, had sent him a little plastic ornament, the kind with a scene inside a water-filled dome casing, which, when shaken, produced falling snow. Although we were still a week from Halloween, it contained a small ill-painted Christmas scene of Santa Claus being pulled in his sleigh by two reindeer.

Philip was over the moon with this treasure. Again and again, he enthusiastically shook it to see the snow fall and then pushed it within inches of my eyes for me to see.

"S-now," I said with deliberate emphasis. I caught hold of his hand that held the ornament and turned it near his own face. "You say it. Lips like this. S-now."

"Ng-gow," Philip intoned, then tore away to shove the ornament into the other children's faces for their admiration.

"I got one of them at home," Jeremiah said, when he saw it. "Here, gimme it, Phil."

Philip wouldn't let go, and this resulted in both boys falling to the ground, limbs flailing.

"Hey, you two, cut it out," I cried, leaping to the rescue of the ornament before it broke in the mêlée. "Jeremiah, stop it."

Reluctantly, Jeremiah pulled himself away from Philip, giving Philip one last kick as he rose.

"Selfish booger. You don't half know how to be a pig, you boog. I wasn't going to hurt your crappy thing anyway."

"You wait to be given something that belongs to someone else," I replied. "You don't snatch. And you certainly don't attack. Clear?"

"Well, mine's better than his anyway," Jeremiah muttered. "Mine's from Disneyland, and it's got a castle in it. Mine don't come from no nigger dime-store and gots a stupid baby picture inside it like that one does."

"Time for morning discussion," I said, physically turning Jeremiah in an effort to reorient him. "You go get the discussion box."

"Baby Santa Claus," Jeremiah continued muttering. "Hey, you boog, that's just right for you. Santy Claus. Bet you still believe in goody-goody Santy Claus coming down your fucking chimney. Don't you, little boog, little piss-in-your-pants boogy baby."

"Jeremiah."

Philip, feeling safe in my presence, wasn't going to miss this opportunity to lord it over Jeremiah. Holding up the ornament to his eyes, he waltzed over toward Jeremiah's place with exaggerated movements, which, of course, had the desired effect. Jeremiah went red with rage and shot out of his seat. Philip darted behind me for protection.

"I think we've had quite enough of your little item here, Phil," and I took it from his hands. "Everyone's seen it and admired it, and now we need to get on with school."

"Ng-oh!" Philip cried in dismay. "Mh-ine."

"Yes, it's yours, but for now I'm going to set it up here on top of the work cabinet. You may have it back when it's time to go home, but for now it's safer here."

Philip howled indignantly for a few moments but gave in when he realized he stood no chance of getting it back. He then snuffled his way over to join us for morning discussion.

At going-home time, however, Philip's ornament was nowhere to be found. When the bell rang, I reached up to get it for him and found nothing there but empty space. Pulling a chair over, I climbed up to see, but the top of the work cabinet was bare.

Philip was inconsolable. "Mh-ine! Mh-ine!" he wailed, dancing first around the base of the cabinet and then around me, his hands upstretched.

I looked everywhere, trying to sound jolly as I did so, but it was becoming obvious that this was no accidental disappearance. Jeremiah was the likely culprit, and I felt like braining him at just that moment, but as I had no hard evidence, I knew I wasn't justified in accusing him. To make matters worse, the buses had already arrived, and I couldn't hold any kind of interrogation, so I apologized profusely to Philip, promising to turn the room on end after he'd left, and said we'd take the matter up in the morning. After that, Philip, still sobbing, was bundled onto the bus.

Once the children were gone, I did make a full-scale search. I pulled out the cabinet to see behind it. I got down on all fours to peer under. Taking the broom, I swept the crevices around the bookshelves and behind the radiator. Nothing turned up, other than two rubber bands, a scrap of paper, and half a dozen dust bunnies. Heart sinking at the realization that it must have been stolen, I pushed the furniture back into place. Morosely, I headed down to the teachers' lounge for a bit of cheering up before doing my lesson plans.

I stayed in the lounge much longer than I'd intended to, which was the primary reason for seldom going down there after school. It was too easy to sink gratefully into a comfortable chair and have an umpteenth cup of coffee, and once I'd succumbed, it was too hard to pull myself out again and get back to work. Consequently, I knew, as I went back to my room, that I hadn't left myself enough time to do my plans here and would have to take them home with me, something I loathed, as then I would have no respite from school.

Going down the hallway to my room, I noticed the door between the hall and cloakroom was closed, which it hadn't been when I'd left. Pausing outside it, I listened. The soft, undulating murmur of Jadie's voice filtered through the door "… and then she got into the sleigh and it went way, way up in the sky. 'We're flying!' cried Tashee. 'Are you going to fight them with me?' 'Yes,' said Tashee. 'Me and Jadie and Amber are going to do it.' And so they ran and got in the sleigh. And it was snowing. Snowing hard. Snowing, snowing, snowing. And they flew up. Up, up …"

Going into the classroom, I slammed the door noisily behind me to make my presence known. The door between the cloakroom and the classroom was also closed. Crossing the room, I paused outside. "Jadie?"

No response.

I tried the doorknob, but it was locked. "Jadie, could you let me in, please?"

No response.

"Unlock this door, please." Teacher's voice.

No sound, no movement, nothing from beyond the door.

"This is going to have to stop happening, or I simply can't let you use that room. Now, I'm going to count to three, and then I want that door opened. Hear me? Here I go. One …"

A soft shuffling and I could hear her approach the door. It still didn't open.

"Two …"

The key turned in the lock and the door slowly opened.

"Now, may I please have Philip's ornament?" I asked matter-of-factly and held out my hand.

"I don't got it."

"If you give it to me now, we can put it back on the cabinet and the boys won't need to be any the wiser about it."

"I *don't* got it."

Dismayed, I regarded her.

"How come you don't believe me? You said you would, but you never do. You're like everyone else."

Putting my hand on her shoulder, I turned her around and propelled her back into the cloakroom. Closing the door behind me, I turned the key in the lock. "Well, if you don't have it, then you won't mind if I look," I said and reached for her coat pockets.

"Stop it. Don't." She broke my grasp. Darting around me, she ran smack into the unyielding door. I caught her again, and it only took a moment to feel the ornament inside her pocket. Even then, however, Jadie refused to relinquish it. Shouting passionately at me, she pulled herself out of my grasp and ran for the door, where the key remained in the lock.

Sprinting after her, I caught her arm. Jadie whirled around sharply in an effort to break my hold again, which she managed to do; however, the violence of the motion also knocked the ornament from her pocket. It fell out onto the linoleum floor, bounced, and then shattered. Plastic shards flew, water splashed out across the floor.

Both Jadie and I froze a moment, the horror of what had happened too intense. "Oh dear," I said at last, lacking any other words.

Jadie burst into sobs. Falling down to her knees, she began to collect the bits, crushing them to her chest.

"Here, let me help you," I said and knelt beside her.

"No!" she screamed and gave my shoulder a mighty push. "No. *You* did it. It happened because of you."

"I'm sorry. Of course I didn't want it to break."

"It's your *fault*. You made me break it. You're awful. You're horrible. I want to kill you."

I rocked back on my heels.

"I want you *dead!*"

"I can see I've made you very angry," I said. "You feel like killing me."

"*Yes!*" she shrieked in rage, leaping back, the shards of the ornament clutched against her.

"That's all right. Your feelings aren't actions. That's why it's all right to have them, even to say them, because feelings alone don't make things happen. You can stand up straight and let them out. Feelings and wishes don't kill."

Jadie paused in her tirade, a startled expression on her face, and then she looked down at her body, perfectly erect. A moment later, she burst into angry tears again.

Fury overtook her. With a strength of emotion I'd never witnessed in her before, she screamed and ran back and forth from one end of the room to the other, growing more frenetic with each lap. Coming to the doors, she'd pound futilely against them, turn and run to the other.

Certainly I had not intended to create this degree of trauma and was more than a little frightened by the fact that I had. My first impulse was to turn the key, open the door, and let her go, as if she were a frenzied butterfly caught against a window. In seeing the depth of the emotion, however, I realized I ought to finish what I had started, so I waited for her to wear herself out.

At last Jadie crumpled to the floor beside the door that led into the hallway. The broken ornament had remained in her hand throughout all of this, and now she clutched it once again to her chest, bending over it protectively, her long hair falling forward to curtain her face off from me. Like that she sat and wept heavily for several minutes. Then weariness overtook her. The sobs ceased. Lifting her head slightly, she wiped her nose and mouth with the sleeve of her coat.

"I think maybe that did you good," I said quietly. "I think you needed to get some of that out of you."

Jadie looked at me.

"Come over here and sit with me," I said and patted the bench beside me.

She hesitated, then finally rose and approached me.

Retrieving the box of tissues from my desk, I took a handful out and reached forward to dry Jadie's eyes. Jadie watched my face.

"Tashee's right," she murmured.

"About what?"

"You are stronger. You must be God."

"You want me to be God, don't you?"

Slowly opening her hands, she looked down at the shattered remains of Philip's ornament. "Yes, I do," she said softly.

"Why is that?"

"'Cause then what they say wouldn't be true."

"What who says?"

"Them. What they say."

I wanted to probe further but felt perhaps our newly won equilibrium was still too fragile.

"Sometimes I want to die, like Tashee done. I think that must be better. Then, other times ..." She fell silent. Fingering through the remains of the ornament, she picked out the cheap little plastic Santa in his sleigh. "Other times, I don't want to die. I just want it to stop. I want me and Amber to ... I don't know. I just want us ..." She fell silent.

Gazing at the Santa, she sighed. "They say hurting's good. You get stronger, when you hurt. They make you strong, so you can kill people. If you don't like someone, they teach you how to make that person die."

"Oh."

"But you didn't die."

"No," I said. "You were angry with me, that's all. Anger is a feeling. Feelings don't kill."

"That's not what Miss Ellie says. She says if I want to make you die, I can."

"No, I won't die."

"That's because you're God, aren't you?" Jadie asked, looking up.

"No. That's because Miss Ellie is wrong."

Chapter Sixteen

To say I went home from work that night unhappy and confused would be to greatly understate the feelings Jadie was beginning to generate in me. I could see only three possible explanations for her behavior. One, she was a deeply disturbed child, her internal world made up of a terrifying mix of hallucinations and fragmented, schizophrenic thought. Two, she had suffered some sort of traumatic event—perhaps abuse or separation or something like that—and had compensated by creating this elaborate fantasy world that protected her from facing the real event. Or three, she was a sane child, caught up in some inconceivably wicked web of murder and torture with no one believing what she said. I had more or less eliminated any likelihood that Jadie's problems were physically based, in that she showed none of the indicators I had come to associate with aphasia or other forms of brain damage, but even here I was forced to keep an open mind.

At home that evening, I found myself restless and distracted, shuffling through my mail, opening letters and only half reading them, pushing the bills into a pile unopened. I wasn't really hungry and nothing in the fridge took my fancy, so I settled for a quick sandwich, which I decided to eat in front of television. The only thing watchable at that time of day was a rerun of "I Love Lucy." Cozily reminiscent of my fifties childhood, it gave me thirty minutes' suspended animation before Jadie returned to haunt me.

Unable to concentrate on the TV any longer, I got up and shifted restlessly around the apartment, straightening things up, doing my dishes from breakfast, and pushing papers around on my desk in the bedroom.

At the bottom of a stack of books beside the desk was the case containing the old reel-to-reel videotape with Jadie on it from the previous winter. I hadn't looked at it since I'd shown it to Jules in the summer, but now I felt an overwhelming urge to see it again, to study Jadie's ghostly figure wavering before the camera, to hear her eerie, high-pitched whispers. Would they have more meaning to me now? Would I understand things I hadn't understood then? Holding the tape case in my hands, I realized, as I looked at it, that my intense restlessness on this particular evening was not so much the result of being unable to leave my concerns about Jadie at work as of not being able to pursue the matter in a satisfying manner. If I was honest, I didn't want to stop thinking about her. My frustration lay in not understanding her.

Sitting there alone in the bedroom of my attic apartment, I was suddenly stricken with yearning for the professional chumminess of the clinic. I ached for the camaraderie of Jules, Jeff, Dr. Rosenthal, and all the others, for the intellectual acrobatics that went on each day around the coffee pot. How had I ever let myself get into this state of isolation?

I toyed with the idea of calling Jules. He was the one I really wanted to thrash this out with. A broad-minded, creative thinker, he was always able to come up with quirky ideas that, even when shy of the mark, were stimulating and kept me thinking. We had worked well together, our thoughts often leap-frogging over each other in rapid succession to produce seemingly disjointed conversations and ideas by the bucketful. But would he remember this case well enough? Would he mind my phoning him up out of the blue? Would he be free? Would it be the same over the telephone anyway?

No. What I wanted was to talk *with* someone, someone I could sit face to face with, someone who knew Jadie, too. This didn't leave many alternatives.

There were dozens of Petersons in the phonebook. Narrowing the likely ones down to three, I tried to call Arkie. Two were wrong numbers. The third had no reply. In desperation, I rang Lucy.

"Yeah, Luce, it's me. How're you doing? Yes, just wondering ... Is Ben home? He's not? Oh, good. Well, I don't mean *good*, but you know what I mean. Just wondering, well ... you wouldn't want to go down to the bowling alley for a bit, would you? ... Yes, I know it's late ... and sort of spur of the moment, but just a couple of games? I need some exercise. And I thought I could bounce a few things off you about school. If you don't mind, that is. Okay? Want to meet me there?"

Lucy was in jeans and had her short hair pulled back into a squat little ponytail. It was the most informal attire I'd ever seen her in, and she looked charming in a farm-girl sort of way.

"Gosh, this *is* good," Lucy said in a half whisper, as we picked up our bowling shoes. "I feel really spontaneous. Ben's going to be so surprised when he finds out. He thinks I never do anything except sit at home and do my lesson plans. Mostly, I don't. Except when I go over to my mom's."

I grinned at her.

We played not two games but six and were still there at 10:30, when they signaled closing time.

"You want to get a Coke?" I asked, as we put the balls away. Attached to the bowling alley was a small bar, which stayed open later. I tipped my head in that direction.

"Yeah, okay," Lucy said brightly. "But golly, I'm going to be tired tomorrow. Aren't you? Have you got your lesson plans done already?"

She found us a small table, and I went up to the bar to get the soft drinks.

"I suppose you did all your plans before you left school," Lucy said when I returned. "You're so well organized. I keep meaning to, but then I get down in the lounge and somebody gets talking ..." Then she shrugged. "But that's okay, I suppose, because the plans give me something to do in the evenings when Ben's not there."

She glanced over. "This has really been fun. I wasn't going to come when you first asked me. I haven't washed my hair and I look awful, but then I thought, well, what the heck? I'm going to be really wild for once. I'm just going to go out and have *fun.* And you know what? It really has been fun. Thanks for asking me."

Touched by her pleasure, I smiled.

"Do you do this kind of stuff all the time?" she asked. "I'll bet you're used to it, coming from the city and all that. I bet you went out a lot up there."

Still smiling, I shook my head. "Not really. I'm not much the going-out type. I just wanted a change of scenery tonight. Things are starting to get on top of me at work, and I find I'm bringing problems home with me."

"You're having problems?" she asked, a fleeting look of alarm crossing her face.

Immediately, I realized she was thinking of June Harriman and I rushed to reassure her I hadn't meant personal problems. "It's Jadie. I'm in a real mess with Jadie." From there, I went on to explain what had been going on over the previous months. Lucy knew a lot of it already, such as the sexual incidents, simply because, being next door, she was the one who had often rescued me in moments of chaos; but now, I also talked about my time after school with Jadie, when she often stood upright, often screamed and shouted. I told of Tashee, Jenny, Miss Ellie, and the others. I mentioned ghosts and spiders. Once I got started, it all just tumbled out.

When I finally took a breath, Lucy lowered her head and peered into her glass. Taking her straw, she prodded the crushed ice that remained. "Gosh," she murmured. "Gosh."

"The thing is, I can't figure out what's going on with her. That's what's so upsetting to me. I mean, what if it's true? What if I'm sitting here, doing nothing because I think she's imagining it, and these horrible, unbelievable, *unthinkable* things are happening to her?"

"Oh, they just couldn't be," Lucy replied. "It'd be murder you're talking about, otherwise."

"Yeah, I know. That's what I keep thinking, but then ... she's so consistent in what she says ... but then it's so farfetched. I keep trying to conjure up what kind of situation could produce this ..."

"But it *couldn't* be real," Lucy replied.

"It'd have to be a group of some kind. A porn ring, maybe. Pedophiliacs?"

"Torey," Lucy said, her voice almost plaintive.

I looked over.

"This is Pecking, for Pete's sake. It's not like up in the city. Jeepers, I don't think that kind of junk even goes on up there. This is California-style stuff you're talking about. Or maybe like what goes on in New York or Amsterdam or one of those other foreign places, where they let people get away with this kind of thing. But for God's sake, Torey, this is my home town you're talking about."

"I'm not saying it is happening. I'm just speculating."

"I know that kind of thing does go on. I'm not that naive, but I just don't think it could happen here. This is a close-knit community. Everyone knows everyone—and everyone's business. I mean, what would the neighbors think?"

A pause came into the conversation. Lucy, growing pensive, stirred the ice in her glass again, then delicately lifted some out with her straw and put it into her mouth. A country-western ballad on the jukebox momentarily intruded on my thoughts, distracting me with its soft, lonely sound.

"You know what I wonder," Lucy said. "I wonder if Jadie could be someone like Sybil. You know, from that book."

"The one with multiple personalities?"

"Yeah. Maybe Jadie's divided herself up into all these different kinds of people. Maybe one part of her's living kind of a 'Dallas' lifestyle and she's made up a fantasy world with those characters. Like maybe all the badness and stuff that she feels inside her she makes over, as if it belonged to Miss Ellie and J.R. and them. The characters on 'Dallas' are no saints, so maybe she's just used them to personify her own negative side. And Tashee ... maybe Tashee's the good, pure part of her, the bit she feels she has to save."

A lot of what Lucy said made reasonably good sense. It was easy to imagine parts of one's psyche being represented by TV characters, particularly in light of the pervasiveness of television in current culture, and there was little doubt in my mind that Tashee, real or unreal, had come to symbolize all that was good in Jadie's eyes. I knew also that the phenomenon of multiple personality was often closely associated with sexual abuse, which would account for Jadie's precocious sexual behavior, as well as provide the traumatic core for such a serious disintegration of self. Some things still troubled me, however. Why, for instance, did the characters she'd chosen to represent her other selves not quite jibe with their personalities on TV? Wouldn't Miss Ellie have been more likely to come out as sweet, caring, and maternal, while J.R. or one of the other less upstanding citizens of "Dallas" have been assigned the evil role? Unless, of course, Jadie's abuser was her mother ... Then again, all her sexual behavior had been directed toward the male anatomy.

The other problem I had with Lucy's theory was the simple fact that multiple personality, particularly in children Jadie's age, is a rare phenomenon indeed. I'd never come across it. In fact, while we all knew about it, no one at the clinic had ever seen an adult with the problem, much less a child. It would be pretty incredible to find such a thing under our own noses. Then, as I sat there with Lucy, my mind going round and round and round, what occurred to me was that whatever Jadie's circumstances, they *were* bizarre, and incredulity was probably playing a major part in preventing us from finding an answer.

The following day, Jadie did not turn up for school. This disconcerted me, given the nature of our time together the previous afternoon. Like most of my special education children, Jadie's attendance record had always been excellent, and, while she was as susceptible to whatever was going around as the rest, there hadn't been much making the rounds. No one even had a cold.

I was further worried because we had reached the last full week in October and Amber's dreaded sixth birthday would be on Sunday. Jadie hadn't mentioned it in the last few days, but I'd fully expected to have the chance to discuss the matter more thoroughly with her and perhaps provide some additional reassurance.

These concerns made me restless company during the morning. When the boys were all occupied, I found myself drawn to the window, where I could see across the playground to her house on the other side of the street. Nothing there seemed out of the ordinary. The blinds were up, the curtains back. But I kept checking anyway. At recess I went down to the kindergarten to see if Amber was there, and indeed she was, playing Doggie Get the Bone with the other kindergarteners, her fair hair flying as she ran, her face laughing and merry. Yet, I still couldn't shake the sense of unease, so at lunchtime, I slipped out of the school.

Almost as soon as I rang the doorbell, Mrs. Ekdahl answered it. She held Sapphire in her arms and looked decidedly surprised to see me. Sapphire, a podgy, round-headed toddler with a very dirty face, whined and struggled to get down.

"She's got a stomachache," Mrs. Ekdahl replied, when I'd explained why I was there. "She puked in her bed last night, so I didn't think I should send her to school."

"No, probably best not to," I agreed. "Do you suppose I could say hi to her?"

The blind in Jadie's room was pulled against the late October sunshine, leaving the room in bright dimness. Jadie was sitting up in bed with a stack of Donald Duck comics next to her.

"Hello," I said.

Surprised, Jadie looked at me.

"Your mom says you're not feeling well."

She didn't speak.

Sitting down on the edge of the bed, I smiled. "Are you feeling a bit better now?"

Her behavior was guarded, as if I were a stranger. Or perhaps simply an intruder.

"I'm sorry you're not in class. We're missing you. This afternoon we're going into Mrs. McLaren's class to make nut cups for the Halloween party next week. I'm sorry you won't be there to help us."

Jadie still did not speak.

"Shall I make one for you? To have at the party?"

Jadie shifted her shoulders slightly, although not sufficiently to produce a shrug.

Flustered by her stark silence, I glanced around the room. It was a typical little girl's bedroom, with all the usual clutter of childhood. Jadie sat amidst tissues and discarded coloring books, crayons rolling around over the bedclothes. Briefly, I was transported back to my own childhood and the days off school with minor illnesses.

Jadie was watching me intently.

"I've brought you something," I said at last. Bending down, I opened a paper carrier bag and took out one of the Sasha dolls. It wasn't the dark-haired one that Jadie had imbued with Tashee's qualities, but rather the one with long blond hair. "I thought maybe you'd like some company. I can't give her to you, because she's part of the set, but I thought that while you need her, you could keep her here at home with you, and then you can bring her back to school when things are better."

Wordlessly, Jadie took the doll and pressed it close into the crook of her arm.

"The lunch hour is nearly up and I need to get back soon, but I thought this doll ... well, if things get hard, you can look at her and know I'm thinking of you."

She continued to regard the doll.

I rose from the bed. "I do need to go now. I hope you get to feeling better."

No answer.

"Okay?"

Gently lifting her hand, she caressed the doll's hair away from its face before looking up at me. Very, very slightly, she smiled.

Jadie's mother was just outside the bedroom door when I came out. She was so close, in fact, that I literally bumped into her. "Oh, I'm sorry," she said. "I was bringing Jadie some clean sheets. She gets herself in such a mess when she's in bed like this."

I nodded. "Thanks for letting me see her."

"I seen that doll," Mrs. Ekdahl said and smiled. "That was real sweet of you to do. I can see why she likes you so much, 'cause you do do the nicest things for her. Her and Amber are always playing dolls together, so that's going to make her real happy."

"I'm glad," I said.

"It looks just like you, that doll. Got blond hair, just like you," Mrs. Ekdahl said. "Jadie's going to like that. Going to make her feel she isn't missing you so much, and Jadie always was one for having her dolls look like people."

On Monday, Jadie was back and quite her usual self. She had the blond-haired doll with her and she kept it with her, laying it on the table beside her as she did her morning work.

"Look what girlie-wurlie's got," Jeremiah said.

"Yes, I know."

"She stoled it. I seen her, 'cause she had it down on the playground before school. And it's one of them dolls you brung in."

"No, she didn't steal it. I've lent it to her for the time being."

"You did?" Jeremiah cried in an injured tone. "You never lent me nothing."

"You want a doll, too?"

"No, I mean nothing of yours from here in the classroom. You never let me take nothing home."

"This was a special circumstance, Jeremiah. I lent it to Jadie for a special reason, and when I feel you have a special circumstance, then I'll lend you something, too."

Jeremiah made a derisive noise. "What would I want fucking school stuff for anyways?"

At the end of the day, I took the boys down to their rides. When I arrived back upstairs, I found Jadie still hadn't departed. She was in the cloakroom, her boots on, her coat down from the hook and lying on the bench. The box containing the other Sasha dolls had been pulled out, and she was involved in silent play with the dark-haired doll, holding it upside down against the wall. When I appeared in the doorway, Jadie started and whipped the doll down.

"You particularly like that doll, don't you?" I said.

She nodded. "But I like the one you gave me, too. I like her best, because I pretend that's you."

I smiled and came around to stand beside her. "This one looks more like Tashee, doesn't she?"

Jadie looked up sharply.

"Shall we close the doors?" Without waiting for a response, I went and did it. "So, how was your weekend?" I asked. "How was Amber's birthday?"

Jadie picked up the dark-haired doll again.

"Did she have a party?" I asked.

"No."

"What about within the family? Did you do anything special for her at home?"

"Yeah. My mom made a cake. It was yellow and it had candles on it." A pause, and Jadie wrinkled her nose. "You know what stupid thing Amber wanted on her cake? Sugar daffodils. *Daffodils.* And this is October, even. But my mom said that was okay for her to want, 'cause it was her birthday."

"Did she get presents?"

"Yeah."

"What kind?"

"My mom and dad gave her some clothes, and she got a My Little Pony, too. And my grandma gave her a tapestry kit, only she's not really big enough to do it. I gave her a Mars bar, but Sapphire didn't give her anything, 'cause she's too little to have an allowance."

"So, Amber turned six on Sunday. She had a cake and presents. Did anything else happen?"

Jadie shook her head.

"She didn't die, did she?"

Jadie turned the dark-haired doll upside down and watched its long hair fall. She cocked her head a little to see the doll's face better.

"Amber's all right," I said quietly. "She's turned six and she's fine."

"No," Jadie replied and there was a brittle edge to her voice.

"She is. I saw her myself this morning down in Mrs. Havers's class."

"*No.* They'll still come. It doesn't have to be on her birthday. It's because she's six now. That's the number they kill you at. That's the number Miss Ellie says is for dying. They're gonna do just like they done with Tashee. I know they will."

"Who?"

"*Them.* I keep telling you. Them. Miss Ellie and Bobby and them."

"But who are they? Where do they come from? How do you get to be with them? Do they take you? Do they come to your house? Are your mom and dad there?"

Jadie looked up, bewildered.

"Do you know?" I asked.

"Usually, I'm asleep in my bed. Miss Ellie comes in and wakes me up. She brings me Coke to drink. For both me and Amber. Sometimes we go out in the living room. Sometimes we go other places."

"Like where?"

Jadie paused, a confused expression on her face. "I don't know where."

"How do you mean?"

"Well, Miss Ellie puts a scarf over our faces. It's at night anyway. I can't see. But she takes us to this other place and when we get there, we drink more Coke, and sometimes Tashee comes."

"I thought Tashee was dead."

"She is, but then she gets alive again, because Miss Ellie puts her bones back together."

"And your parents? Where are your parents when all this goes on?"

"Asleep?" she asked, uncertainly. "I think maybe they're in their bedroom asleep. That's why we always got to be real quiet when Miss Ellie and them come, 'cause I don't think she wants to wake my mom and dad."

"But why don't you wake them? If you don't like all this, why don't you just scream when Miss Ellie comes, and that'd wake everybody up."

"Oh, I couldn't. Miss Ellie'd make them die. She might make me die." Jadie paused. "You can't never do anything Miss Ellie don't want you to. Not ever. 'Cause if Miss Ellie's spiders ever seen you were doing that, nobody'd be left alive."

Chapter Seventeen

One of the nicest aspects of working in the Pecking school was everyone's general acceptance of my children. This was the first place I'd worked where I felt my special education class was genuinely integrated into the life of the regular school. We were included in all the activities and always given genuine and meaningful ways to participate, not simply token ones. Indeed, it was usually taken for granted that we would pull our weight, which was probably the greatest compliment of all, because it made us no longer "special." As a consequence, our class was given its own part to play in the traditional Halloween activities at the school, which included a costume parade through the halls, followed by an afternoon-long party in the school gym. Each classroom was making its own contributions toward the decorations and party food. The sixth-graders, for instance, had carved pumpkins and were making black cat cupcakes. The fifth-graders designed the paper table-cloths and made spider-web pizzas. My class offered up our finally finished tissue paper pumpkin as a wall decoration and were assigned the job of making enough popcorn balls for the whole school.

The morning of the party, which was a Thursday, didn't dawn quite as I had expected. For a start, Brucie was absent, which meant his mother didn't bring in the popcorn popper that she'd promised. So there I was with six pounds of popcorn to be popped and no way to do it. Second, Jeremiah didn't arrive.

"Ng-ah-ah!" Philip cried excitedly when he came into the room.

"I'm sorry," I said, "could you try that again?"

"Ng-ah-AH!" and he gestured wildly. Philip was now receiving intensive speech therapy and being taught sign language in an effort to help him communicate more successfully. Unfortunately, he hadn't quite got the idea and assumed any gestures would work. His hands and arms flailed frantically.

Just then, Mr. Tinbergen appeared in the doorway. "They've put Jeremiah off the bus. He was causing his usual ruckus—you know how Jeremiah gets—and Fred said he'd just had enough. He turned the bus around, took him home, and dumped him off."

"Oh jeez," I muttered. "And today, of all days."

Jeremiah had long-standing problems coping with the half-hour bus ride to school. In years gone by, his excessive behavior had often been dealt with by returning him home, and this response had been moderately successful. I, however, had vetoed it when I'd come, as it seemed self-defeating to me. If anyone needed the structure and stability of the classroom, it was Jeremiah. So we'd been using a strict reinforcement system, whereby he earned tokens for behaving well and lost them for troublesome behavior. On the other hand, I could sympathize with Fred, the bus driver, who commented on occasion that if he actually took a token away every time Jeremiah misbehaved, Jeremiah's daily token balance would average about minus twenty-seven.

The class seemed empty with just Jadie, Reuben, and Philip, but we didn't have much choice but to get on with things, so I took them down to the teachers' lounge with me, where we spent the first ninety minutes of the day making batch after batch of popcorn in a small pot on a hot plate. At recess, I hopped in my car to run out and get Jeremiah.

He knew I was coming, because Mr. Tinbergen had phoned earlier; so there he was, sitting cross-legged in the dust at the top of the track that led back to his house.

"Fucking bus driver," he said to me as he got into the car. "Fucking bastard. You know why he hates me? 'Cause I'm an Indian kid. 'Cause I got brown skin and he's got white skin. That's why he don't take no care about my feelings."

"Do you really think that?" I asked.

"Look, what d'you expect? I'm poor. I don't got nothing good, like you got. My folks don't got no

Lincoln Continental, like this."

"It's a Fiat, Jeremiah, not a Lincoln Continental."

"Well, it *looks* like a Continental. Can't blame me for that. I need glasses. My folks so poor they don't even get my eyes checked."

The temptation was to mention that he was blaming everyone for his behavior but the culprit, but I didn't. He knew. I knew. He knew I knew. Some things are best left unsaid.

Then worse happened. Just as we got inside the classroom, Jeremiah gave a wild scream and fell to the floor, as if in a faint. "Oh *no!*" he wailed. "I forgot my costume!" And he then did something I'd never seen him do before. He burst into tears.

I think I'd seldom felt so bad for a kid. Helping him off the floor, I walked him over to the table.

"I was gonna win," he sobbed. "I was gonna be best." I tried to comfort him, but he was inconsolable.

Jadie, sitting across the table from us, continued molding her popcorn balls for several moments and said nothing. Then, slowly, she leaned forward. "I can get him a costume," she said, her voice soft.

I looked over.

"My aunt came last week from Lower Falls and she brung me and Amber costumes to go trick-or-treating in. But Jeremiah can have mine, if he wants. I'll give it to him."

Jeremiah's face brightened instantly. "Hey, what kind of costume is it? Is it good?"

"But what about you?" I asked. "Will you still have something to wear this afternoon?

She shrugged.

"Hey, man, if this girl wants to let me wear her costume, don't go making her feel like shit for it," Jeremiah said. He swiped roughly at his still-wet cheeks. "Man, this girl wants to be a *friend.*"

"But what about you, Jadie?" I asked again.

"There's no rule says you gotta wear a costume to the party," Jadie replied.

"There is to go trick-or-treating, man," Jeremiah said. "You can't just go as a kid. They wouldn't give you no candy."

Jadie shrugged. "That's all right. I don't want to go. Neither me or Amber goes. That's because Amber don't like to go out after dark. She gets scared. She even has to sleep with the big light on in her bedroom. So, you see, we just don't like that kind of stuff. Besides, candy rots your teeth."

We spent the rest of the morning desperately trying to finish two hundred popcorn balls. About 11:30, I allowed Jadie to run home to get the costume for Jeremiah, and she returned with what I assume was supposed to turn the wearer into a leopard. Hard to know, though. The costume consisted of what appeared to be black-and-yellow-spotted long johns and a mask that could have been anything from a freckled dog to a bear with measles.

Jeremiah had to try it on immediately and to his dismay found it was at least two sizes too big and, moreover, tailless. To remedy the fit, I took large rubber bands and fastened up the arms and legs, then stuffed pillows from the reading area down his front.

"Hey!" he cried with delight. "Looks like I just ate somebody, huh? Grrrarrgh!" And he leaped up on Philip's back, but the pillows gave him a surprise, bouncing him right back off again. To distract him, I suggested he search through the scrap box to find something to make a tail.

The afternoon quickly fell victim to Halloween mania as shrieking, overexcited scarecrows, hobos, and witches tore up and down the school corridors. My crowd were as bad as the rest. Having buttoned Philip into his bunny costume, buckled Reuben's pirate's belt, and restuffed Jeremiah's stomach, I turned them all loose to run and scream with the others. The only exception to all this excitement was Jadie, who had taken the big tub of crayons and a coloring book and was sitting at my desk in the cloakroom, coloring a picture of horses in a field.

"Are you sure you don't want to join us?" I asked, as I prepared to capture the boys and get them in line for the parade.

"I'm sure," Jadie said without looking up.

"You don't have to go in the parade, you know. You could just stand in the classroom door with me and watch."

"No."

So I left her to her coloring.

The corridors of the school reverberated with undiluted joy as the children marched up and down, each class joining as the parade wended by their room. Then, onward to the gym.

Jeremiah won his prize. In fact, all three boys won something, but Philip and Reuben received only badges saying "Join He-Man. Fight Cavities," which they proudly stuck to their costumes. Jeremiah got not only a badge but also an eraser in the shape of a jack-o'-lantern.

"Lookit *this!*" he cried. "I got the best tail prize! I got the prize for the best tail in the *whole* school. He didn't even know I made it myself. He probably thought it was store-bought. It was *that* good."

Raising my head to see across the bobble of heads in the gym, I caught Mr. Tinbergen's eye. I smiled. He winked.

Once the boys were involved in party games, I asked Lucy to keep an eye on them for a bit and slipped back to the classroom. Jadie was still at my desk, still coloring.

"They've started to play games. Don't you want to come down?"

"No," she said quietly, most of her attention still on the coloring.

"What's the matter? What don't you like about this?"

"Nothing's the matter. I just don't like it, that's all."

"But why? Usually you like parties. You always enjoy the games we play on people's birthdays."

"I don't like Halloween."

"Is it the costumes? Do they frighten you?"

"I just don't like it."

Grateful to be out of the deafening noise of the gym for a moment, I sat down on the right-hand bench and leaned back against the wall. Fleetingly aware of what an exhausting day it had been and how it wasn't over yet, I sighed. That made Jadie look up. She didn't lift her head, only her eyes, but briefly our eyes met. Then she returned to her coloring.

Silence enveloped us. The joy in the gym was audible, but barely, just a pleasant bit of embroidery on the silence. After a long stretch of cold weather, it was warm and sunny outside, and this, combined with the school's ferocious central heating, made the small room warm and stuffy. I found myself unexpectedly sleepy.

"I could tell you how it happened," Jadie said, her tone conversational. She didn't look up.

Pulled back from the brink of closing my eyes, I glanced over.

"If you wanted me to, that is," she added.

I didn't know what she was referring to, but I nodded anyway. "Okay."

"See, it was Halloween that other year. When Tashee was six."

I nodded again.

"Me and her were both six. I'd been six in December and her birthday was in August. I knew it was important to be six. Miss Ellie kept saying that. She said it meant big things, 'cause me and Tashee were both six. She said everybody was going to be strong that year. She said we were going to get these wishes. Something about sixes and how you could make things come true. I didn't understand it exactly, but I thought it meant I might get a

Barbie house for Christmas. That's what I wanted, but my mom said it cost too much money. I thought 'cause we were getting lucky out of sixes, I was going to get a Barbie house."

Jadie paused. Her voice remained soft, her words flowing in a smooth, conversational way quite unlike her usual speech in the classroom. Even alone with me, there was usually much stopping and starting. Now she stopped, pensive, her eyes on the coloring book, as if assessing the picture she'd been working on.

"Then ... it must have been September, I guess ... I don't know really, 'cause I didn't know the months so good then, but ..." She paused again, her brow wrinkled, her expression inward, as if concentrating hard. "Tashee and me were laying on the big table. We had our little dolls, and Miss Ellie told J.R. to take them and put them on the table behind us. So he did, and then Miss Ellie and Pam and everybody came around and first they kissed the dolls and then they kissed either me or Tashee, but we couldn't see which dolls they were kissing, because the dolls were behind us. Tashee started crying, but I didn't, because I didn't know what was happening. Then J.R. took the candleholder and he hit Tashee's doll and its head broke. That's when I knew Tashee was going to die."

I wasn't quite sure how to react. Indeed, I wasn't even quite sure what she was telling me, because it didn't make complete sense to me.

"It could have been me," Jadie said pensively, and for the first time she looked up from her coloring book. "I could have died. I was six. But my doll didn't get smashed, so I stayed alive."

"And she did die?" I asked.

Jadie nodded. "Yeah, like I told you."

I sat, speechless. I felt paralyzed, my feelings numb and unreachable. Nothing in my experience, in my previous work, had equipped me for this.

"When Miss Ellie put the knife in and the blood came out, like I was telling you, she caught it in a cup. We had to drink it. See, that's where the power of the six was. It was warm. It was ... sort of oily tasting. Kind of like if you take a sip of salad oil or something. It sort of slipped on your tongue."

Chapter Eighteen

I'm not sure how I got through the rest of that day. Emotions never really came back to me. A dull, nauseous feeling was there instead, making my head muzzy and my throat tight. More than once I thought I was in real danger of vomiting.

The kids screaming in the gym were too much to take. I returned tense and irritable and wished they would stay away from me. They wouldn't, of course, and I got through the remainder of the party with my teeth gritted. Jadie, on the other hand, seemed absurdly calm and bantered cheerfully with Jeremiah when we came back to the room. Lucy saved me. Realizing I wasn't feeling well, she volunteered to take my children with hers when the going-home bell rang, and she did, seeing them all down to the playground, including Jadie.

After they left, I fell wearily onto one of the benches in the cloakroom. Covering my eyes momentarily with my hands, I rested there a moment, then lowered them. All around me was the quiet familiarity of the school, the sound of the clock, the smell of the floor polish, the distant din of children on the playground; yet it was as if I were in some alien place, unable to move, unsure of what to do next.

What *was* happening with Jadie? Was she being abused? Were her stories true? *Could* they be true? Had some real child been murdered and Jadie made to drink her blood? The instant that thought came to me, the conversation with Hugh in the summer flashed back into my mind. *Satanism.*

Satanism? My concrete knowledge of such things was restricted to newspaper articles of cattle mutilations and the Manson family murders. I'd never been particularly interested in such subject matter. There were enough ordinary evils in the world to joust with; I'd never been attracted to the thought of worse and more unassailable ones. More to the point, I don't think I could really believe in all that. I had no trouble in accepting that there were dangerously disturbed individuals capable of perpetrating unspeakable acts, and I had had enough contact with the fringes of society to accept that counterculture forms of religion, such as paganism and even devil worship, attracted a fair number of people, but I could not bring myself to believe there were large, wide-ranging networks of people regularly carrying out ritual murder and mayhem. These stories I'd always felt were mythic, the results of popular horror films and books and a few charismatic, headline-grabbing psychotics.

In terms of Jadie, I found it almost impossible to contemplate a connection with satanism. Even back when Hugh had first mentioned it, the idea had gone right out of my mind, simply because it seemed so farfetched. Now, alone after school, I touched the idea cautiously, like a tongue in a newly formed tooth socket, drawn to it, yet repulsed. Could Tashee have been a real child? How would Jadie have known about the taste of blood? What about the smashed dolls? Why would she make things like that up? How could she create such details, if she didn't have firsthand knowledge?

Then as soon as those questions raised themselves, I was assailed by doubt. These were the things horror movies were made of. Indeed, some things Jadie had spoken of, like Miss Ellie putting Tashee's bones back together and making her come alive again, could be extrapolated from the scenes of some quite popular and readily available horror films. Even the murder of a child and the drinking of its blood were pretty standard fare in some of the worse films. How would watching such movies affect an already disturbed child? Jadie had evidenced the year before that she was familiar with the operation of a video recorder. Did she have access to a collection of horror films, or worse, some of the pornographic ones? Was that why she had asked me if I had seen Miss Ellie killing Tashee on my TV, too?

Perhaps the worst part of all this speculation was the realization that whatever conclusion I came to, at this point I could do nothing. Horrific as it all sounded, I had no concrete evidence that anything was happening, and unless Jadie herself was willing to make accusations, I could not officially do anything. Much as I wanted to act, I knew that patience and alertness were all that was left open to me.

Friday found everyone tired and grumpy. Jeremiah had stayed up to all hours, doing God knows what, although how much of this was due to Halloween and how much to Jeremiah's usual lack of parental supervision was hard to say. Jadie, too, complained of having stayed up too late and was now subdued and hollow-eyed. Change in routine made Reuben restless and distractible, and Brucie was cross about having missed the party. Philip, victim of Halloween excesses, did not come to school at all.

One of our regular class activities was journal keeping. All the children, except for Brucie, who had little control over a pencil or crayon, had a journal, and every day a certain amount of time was given over to writing and/or illustrating. I encouraged them to record their feelings, then ups and downs, their hopes, wishes, and dreams, as well as daily events. I tried to keep it an open, safe place where the child could express anything—even a negative opinion of me and my teaching methods—without fear of retaliation. I, in turn, went through the journals nightly and left notes back to make it a form of useful communication.

Morning recess had been a trial that Friday. A pall of dank, dark, very Novemberish weather had descended on us in contrast to the bright day we'd had twenty-four hours earlier. It had been my turn at recess duty, so I'd stood out, shivering with the rest. Everybody seemed in a foul mood. Not only were my children prickly, but I pried apart two fifth-grade boys who were determinedly smashing each other's faces into the asphalt, and I mopped blood off a first-grader, who had been tripped by an older child. Jeremiah fought with everybody in sight and finally finished recess in Mr. Tinbergen's office. And some kid whose name I couldn't remember was sick under the swings.

Because of the unsettled nature of the day, I decided to allow the children to work on their journals immediately after morning recess instead of doing the activity planned. This was greeted with cheers from Jeremiah, who loathed the post-morning-recess period, because it was usually a time for serious academic work. Jadie and Reuben took their journals out with a little more decorum.

For the first fifteen minutes, I sat with Brucie, doing one-to-one work while the others were busy. Our goal of getting him to dress himself wasn't progressing too speedily, and after two months, he could just about manage his underpants. Thus, I spent a scintillating quarter hour repeatedly pulling Brucie's pants down for him to pull up again. His patience for this pastime exceeded mine, so when his interest finally began to wane, I gratefully turned him loose to scribble on a piece of newsprint with a crayon.

Coming over to Jadie, I pulled out the chair next to her and sat down. She hadn't written anything in the journal but was, instead, making a picture with felt-tip pens. The first figure, carefully drawn, was of a standing cat. Next was a bell-shaped figure with eyes, legs, and nothing else. The next figure was even less distinct, and as she progressed, she drew as if she'd been powered by clockwork and was slowly running down. Each figure grew smaller and less distinct.

"That looks interesting," I said.

"It's supposed to be my family," Jadie mumbled, her voice sounding weary, as if she weren't too pleased with the results.

"Ah, I see."

"That's Jenny," she said, pointing to the cat. "She ain't with us anymore, but that don't mean she ain't part of the family. She is, 'cause I still remember her. She was my best pet."

Jadie paused, laying the pen down and sitting back. "She had stripy fur. Did I tell you that before? Sort of gray-brownish with black stripes on it. I looked it up in a book at the library once, and it said you call those kinds of cats tabbies. And she had an orange nose and pink lips. That was my favorite part, her pink lips." Jadie picked up a pink pen to amend the picture.

I was anxious to discuss the human figures in the picture, but I managed to keep quiet while she lavished attention on the drawing of the cat. At last she laid the marker down. "And who's this?" I asked, pointing to the bell-shaped figure.

"That's me. And that's Amber. And that's Sapphire. And that's my mom and my dad," she said, pointing to each figure in turn. She paused and again touched the last two figures, which were nothing more than minute blobs on the paper. "I didn't do them so good, because I got sick of drawing. I don't really feel much like doing this today."

"Yes, I can tell."

Jadie didn't respond.

Leaning forward, I examined the picture more carefully. "What made you feel like drawing a picture of your family in your journal today?"

She, too, leaned forward to look at it, but she didn't answer.

"What I notice is that you and Jenny are the only two important ones in this picture. Everyone else gets smaller and smaller. Your parents are much smaller than you. Do you feel like you're the big one sometimes?"

Jadie shrugged. "I dunno." A pause. "I feel like I'm the one who's got to take care of everyone."

"Usually that's the mom and dad's job, isn't it?"

"Well, maybe they're not there. Maybe they're far away. Somewhere else. Then someone else in the family's got to do it."

"Is that what happens in your family sometimes?"

She frowned but didn't speak.

I examined the picture in more detail. "You know, the only one in this picture who has a mouth is the cat. Look, you haven't drawn a mouth on you or Amber or anyone else."

"That's 'cause everyone's ghosts there, that's why."

"Oh."

"Ghosts can't talk. They can talk to other ghosts and that's how come Jenny can understand me, but ghosts can't talk to people. People can't hear them, so they don't really need mouths."

"I see. You're saying there's no point to talking, because people don't hear you anyway."

She nodded. "That's right."

The following week started very quietly. Sated by their Halloween excitement, all five settled down and worked hard. There were few disruptions.

Jadie, like the others, seemed more settled. She hadn't been in after school since the Monday before Halloween, and we went the first four days of that week with no visits. Then, on Friday, while I was cleaning out the rabbit's cage, she turned up.

"Do you mind if I play with those dolls?" she asked from the classroom doorway.

"Sure, that's all right. I'm just about done here anyway. You go ahead, and then I'll be in shortly to do my plans."

Jadie had located the key in my desk drawer and locked the door into the hall by the time I came into the cloakroom. Shutting and locking the other one, she returned the key to my desk and then went to pull the box of dolls up onto the right-hand bench. I settled down to do my plans for Monday.

Several minutes passed in total silence as Jadie bent over the box and pawed through the contents. The boy and girl dolls were all laid out, except for the blond-haired one, which Jadie still had at home, yet these didn't seem to satisfy her. She pawed deeper into the box, extracting handfuls of doll clothes and laying them on the floor. Then she came across one of the baby dolls. On previous occasions Jadie had never shown any interest in the baby dolls, and as a consequence, this one still wore the clothes put on it by some long-ago child. Now, however, Jadie lifted the doll up and inspected it.

"My sister's a baby," she said casually. "She's one now, but that's still a baby."

"You mean Sapphire."

"Well, my other sister's not a baby, is she? She's six." There was a note of annoyance in her voice.

A pause.

"Me and Amber, we're big. We know things. We understand things. But babies don't. Babies know hardly anything."

Bending over the doll, she started to remove its clothing, her fingers delicately attempting to unfasten the minute buttons on the cardigan. "Babies, really, they're sort of like animals. You got to do things for them all the time. And you got to be nice to them, 'cause they don't understand when you're being mean."

"Do you like babies?" I asked.

She shrugged. "Not a lot. They're too big a bother."

At last the cardigan came off and Jadie held the doll up to examine it. Then she laid it back in her lap and continued to undress it. When she finally undressed it completely, she removed its diaper. "Hey, look!" she cried. "It's a boy! Look here at what it gots. A peanut." Looking up, she giggled coyly. "That's what I call it sometimes. A peanut."

I smiled good-naturedly.

"None of them other dolls got this, none of them big boys. They're just dolls. But look at this baby. Look what it gots."

Jadie regarded the doll's tiny penis for several moments and then touched it gingerly with her index finger. Unexpectedly, she blew a loud, derisive raspberry. "That's what I think. And you know what I'm going to do? This." And she spat heartily between the doll's legs before flinging it across the cloakroom. The doll hit the opposite wall with a resounding thud and fell to the bench below.

"Seeing that penis seemed to make you feel very angry," I ventured.

She had a strangely defiant expression on her face, although it was inward and not directed toward me. "They make us play peanuts," she murmured, her voice brittle. "J.R. and Bobby and them. They take out their dickies and then everyone says, 'Peanut, peanut, who's got the peanut?' and me and Amber, we got to ..." Her voice trailed off.

Oh God.

"Actually," she said, "I hate them." She glanced in my direction, I suspect to gauge my reactions.

Not trusting my words, or, for that matter, even my voice, I simply nodded.

The silence came then, washing in around us, but it wasn't divisive. There was an unexpected sense of fellowship. The silence soothed, spanning the distance between us and joining us.

"I don't want to see them take Sapphire," Jadie said at last, her voice quiet. "And they're going to. I guess they already have."

"What do you mean?"

"Well, the other night, last week, they put her upside down on the stick." Jadie twirled her hands in demonstration. "Me and Amber, when we go upside down, we have to put our legs around the stick and they tie them, but Sapphire was too little for the ropes to reach, so they did her like this." Jadie looked over to see if I understood her gestures.

"When you're on the stick," Jadie continued, "the men come around and put their dickies in your pranny or sometimes up your bottom. But the other night, when Sapphire was on the stick, they put their fingers in instead. I think 'cause she was too little. But everybody had to do it, even me and Amber." Jadie lifted her left index finger and regarded it. "When it was my turn, I kissed Sapphire afterwards, to make her feel better. I wanted her to know I was sorry, that I wasn't doing it 'cause I wanted to."

Stunned into silence, I just sat.

"I hate 'em doing that to me and Amber, but with Sapphire, it's just too much. It hurts a lot.

I know, 'cause it hurts me, and she's just little. She's only a baby and you're supposed to take care of babies. Even when they cry."

"That shouldn't be happening. That definitely shouldn't be happening. Not to Sapphire, and not to you or Amber either."

"Miss Ellie says we gotta. They don't do it every time, but when they got their faces on, you know it's going to happen."

"No, you don't 'gotta,' Jadie. That's wrong, what they're doing. Putting fingers in your vaginas? And in your bottom? And men putting their penises in. That is what you're saying in all this, isn't it?"

Jadie nodded faintly.

"That is something they should not do, and I'm very glad you've told me."

"You believe me?"

"Yes, I definitely do."

An expression of such obvious relief broke over Jadie's face that I was instantly overwhelmed by regret for not having pressed this matter harder, sooner.

"What we need to do now is stop them," I said.

The relief still relaxing her features, she smiled and nodded. "Yeah. You can stop them, can't you? I told Amber that. I said if we told you, you could make them stop."

"You bet I can. And the first thing I think we need to do is go down and talk to Mr. Tinbergen. That'll probably be the best place to start."

Bewilderment overtook Jadie. "Mr. Tinbergen? What do you mean?"

"Well, first we'll talk to Mr. Tinbergen and then—"

"No!" she cried, cutting my words off. *"No!* We can't *talk* to anybody. We *can't* tell. Just you. You're the only one I want to know about it."

"Jadie, I have to tell."

"No."

"Jadie, I have to. To get help. Those people are doing something very, very wrong to you and Amber and Sapphire and we must stop them."

Jadie went into an absolute panic, leaping up from the bench in terror. *"No!* You *can't* tell anybody. Don't you understand? I'll die! I mean it, I'll die. *You'll* die! Oh, please, you can't tell anybody else. You can't! Please don't. Please, please, please, please!" In a frenzy, she ran for the door, then realizing it was locked, ran back for the key, rumbled with it, dropped it. This proved too much for her and she sank to her knees, sobbing.

I rose from my place and approached her. "Lovey, come on," I said and physically lifted her from the floor. She trembled in my arms.

"Please, *please* don't tell anyone else. Don't tell them I told. I'm going to die, if you do. Please, don't. Promise me. Please, please promise me."

"All right," I said, overwhelmed by the intensity of her distress and not knowing what else I could say.

"I just want *you* to make it stop," she said amidst her tears, "but I don't want you to tell anyone else. I shouldn't even have told you. If Miss Ellie knew I did, she'd make me die."

"The problem is, lovey, this isn't the sort of thing I can stop by myself."

"But you *can*. I know you can. You're God."

"Oh, sweetheart, I'm not God. I'm a person, like you are. I need help sometimes, too."

"But I want you to be God," she said, dissolving into tears again.

I felt like crying myself, then.

Chapter Nineteen

Once again, I found myself sitting alone in the cloakroom, feeling overwhelmed to a point of nauseous numbness. There was only one question: what was I going to *do?* And it seemed damned near unanswerable.

There was little doubt in my mind that Jadie was being sexually abused, although the wild framework within which she set her account remained a mystery to me. If what she said was true, I was obliged by law to report what she had told me. Turning my head, I gazed at the half-ajar door through which Jadie had departed. What should I do? If she told me what she had in confidence, clearly expecting it to go no farther, did I have the moral right to take it farther without her permission? On the other hand, how would I live with myself, if I knew a child was being brutally abused and I allowed the abuse to continue even a moment longer?

Then, as always, the suspicions began to creep back. Despite Jadie's graphic account, I had no facts. I didn't know who was involved. I didn't know where it was happening. I didn't even know for certain what was happening, other than the specific abuse. Why was Jadie always so hazy on the details? Where on earth were her parents? Just who, precisely, were all these people she referred to? Where did they come from? Where did they disappear to when their sessions with Jadie and Amber were over? I had reported other cases of suspected abuse in my career, and I knew the kinds of details the police would require. I didn't have them in this case. I could tell the police, but what, realistically, could they do, if I didn't know who was committing the crime?

Worse, I worried about what effects my reporting would have on Jadie. In all likelihood, it would destroy our relationship, if for no other reason than that I had so blatantly betrayed her trust in me. Would she stop talking to me about what was going on? Would she talk to the police or to social workers about what was happening?

Then came the old worry. Could a disturbed child create all this? Might it be an unconscious cobbling together of TV shows and pornographic videos? Might the abuse itself be very different, committed perhaps at a completely different time, perhaps by a bunch of neighborhood boys, and transformed in Jadie's mind?

I went home in a state of complete emotional devastation. What could I do? How did I cope with this? Should I keep it private between the two of us until I knew more? Should I seek advice from professional colleagues? Should I tell someone in authority? It was this unspeakably difficult state of *not knowing* that was crucifying me, and the extent of what I did not know seemed limitless.

All evening I agonized, unable to distract myself with anything. When bedtime came, I knew there was no hope for sleep, not until I was too tired to think, so I went out into the living room and turned on the TV. Johnny Carson was on, and I watched the usual line-up of half-witted comedians, fading stars, and authors flogging their books. Among this last group was a woman who claimed telepathy with animals. After giving several mind-boggling examples from her book, she asked for a live animal on stage. A Pekingese was duly supplied and she quickly rattled off its complaints, to which the amazed owner concurred. At this point, I got fed up and turned the program off.

I still couldn't sleep. I lay in the darkness, listening to the silence, and Jadie quickly overwhelmed me. Always able to create bright, precise mental pictures, I could all too easily follow Jadie and her sisters into the shadowy world she had described for me. The characters of "Dallas" sprang to life in lurid, menacing fashion, clutching Sapphire and Tashee's broken doll.

No. I made a strong effort to pull my thoughts away. *No. No. Think of something else.* The woman with the Pekingese on Johnny Carson. I forced pictures of the reluctant dog into my mind. I pondered what the woman might have been doing when she claimed to be able to communicate telepathically with the dog. Was the dog picking up minute behavioral clues? Was she? Had she trained him ahead of time, making it no more than a fancy parlor trick? Or was she really reading the dog's mind? I considered the likelihood of anyone's being able to do this. My thoughts broadened from the specific to the general and then went laterally. Telepathy with dogs to telepathy in general. Could people really do it? Telepathy to psychic powers. I recalled a book I'd read once. Psychic powers to occultism. Occultism to satanism. Satanism to Jadie. I'd come full circle.

Satanism. The thought assailed me with the same force it had that afternoon of the Halloween party. Halloween. *Halloween.* Abruptly, it occurred to me that Jadie had said "last week" in terms of Sapphire's molestation. Had it been on Halloween? Six. Miss Ellie had said six was an important number. Having read the Book of Revelations, I knew 666 was the number of the beast, often assumed to be Satan. Was there a connection?

Electric with this insight, I realized the time had come to learn more about satanism. Without knowledge, I could do nothing. But where? How? I knew there was nowhere in Pecking to find the kind of in-depth information I was going to want on satanism. Moreover, I wasn't sure I wanted to call attention to myself by asking for such material locally. The only place I could think to start was with the bookstore Hugh had mentioned up in the city. So I resolved to get up early and make the four-hour journey northward in the morning. Assuaged by having found a course of action, I was at last able to fall asleep.

Hugh came with me to the bookstore, and I was grateful for his company. A good deal of my bravado had left me by then. What had seemed an impeccably sound theory in the middle of the night seemed a bit silly in daylight, and I was feeling decidedly sheepish about going into the bookstore. I would have been quite comfortable inquiring about a book on astrology or even something a bit kookier, like channeling, but satanism went right off my kook scale.

I didn't need to worry much, however, being with someone like Hugh, who seemed able to discuss anything with anyone, often in loud, ringing tones. "Hey, Brenda!" he called out when we entered the store. "Remember me? Yeah, Hugh! Remember?"

The girl behind the counter looked up. It wasn't clear if she did remember, but she smiled in a friendly fashion.

"This is the one I was telling you about," Hugh said to me. "Brenda's the witch."

This wasn't too hard to imagine. Brenda had waist-long, black hair and pale, unmade-up skin. Although she was young—probably no more than in her early twenties—she wore relics of sixties hippy fashions. I eyed her; she eyed me. We both smiled cautiously.

"This is my girlfriend, Torey. She's looking for stuff on the occult. You know, satanism and all that. I said this was the best place to come."

Brenda brightened at this, clearly taking it as a compliment. "Yeah, okay. Over here. I'll show you the section where we keep all those books. You been into this sort of thing long? Or are you just getting started? I could recommend you some good books. You ever read Crowley's stuff?"

I shook my head. "No, I don't really know much about it."

"Well, Hugh's right, you know. You have come to the right place. We've got this shelf and this shelf and over here." She was a pretty girl in a wan sort of way. As I watched her wend her way among the bookshelves, I wondered what being a witch meant to her.

"If I ..." I paused a moment. "Well, say if I wanted to meet someone who's into this kind of thing ... Would I be able to find someone in the city?"

She searched my face, then gave a faint lift of her shoulders. "Yeah, probably." There was an undercurrent to her words, on the nature of a challenge, and I knew I'd have to prove my interest in some way, if I wanted to pursue that direction. I didn't really. I was only curious about how plentiful and easy to find these groups might be.

"Basically, I just want something that can give me the facts. I don't know anything about it, other than what I've gotten from the press, and I thought I'd like to be better informed."

"That's a good idea," Brenda replied. "It's not the way everyone says. Most of what people read is made up by the newspapers. Like, it sells newspapers, you know? But satanism's not anything bad. It's a kind of religion, like, and people ought to have the freedom to believe whatever their hearts say is right for them."

We browsed for more than an hour in the store. Never having been inside such a place, I found it very interesting, and the scope of the books took me by surprise. In the end, I settled on what looked like a type of primer on satanism and on a lengthy account with several pictures that told of a series of murders thought to be carried out by a network of satanists on the West Coast.

Afterward, Hugh and I retired to a nearby bistro for lunch. He knew why I had been looking and had taken a lively interest in browsing through the occult bookstore. Now, however, he paused pensively over his sandwich.

"Do you really believe in the devil?" he asked.

"I don't think that actually matters much. It's whether the people surrounding Jadie believe he exists."

"But do you?"

I shrugged. "I believe in evil. I don't really think there's an external entity, I suppose, but I don't know. It's the kind of thing I keep an open mind on."

Hugh turned his attention to his french fries, eating them one by one.

"Why do you ask?" I inquired.

"There're a lot of people for whom the devil's a very real thing. You get into this too much, and you're not going to have any trouble finding support, especially in a small place like Pecking. You get in some of these more conservative churches, the ones with the fundamentalist views. and they're already seeing occultists behind every rock. And you go into one of these little backwoods police stations making the kinds of allegations you're coming up with and they're going to go wild. Sitting a hundred years coping with parking tickets and drunks and something like this comes along, they're going to leap into your arms. Man, this is *interesting.*"

"Good gracious, Hugh, the last thing I'd want would be to make some kind of media circus out of this. It's not a moral crusade. I've gotten caught up in something I don't even believe in, and I'm still not sure I do. But it's Jadie ..."

Hugh nodded his head thoughtfully. "Yeah, I know," he said. "But be sure and listen to what you're saying, Tor. It's all right to go making jokes with Brenda down at the bookstore. She's sweet, but she hasn't got the brains God gave a goose, and so you expect it out of someone like that, but ... not out of someone like you. I mean, listen to what you've cooked up, for Pete's sake. It sounds like the plot to a bad novel."

I stayed over with Hugh, planning to drive back on Sunday. On impulse, we decided to go ice skating early Saturday evening. Afterward, still in our jeans, we risked going into a fancy Mexican restaurant for chimichangas and then took in a movie. Thriving on the change, I enjoyed myself tremendously and Jadie was eclipsed.

Once back in Hugh's apartment, however, I was unable to keep away from the books I'd bought. Just a few chapters, I pleaded, and then I'd turn the light out. Exhausted from our activities, all Hugh wanted was sleep, so I picked the thicker of the two books up and went out into the living room to read. Stoking the embers in the fireplace back into flames, I added another couple of logs and settled into the armchair.

The premise of the book was that a series of murders committed in various locations around the West were not isolated incidents but the work of a large, loose network of Satan worshippers. The first section dealt in appallingly graphic detail with the murder of a young woman, whose body was found in a church. Revulsion is not an adequate word for the feeling that came over me while reading. The violence, alone, would have been enough to put me off in normal circumstances, but this went far beyond that. I felt dirty having the book in my hands. Closing it, I set it on the table beside me, but found I still felt tainted by it. A need to destroy the book overpowered me.

Rising from the chair, I pulled the fireguard back and grabbed the book with the full intention of throwing it in. I paused. Hey ho. Was this me? The rational, more down-to-earth side of myself struggled forward to remind me that I'd paid almost five dollars for this thing just that afternoon and had read less than a hundred pages. Intellect, however, didn't stand much of a chance. Burn it I did. It was the only way of relieving that need to get it away from me.

By Monday I'd come back to my senses. Pulling aside the kitchen curtains while I was eating my breakfast, I gazed out over the Pecking rooftops. It was a dull, mid-November morning, heavily overcast and absolutely still. From the height of my attic window, I could see past the bare trees, past the houses to the plains beyond. They stretched away, yellow-brown, until they met the sky. Devils and devil worship, murder and mayhem all seemed a long way removed from Pecking, bathed in pale gray morning light.

Now, in daylight, I was having difficulties giving credence to the idea of something as outlandish as occultism being involved in Jadie's problems. I hadn't needed Hugh's reminder of the willingness of certain groups to jump at proof of the supernatural. As I sat eating my breakfast and studying the view from the window, my thoughts were drawn back to another time, another place, and another Devil's child. He was twelve, his name was David, and he suffered from a chronic and very debilitating form of childhood schizophrenia. I was in a small town then, too, in an area of strong, fundamental religious views, which were shared by many of my colleagues on the staff; and I remembered encountering David's physical education teacher on one occasion outside the school. "There's no point in doing therapy," he'd said. "There's not much any of us can do for David until he accepts Jesus. But our whole church is praying that the Lord will take pity on him and cast his demons out." And I remembered going back to class the next day, to David, who often fell writhing to the floor when in the grip of his hallucinations, and it was easy to believe demons possessed him. It was easier still to want the Lord to take over the back-breaking, heart-wrenching job of helping David. Was that the case with Jadie, too? Was I looking to shift the responsibility elsewhere, to free myself from the hopelessness of working with a psychotic child?

On playground duty, we worked in threes, one teacher at the back of the school where the playing field was, one on the side where the long span of asphalt ran alongside the building, and one in front where the swings, monkey bars, and sandbox were. I usually supervised this last area when it was my turn at duty. There weren't any regulations as to where the children could play, but they tended to divide themselves roughly by age, so that I usually had the youngest on my patch. Even by seven or eight, most usually gravitated around to the side of the building to play ball games or hopscotch.

On Thursday of that week, it was my turn out on the playground, so morning recess found me leaning against the wall of the building, where it was warmest. It was a pleasant day for that late in the year. Weak sunshine shone through high, diffuse clouds, and although it was cold enough for gloves, it was not bitter.

Most of the period passed peacefully. Jadie and Jeremiah were out of sight, around the corner of the building. Reuben and Philip were together on the swings, and Brucie sat slumped in the sandbox, being solicitously entertained by a kindergartner. I stood alone, scanning the kids, my attention not focused on much of anything. Then, all of a sudden, a great caterwaul rose up from the vicinity of the monkey bars. Pushing myself off the wall, I went to investigate.

"Amber Ekdahl's hurt herself!" one kindergartner yelled. "She's got blood all over."

I pushed through the throng of children to find Amber wailing, hands over her mouth, blood flowing through her fingers.

"She fell off the monkey bars from way up there," one little boy said, gestering. "She should of been more careful, huh?"

"Come on, lovey," I said and tried to encourage Amber to her feet. She wouldn't budge. Finally, I pulled her up through the bars and carried her into the small first-aid room adjacent to the front office.

The injury to Amber's face was a lot less serious than it had first appeared. There was a nasty scrape across her nose, a cut beneath it, and quite a large cut on her upper lip, but nothing was broken, and the cuts all responded well to a cold, wet cloth. Once away from the hysteria of the other children,

Amber calmed down immediately, taking the cloth from me and holding it in place without any further fuss. This matter-of-fact response to the injury impressed me.

"You're being very brave about all this," I said. "I bet it hurt."

She nodded.

"You've hardly cried at all, and you seem to know just what to do. That's good thinking for someone who's just six."

"I am brave," she garbled through the cloth.

"Yes, I can tell."

"I'm like She-Ra, Princess of Power. She's the bravest girl in the whole universe."

I smiled down at her.

"She's always beating Hordak. He's the evil person. And that's why I like her. He tries to get her, but she always wins."

"Is that your favorite TV program?"

Amber nodded enthusiastically.

I took the cloth from her and rinsed it out before handing it back. "Do you watch much TV?"

"Yeah. I like TV."

I eyed her. "Do you ever watch 'Dallas'?"

Her brow furrowed, then a slight shake of the head. "I think that might be a grown-ups' program. Mostly I watch cartoons."

"Just wondered. Jadie seems to watch it."

"Jadie watches lots of junk. My mom always yells at her."

I had perched Amber on the tabletop while I cleaned her face, and now she sat, swinging her legs back and forth in a relaxed fashion. Taking down the bloodied cloth, she examined it. Her lip had already swollen to twice its usual size.

"I'm a little curious," I said, trying to keep my tone conversational. "Does your sister's friend Tashee come over to your house very often?"

Amber's eyes went wide and she regarded me oddly, then she smiled. "Tashee's not real. Didn't you know that? Tashee's just pretend, someone Jadie talks to."

"A make-believe friend? She's not a real little girl? Does Jadie have any other friends like that?"

Amber shrugged. "Jadie don't act like everyone else. My mom says its 'cause she got borned the wrong way."

"I see." Inspecting her face one last time, I judged all the bleeding to be stopped, so I took the cloth from her. "Well, there you go. I think we have you fixed."

"But what about my knee? I hurt my knee, too. Look. See? It's blooded right through my pants."

In the mayhem caused by her facial injuries, I'd completely forgotten about her knee. Lifting her down from the table, I bent and attempted to pull the leg of her rather too-small jogsuit up, but I couldn't get it high enough without hurting her. "I think you're going to need to pull your pants down from the top."

"I'm not supposed to take my clothes off at school. I'm always supposed to ask my mom about these things first."

"Amber, I'm sure it's quite all right in this

instance. I can't get to your knee otherwise." I reached over and pulled the pants down myself.

In doing so, I exposed a faint mark on her skin, partially obscured by the waistband of her underpants. "What's this?" I asked in surprise. Putting a finger out, I gently eased the band down. The mark was a pale red and raised, a healing scar, and it was familiar—a cross with a circle around it. "What is this?"

"X marks the spot."

Chapter Twenty

I go dead calm in crises. No matter how frightened or emotionally wrought I may be feeling immediately prior to it, the moment a situation pushes over into a state of genuine emergency, I'm flooded with an internal anesthetic. With it comes a sense of time winding down to move very slowly, each moment taking on sharp, freeze-frame clarity, and I get a faint sensation of being outside myself.

When I first saw the mark on Amber's abdomen, a rush of adrenaline overtook me, making my ears roar and my heart rush. Here it was, the concrete evidence to substantiate Jadie's claims. A moment of abject terror hit, as it came home to me just how horrifying this case was likely to be, how I was going to be right in the middle of it through all the police action, the courts, the social service intervention, and the undoubted media attention such matters attract, and how from this moment on, I would not be able to turn back the clock and uninvolve myself. Then came the calm. The noise in my ears faded; I could no longer feel my pounding heart. Amber took on unusual clarity.

"I think we need Mr. Tinbergen to come in here."

At once, Amber began to cry.

"No, it's all right, sweetheart. You haven't done anything wrong. I just think we better have Mr. Tinbergen take a look at this."

"What for?" she asked plaintively.

Then came confusion. Recess was over, so I had to make arrangements for Lucy to take my group temporarily. I had to stop and tell Alice that Amber was in the office, and all the while we were looking for Mr. Tinbergen.

At last Mr. Tinbergen was located in the boiler room with Mr. O'Banyon. Back in the small first-aid room, I closed the door behind him and then approached Amber. "This has been put here deliberately," I said. "It's healing over, but someone has intentionally carved this symbol on her."

"How did this happen, Amber?" Mr. Tinbergen asked.

"I don't know," she whimpered.

"Oh, come on, honey. I can't think you really don't know."

This reduced her to a wail.

"'X marks the spot,' that's what she said." I turned to Mr. Tinbergen.

He smiled in a warm, fatherly fashion and leaned forward to push wayward strands of hair from Amber's face. "No one's going to be angry with you, sweetheart. We're here to help you, so it's very important that we know what's happened."

"I'm not supposed to tell," Amber said through her tears.

"I'm sure it'll be perfectly all right to tell Torey and me. Come on now, sweetheart."

Amber cut a pathetic figure. Like Jadie, she was attractive in a rather atavistic way, with her long, uncombed hair and her dark-lashed eyes, however, her paler coloring gave her a washed-out appearance and her ill-fitting clothes made her look less the untamed creature Jadie often seemed and more simply uncared for. Now, lumbered with the scratched, bloodied nose and a ballooning upper lip, she looked like a war orphan.

"Why are you not supposed to tell?" I asked. "Has someone warned you not to?"

There was a long pause. Amber cautiously daubed her streaming nose, but apparently it hurt too much, because she took the tissue away and let it run. Mr. Tinbergen and I stood, tense, alert, and silent.

At last Amber nodded. "My mama did."

"Why is that?"

"'Cause my sister done this. 'Cause my sister took one of the knives in the kitchen and cut me with it."

"*Jadie* did that?" I asked, stunned.

Amber nodded. "And my mom says if we don't keep good care of Jadie when she does awful things, they're gonna come and take her away. She said I shouldn't ever tell what kind of things she does." Amber dissolved into tears again. "'Cause if she gets tooken away, it's gonna be my fault."

Mr. Tinbergen looked over at me to see my assessment of this matter. I widened my eyes to convey my own surprise at this unexpected turn of events.

"Please take off your shirt," Mr. Tinbergen said, and when Amber did, he thoroughly examined her back and arms, looking for evidence of other marks. There was none. He then had her remove her pants; however, aside from the bruised knee and the encircled X, there were no other marks there, either. "I think we need to see Jadie," he said and rose to go get her.

Alone with Amber, I looked at her. "Is that *really* how you got that mark?"

Warily, she glanced in my direction. "Yes," she said, her voice barely above a whisper.

"We need the truth here, Amber. The *real* truth."

Her eyes filled with tears again.

"You must tell us what really did happen there. I want to know the truth, and I'll find it out one way or another, but it'd be best if you told me yourself." My words came out sounding like a threat, and despite my sympathy for Amber, I suppose that's how I meant them.

"Jadie done it."

I didn't speak.

"Jadie does awful things. Once, she killed our cat." Amber looked up at me. "But she can't help it. That's just the way she is."

When Jadie entered and saw Amber standing in her underwear, her face went gray. She wavered on her feet and for a moment I feared she might faint.

When Mr. Tinbergen asked for an explanation, Jadie gave no response. Indeed, she gave no word, no nod, no sign of any sort that she'd even heard the question.

"Jadie, the time's come for us to talk to Mr. Tinbergen about what's going on," I said.

"No," she mouthed, although the word had no sound. Tears came immediately to her eyes and spilled down over her cheeks, and she made no effort to check them. She only lowered her head.

"Come on, Jadie. We must talk about things." I rose to my feet to come toward her.

"No," she cried and it was a plea.

"There's no reason to get upset, sweetheart," Mr. Tinbergen said tenderly. "Like we said to Amber, we're not going to get mad at anyone. We just want to find out what's happened."

Head down, face crumpled into tears, Jadie didn't respond.

"Amber says you did this," Mr. Tinbergen continued. "Is that true?"

There was a tiny pause, like an abrupt intake of breath, and then Jadie raised her head. "Yes. It was me that done it," she said, then she began to cry bitterly.

"We-e-elll," Mr. Tinbergen replied in a fatherly way and reached his arm out to her, "that was a *very* naughty thing to do, wasn't it? And I can see you know it was wrong. You're not ever going to do anything like that again to your little sister, are you?"

Jadie continued to weep inconsolably.

"There, there, there," he said and hugged Jadie to him with one arm. With the other, he reached out to touch the mark on Amber's abdomen. "I'm sure your mommy and daddy have gotten after you quite enough for this, so nobody's going to get mad about it here. Besides, it doesn't look very serious. Just a scratch, really. And nearly healed." He looked at Amber. "This was a very, very silly thing for your sister to have done to you, wasn't it?"

She nodded.

"All right, then. You get your clothes back on and both of you may go."

After the girls had departed, Mr. Tinbergen turned to me. "I think you were right to query it. These days you never can tell. Better safe than sorry, hey?" He paused. "But I don't think this was very serious. I daresay, I did even worse things to my brother when we were kids. Got him through the shoulder with a penknife once." Mr. Tinbergen laughed. "Accidentally, of course, but then we should probably never examine the motives of siblings too carefully." And he laughed again.

Deeply troubled, I returned to my class. I didn't know what to think now. While the degree of Jadie's disturbance had always been an issue in interpreting the things she told about, it had never crossed my mind that she, herself, might actually be the perpetrator. This threw everything into an entirely different light, and I was horrified by the implications. The worst of all for me was Amber's chance remark about Jadie's killing a cat. Had that been Jenny?

My instinct was to confront Jadie regarding all this, and had we been going back to a situation where we were alone together, I probably would have. Instead, we returned to the hurly-burly of a class upset by the unexpected change in routine my time in the first-aid room had caused, and I had my hands full getting everything back under control. The desire to confront her faded very quickly, to be replaced by a weary sense of confusion, wherein nothing made much sense to me. I realized that any confrontation I might bring about would be more to assuage my own feelings of having been duped than to help Jadie.

Jadie seemed aware of the intensity of my emotions and openly avoided me for the remainder of the day, which only reinforced my feeling that I had been the fool in all this. I left her alone, however, because I knew Jadie too well to think I could make her talk when she didn't want to.

Friday followed the same pattern. Jadie approached me only when I was well surrounded by the boys and, thus, unable to have a private conversation. Otherwise, she made herself scarce.

The following Monday, I had a case meeting after school over Brucie. His parents, his pediatrician, Mr. Tinbergen, and Arkie were there, as well as a new speech therapist, who would be working with him. When the meeting was over, I cornered Arkie.

"Listen, I have to have a chat with you over Jadie Ekdahl. I really do."

"Eeee," Arkie replied, pulling her lips back in a grimace. "Bad time. Super bad. Up to here at the moment. Could it wait 'til the end of the month?"

"I don't think so. I'm pretty desperate."

"You're determined to get that dinner out again, aren't you?" And she laughed. "Tottie's? Friday night? That okay?"

Frankly, I would have much preferred the peace and quiet of my classroom, but realizing that to see her at all would require an after-hours meeting, I agreed.

After everyone had left, I remained a while longer, making notes of the conference for Brucie's file and then putting away the materials we'd used. Then I pushed the chairs back in around the table, turned off the lights, and left, too.

Down in the parking lot, I headed around the side of my car to put my books into the passenger seat. In the process, I very nearly tripped over Jadie. She was sitting on the ground in the narrow space between my car and the one parked next to it, her back against the other car's rear door.

"Good grief, you frightened the life out of me," I said. "What are you doing there anyway? You could have been badly hurt, if I hadn't seen you in time."

"I would have moved," she muttered, but she didn't move. Lightly dressed for a November evening, she remained with her legs drawn up close to her body.

We regarded one another.

"Can I talk to you?" she asked at last.

Looking back over my shoulder at the school building, I knew Mr. O'Banyon would already have locked the doors. "You want to get into the car with me?"

"I don't want no one to see me."

"Well, get in and we'll drive somewhere." So quickly she scuttled up and opened the door.

I didn't know where to take her. In previous years, I'd always been able to fall back on the anonymity of a McDonald's or such place when in retreat with an unhappy child. In Pecking, there were no fast food restaurants. I was reluctant to go into one of the local cafés, where we'd draw attention to ourselves and most likely be recognized. So, for ten minutes or so, I simply drove around, completing the circuit from Main Street up to First and back again several times. Silence wrapped around her like a garment, Jadie laid her head against the shoulder strap of the seat belt and gazed out the window.

After the umpteenth circle, I was desperate to stop. Pulling into a gas station on the southern edge of town, I hopped out and bought us two cans of pop from the soft drinks dispenser.

"Here," I said, getting back into the car. And with that, I pulled the car around into the gigantic parking lot that fronted the supermarket. I turned off the ignition.

Jadie inspected the can of pop. "I don't like orange," she said.

"You like Dr Pepper better? Here. Trade me."

"My mom doesn't let us have pop before dinner."

"Very well. I'll drink them both, then."

She didn't hand the Dr Pepper back.

Silence.

"You want to talk?"

Jadie leaned forward and peered into the little hole left by the pull tab. Night was nearly upon us and the huge sodium lamps in the parking lot bathed us in a pale, orange glow.

"We're going to have to go soon," I said. "I don't feel at all comfortable about your being here without your parents knowing."

"They won't miss me. I told them I was going over to Rachel's."

Silence again.

I finished the orange pop, being pulled back by the taste to childhood summers spent on the banks of the Yellowstone River, and the bottles of orange NeHi my grandfather used to buy me when he took me fishing.

Gently, I squeezed the aluminum can and a metallic crackling broke the silence. "I didn't tell Mr. Tinbergen anything about what you've told me, if that's what you thought."

Barely raising her head, Jadie looked sidelong at me.

"Has that been bothering you these last couple of days?" I asked. "Did you think I'd told? Did you think the whole game was up? No, I didn't. I promised I wouldn't, and I kept my word. We found that mark on Amber by accident, so Mr. Tinbergen still doesn't know what you've told me."

Jadie turned her attention back to the Dr Pepper. Agitating the can gently, she sloshed a bit out onto the top. Then she lifted the can and sucked the pop off with a noisy slurp.

"When I saw the mark, I showed it to Mr. Tinbergen, because I thought it might be a good way to get things out into the open without your being implicated. See, I thought that nobody would get mad at you, if I was the one who discovered the symbol on Amber and … But …"

Jadie's entire attention seemed absorbed in sloshing up the pop onto the can and then slurping it off. After listening to so much of this, it took saintly patience not to rip the can from her hands. The noise itself was annoying enough; her recalcitrant silence capped it off. Irritated, I turned the key in the ignition.

Jadie looked up abruptly.

"I'll drop you off in the school parking lot."

A disconsolate expression crossed Jadie's face. "You don't believe me, do you? You believe Amber."

"Don't believe you? You haven't said anything for me to believe. The only thing I don't believe is that you want to talk. If you did, you'd talk. But as for what we're doing at the moment … well, missy, it's after school hours. Time for you to be at home with your family. Time for me to be doing my own things."

"I didn't do that mark on Amber's stomach. Sue Ellen done it. Amber's going to die, just like Tashee did, and Sue Ellen had to make the mark. She done it with the knife, that one I told you about, the one that's shaped like this." With a finger, Jadie drew a crescent on her jeans. "And it's got this twisty design on the handle and curves up with this special sharp point for cutting. It's what they put in Tashee. In her throat, right here."

"Then why did Amber say you did it?"

"'Cause she had to. 'Cause that's what they tell her to say."

"Then why did *you* say it?"

Lowering her head, she pulled her lips back into a tight grimace. "'Cause I had to," she whispered.

The silence, diseased, oozed back in around us. I sighed. Turning the ignition off again, I gazed wearily out across the empty parking lot. There were only seven other cars in the lot, all clustered down in front of the supermarket, which, without exaggeration, was probably a quarter of a mile away.

"Do you believe me?" Jadie asked, looking over.

"To be truthful, Jadie, I don't know what I believe anymore."

"You don't, do you?" she muttered gloomily. "You think I'm making it up. You think I'm crazy."

"I didn't say that. I said I don't know what I believe, and at the moment, I don't."

Crossly, Jadie thumped the side of the Dr Pepper can, making the liquid leap up and spill across her hand.

"Amber says you killed the cat."

"I *didn't!*" Jadie shrieked out, as if electrified.

I regarded her.

"I *didn't!* She's lying. Can't you see she's lying!" Jadie broke into tears. "I'm the one who tried to *save* Jenny. It was because of Jenny that I told you."

"But Amber's only little. Why would she lie about something like that? How would she even know to?"

This seemed too much for Jadie and she sobbed heavily, bending forward in the seat.

Turning my head, I looked out across the parking lot. We were on the farthest eastern edge, where the asphalt simply petered out and the buffalo grass took over.

"She said it, 'cause she thinks I did," Jadie said at last, her voice ragged. "'Cause Miss Ellie said I did."

I turned back to look at her.

"I was on my back on the floor and they laid Jenny on top of me. Bobby and Clayton were holding her. I didn't have no clothes on, and Jenny was on my tummy. But I was screaming and Miss Ellie told me not to, but I wouldn't stop. They were tickling my pranny with her tail, and I thought they were going to stick it inside and I didn't want them to do that. I thought Jenny was going to scratch me. So Miss Ellie made J.R. and Ray come up and hold on to Jenny's other two legs. Each of them had her legs and they started to pull." Jadie began to sob again and didn't catch her breath for a moment or two. "They just kept pulling 'til she came apart. 'Til the blood started running down on my tummy and her insides came out. And Miss Ellie said it was my fault."

I drew my lower lip in between my teeth and bit it, concentrating on the pain, willing the pain to overwhelm the rising sense of panic. The confinement of the car intensified my feelings. I was acutely aware of being unable to jump up and run away, which I dearly longed to do.

Beside me, Jadie fought for control of her tears. She squeezed her eyes shut and pressed her fingers tightly against her temples.

"Jadie, you *must* tell," I said, when I could finally trust my voice again. "This can't go on. It needs to come out into the open."

"I *can't* tell."

"You can. If the things you're telling me are true, then we must stop them. I can't do it alone. I can't do it without your help, but it has got to stop. These are wrong, bad, *terrible* things and they should never be happening to anyone."

"I *can't* tell," she said again, plaintively, the tears thickening her voice.

"Then, if you can't, let me tell."

Jadie didn't answer immediately. Instead, she lowered her head and stared at the can of pop still in her lap. I sat quietly, listening to the tinny dashboard clock going pink, pink, pink around the dial.

"I can't tell," Jadie whispered at last.

I turned to look at her. "You won't die. Whoever told you that is wrong. Nothing will happen to you that is any worse than what already has. Nothing will be as bad as what Miss Ellie is doing to you."

"But the police'll come. They'll put us in jail."

"Little children don't go to jail, lovey."

"But they can make my mom and dad go to jail. They can make me and my sisters go to live in a children's home and never see our folks again."

Extending my hand, I gently pushed the hair back from her cheek. "Is that what's worrying you?"

"Would that happen?"

"Are your mom and dad part of this? Do they know what Miss Ellie's doing?"

"I think my mom and dad are always asleep."

"Well, it's a policeman's job to make sure people follow the laws of the land. One such law says that hurting children is wrong, so if someone really was hurting a child, the police would make him or her stop. This doesn't necessarily mean they would go to jail. That's not for the policemen to decide. There are judges and other people, who get together in a court and try to decide what's best for everyone."

"What happens to the children?"

"Well, they need a safe place to stay. Usually, it's a foster home. Like Philip lives in. Usually there's a foster mom and a foster dad to take care of the children and help them get over what's happened to them."

"I don't want that. I want to stay with my family."

"Well, if your mom and dad aren't part of this, then you probably could."

"But would we get tooken to a children's home first?"

"There might be a bit of time away, but probably not in a children's home. Probably just in a foster home. Like Philip has, and you know how much he likes his." I paused to regard her. "Really, Jadie, it'd be better than what's going on now, wouldn't it?"

"I don't want to get tooken away. I don't want Amber and me and Sapphire to get put in different places. I don't want not to be able to see my mom and dad. I don't want anyone to go to jail. I don't want nothing, except for it to *stop*. That's all I'm asking." She raised her head and looked over at me. "This isn't fair. Why do I have to decide this?"

I gazed into her eyes, the purity of their blueness obscured by the orange-shaded gloom of the parking lot, and I felt deep anguish, because I knew I had no answers. Child abuse is such a patent evil that exposing and rectifying it should possess only black-and-white clarity—abuse identified, child rescued, perpetrator gets what's coming to him. Sadly, I knew it was never so. The reality always included the ruins of small, shattered lives, destroyed relationships, and broken hearts. Good and evil are not absolute, but relative.

Chapter Twenty-One

The hanging plants were restaging "Day of the Triffids" over the table to which Brad, our waiter for the evening, escorted me. Not having Arkie's guts, I failed to mention to him my preference for tables occupied only by humans and was seated next to a monstrosity of a cheese plant with a menacingly inclined main stem. Gently, I tried to rearrange the trailing strands and hooked the worst of the spider plant's offspring over the back of the booth. The cheese plant seemed to take offense at this and leaned a little closer to me, so I stopped.

"Jeee-sus," Arkie muttered, when she arrived. "This is like a night out in the Congo. I should have brought my machete."

"Shush," I whispered and gestured toward the cheese plant. "We're outnumbered."

As with our previous visit to Tottie's, Arkie and I quickly fell into amiable conversation while browsing through the menu and wine list. We put in our orders and the repartee continued until well after our food arrived. Wistfully, I wished it could continue all evening.

"To say I'm having problems with Jadie is a bit of an understatement," I began.

"Yes," Arkie agreed. "I sussed that. I think we all have. Glen was just mentioning it to me the other week, saying you've got something going with her."

"Mr. Tinbergen said that?"

Arkie nodded. "I think he's worried. I mean, what with June Harriman last year and all that, he tends to get concerned about his teachers pretty easily. It's understandable. But I told him he probably didn't have anything to worry about, as far as you're concerned. You've had a lot of experience, and if you got into trouble, you'd have the good sense to ask for help. You wouldn't try to solve the world's problems on your own." She looked over. "And I assume I told him right."

I found this information embarrassing. Mr. Tinbergen was worried about *me?* Did I appear that out of control?

"You aren't getting in over your head, are you?" Arkie asked.

"No, *I'm* okay. It's Jadie Ekdahl ... I keep thinking that I finally understand what's going on with this kid and just about get to the point where I think I can help, then poof! Like a house of cards, all my assumptions fall flat and I'm back at the beginning again. I don't think I've ever come across a situation where I've changed my mind more times. Or where I've felt more helpless."

"I think what's worrying Glen is that you're not talking to any of the rest of us about this. It's going to be frustrating, if that's what's going on, but you shouldn't try to do it on your own."

I fell silent. She was right, if she meant I didn't sit around down in the teachers' lounge, discussing Jadie the way Alice discussed Ben Soames's hopeless table manners or Lucy bemoaned Matthew Grinstead's inability to understand subtraction. Arkie wasn't right, however, about my not giving anyone else a chance. What did she think I was doing here and now?

Arkie perceived my discomfort and smiled reassuringly. "So, I'm all ears." She leaned across the table and touched my arm. "How can I help?"

"She's abused."

"Yeah, I remember you saying you thought that some while back. Have you got something we can take to court?"

"No. Not if Jadie doesn't back me up."

Arkie's brow furrowed.

"It's damned slow business getting facts out of Jadie, for one thing. She can be incredibly specific about some things, things you'd never imagine a kid her age could make up, so you just assume they've got to be true. Then you ask her about the basic stuff—who, where, when—and she never seems to know any of this. I mean, what I've got is a girl who can tell me in excruciating detail how she and her sisters are molested, but she can't tell me who's doing it."

"She doesn't know who's abusing her? Is it a stranger?"

I shook my head. "No, she just has different names for them. Code names, I think. That's these 'Dallas' characters I've told you about before. What she's talking about is very, very serious abuse, but she only knows them by these names."

"They're real people?" Arkie's voice had a skeptical tinge.

"Well, I *think* they're real people." A pause. Arkie had gone back to her meal and I sat, watching her, my brain revving up, like a car at a stoplight. "What I'm going to say here ... I know I'm going to sound a little far-fetched." I reached for the wine bottle and poured myself a second glass. "But if I'm going to be credited with having the good sense to ask for help when I need it, I'd better say it."

Arkie looked up, fork poised halfway to her mouth.

"Some of the things Jadie talks about ... well, I was up in the city last summer and talking with my boyfriend ... and I got this book at a bookstore there ... and just sort of putting things together ... I'm wondering if she isn't being abused in some kind of ... well, ritualistic way."

"*What?*"

"I know it sounds crazy, and this is why I haven't been talking much to anyone about what's going on. I feel crazy just for thinking it."

"You mean like Moonies or something?"

"Like satanists. See, there's this symbol Jadie is always drawing, and my boyfriend was the one to mention that it's a Black Mass symbol. And then a couple of weeks ago, I was up in the city and went to this occult bookstore. I got a couple of books on satanism and in this one ..."

Arkie's fork went down with an audible clink.

"Some of what Jadie talks about fits what they say in this book. Some of it doesn't, admittedly, perhaps most especially the fact she's never mentioned Satan or a master or that sort of thing. This woman, this Miss Ellie, seems to be the leader of this group Jadie's involved with. But a lot of what they say in this book ... well, it could explain some of the gaps in Jadie's stories. Like, for example, they talk about how these groups often drug kids, legal drugs as well as illegal ones, and Jadie's always saying how Miss Ellie wakes them up at night and gives them Coke to drink. Maybe they're being drugged before they're taken to wherever it is, and that's why she never remembers how she gets there."

"So what do you think this means Tashee is?" Arkie asked. "You think Tashee is a real girl? This—'group'—has murdered a real six-year-old without anyone else ever knowing it? Without anyone ever reporting her missing? Without any evidence at all? Wouldn't there have been a birth register? Wouldn't she have been in school somewhere?"

"Well, in this book they talk about 'brood mares,' women who have babies specifically to be used as sacrifices ..."

"We're not talking about a baby here, Torey. We're talking about a six-year-old girl. A first-grader. Someone old enough to have undoubtedly encountered doctors, teachers, and countless other outside adults. Old enough to be missed and yet not so old that she'd be classed a runaway. If these people were genuinely into human sacrifice, I would have thought a child of that age would be a particularly bad choice."

Arkie's expression was glazed with skepticism, her tone of voice vaguely patronizing, and I was quickly being overwhelmed by humiliation. How close I was treading to the lunatic fringe had always been something I was aware of. When reading the book on satanism that I'd bought at the occult bookstore, I had often found myself suspicious of the content. Certainly, it had an answer for everything, particularly substantiating the use of humans as sacrifice, saying that these were either offspring of the "brood mares" or fetuses from abortion clinics. Bodies were disposed of by sympathetic undertakers, who included them in freshly dug graves, and so on and so forth. In fact, I found myself unsettled by just how pat all the solutions were. I think I would have been able to believe more easily if the authors of the book had occasionally said that they thought these things were going on, but they didn't know how the satanists kept getting away with it. Yet, in the privacy of my own thoughts, I was willing to give it all the benefit of the doubt, particularly in light of some of the things Jadie had talked about. On the other hand, hearing myself actually say this stuff aloud, I was only too aware of how ridiculous it sounded. The fear of being thought silly, or worse, unprofessional swamped me.

"I mean, not that I necessarily *believe* any of this," I added hastily. A sigh. "I don't know. I'm grasping at straws at this point."

An expression of tremendous relief crossed Arkie's face, and she dropped her fork in mock collapse. "God, you really had me scared there for a second, kid. I was thinking, 'Oh shit, she's gone native on me.' Know what I mean? Good-bye *New York Times*. Hello *National Enquirer.*"

I laughed, too.

A pause came between us and grew into silence. I looked down at the food remaining on my plate. As before, it was nothing more than a sandwich with pretensions. Frankly, I would have preferred a steak, calories, cholesterol, and all, to this green version of the emperor's new clothes.

"I suppose I think like you do," Arkie said at last, "that there must be some truth at the bottom of this. But what? I'm not sure. The only thing I can think is that Jadie has fragmented the abuser. Perhaps it's Dad. Or Mom *and* Dad. And she just can't face it. She's created this assortment of personas to help her cope with Mom/Dad as abuser and as loving parents. And I agree with the basic difficulty: that we can't go charging in there to do something until Jadie somehow indicates who's the guilty one."

"You don't think there's any possibility—faint possibility—that Jadie might be telling the truth about these people and there are a lot of them?"

"You mean the possibility that Larry Hagman is dancing around her living room? Do *you*? Cutting out all the sensational newspaper reporting, all the seamy books and horror films, now, have you, with your experience, your background, your travels, actually ever encountered evidence—concrete evidence, not hearsay—of something like this? As opposed, say, to the number of times you've come across schizophrenic-type children obsessed and often hallucinating about blood, gore, monsters, or whatever?"

I had to admit I hadn't ever.

"More to the point, you could never keep a large group underground in a small town like this. Not the way everybody knows everybody else's business."

"But it does happen," I said.

"Sure, it does. I'm not saying it doesn't, but we're the professionals here, Torey. There's God knows how many folks out there to worry about witches and ghosts and aliens from outer space and all the mischief they get up to. But it's your responsibility and mine to remain rational, to judge each of these incidents by educated standards, and then see this child gets the treatment she so desperately needs."

I nodded.

"The real problem in Jadie's case is that she is one heck of a sick child," Arkie said. "When Glen told me about that mark on Amber, my stomach turned. I mean, can you imagine her doing that? Holding Amber down and cutting her like that? And, of course, the other question I think we're forced to ask ourselves is how safe are we with this girl in a public school? Here's a kid hallucinating about people coming off the television and molesting her baby sister. About seeing a little girl murdered and then magically put back together. About playing with this little girl's ghost. Indeed, about becoming a ghost herself. And now, this incident with Amber. I mean, if you were a parent, how thrilled would you be to have your boy or girl in the same school as a delusional child with access to knives?"

Contemplating Arkie's words, I realized there was a great deal of sense in what she was saying. Indeed, it felt good to be back on familiar ground, dealing with a disturbed child. No doubt Jadie was deeply psychotic and I hadn't encountered anything of such a distressing nature before, but this was work I knew I was good at. In fact, it was the mystery of mental illness that had always attracted me to working with it. The similarities among types of disturbances was enough to give a toehold, yet each individual's problems were always challengingly unique, providing me with an ultimate sense of mastery on those occasions when I could successfully intervene. As Arkie talked, my mind began chasing quickly down the maze of possibilities for such a complex disturbance in an eight-year-old girl.

"The only thing I can think of," Arkie was saying when I tuned back in, "is to call a conference with her parents and insist they take her back to the mental health clinic. They were going there for a while when Jadie was about five, but they broke it off because of the trouble in traveling weekly between Pecking and here. That, and, of course, the fact that Jadie wouldn't talk to the therapist. Seemed a bit of a waste of money at the time. But none of us appreciated what a disturbed child the mutism was cloaking. I think we now need to impress upon Mr. and Mrs. Ekdahl that this isn't something Jadie is going to grow out of. I think we might even mention the possibility of short-term psychiatric hospitalization if Jadie doesn't show signs of improving. That might be one of the best ways of tackling the situation, if it's abuse related."

"Yes, that might be a good idea."

"And this should take some of the burden off you. If she can establish a good relationship with a therapist, a lot of this counseling role you've fallen into should be lessened."

I nodded.

Arkie leaned down and retrieved her handbag. Taking out her Filofax, she paged through it. "Who I'd really like to have see Jadie is a woman named Phyllis Ruiz. She's a psychiatrist at the mental health clinic who's had a lot of experience with severely disturbed children, and she holds some very enlightened views. Not just pills and theory. You'd like her. I'll see if I can contact her on Monday and find out what her schedule's like." Arkie snapped the diary shut and looked over, grinning. "There. Great. I always feel better when I've settled on some concrete action, don't you?"

* * *

The weekend of Thanksgiving arrived, and the whole school was involved putting on a Thanksgiving "pageant," as Mr. Tinbergen liked to call it. The third- and fourth-graders were doing a play they had written about Pilgrims, while the rest of us contributed songs, dances, and poems. My group were to represent the Native American point of view, all except for Brucie, who had been aptly designated a pumpkin and simply had to sit on the stage in his orange costume while the rest of the children sang and offered up their baskets of food.

Monday and Tuesday afternoons included time spent making Indian outfits and running through rehearsals with the other classes in the auditorium.

"I'm the only *real* Indian in this," Jeremiah said as we sat around the table and cut out construction-paper feathers for the headbands.

"Actually, quite a lot of the children in this school are native, Jeremiah."

"Yeah, but I'm the only one in this here class. Look at him, he's gonna make a boogy-looking Indian. Look at his black booger's face," and he pointed a finger directly onto Philip's nose.

In all honesty, I thought they were going to make a handsome band of Indians, Philip included. It would have been Brucie, with his white-blond hair, who would have ruined the appearance.

"My dad's got a real headdress," Jeremiah said. "My real dad, that is. Not the guy who's living with my mom now. He's just some dude that don't got nothing interesting. But my real dad, he's got a headdress that hangs clear down to here." Jeremiah leaped from his seat to demonstrate the length with his hands.

"That must be beautiful."

"Maybe he could lend it to me. Maybe I could wear that in the pageant."

"Nice idea, but I think we'll stick to these."

"Why? Man, lady, these don't look like nothing. Boogy, little baby things, these." He flicked a paper feather in Reuben's face.

"My friend, Tashee, she used to have a pair of real Indian moccasins," Jadie suddenly piped up. Her comment was clearly meant for Jeremiah, as she slid her chair back from the table and lifted her foot toward him. "They had beads right across the front, here, and the tops folded over. They didn't look anything like those moccasins you can buy in the shoe shop."

Raising my head slightly, I glanced over at her. Jadie still did not speak spontaneously a great deal in class, although she was given to occasional conversations with Jeremiah, some of which could be quite lengthy. This, however, was the first time I'd ever heard a reference to Tashee outside the confines of our cloakroom sessions, and it caught me by surprise.

"Yeah, well, you think that's great?" Jeremiah replied, nonplussed. "My real dad, he's got a spearhead. A *real* spearhead, from long ago. The kind they used to tie onto these long poles." This image proved too tempting for Jeremiah, and he held up one of the paper feathers, spear-style. "They had 'em on these long poles and then they'd go

AGGGGGHHHHHHHH!" And with that Jeremiah leaped across the table, plunging the feather against Philip's shirt. Philip, quickly catching the mood, grasped at the invisible wound and fell from his chair to have death spasms on the floor.

"Enough, you guys. Back in your seats."

"Man, lady," Jeremiah muttered, "you never let us have no fun."

At the end of the day, the children carefully folded their costumes and laid them on the counter at the back of the room in readiness for the pageant on the following afternoon. On top were placed the paper headbands and the few props we'd acquired.

Jadie was still arranging her things when I went back to the sink to wash the glue off my hands. She attentively smoothed the wrinkles from the cloth of the squaw's dress.

"It's going to be fun tomorrow, isn't it?" I said. "Are you looking forward to it?"

She shrugged.

"Is any of your family coming?"

"Yeah, my mom is. And Sapphire, of course."

"That'll be nice."

Just then the going-home bell rang. Jeremiah whooped and dashed for the door. Nearly a year together and the best I'd ever gotten from him was a pause to say good-bye before he bolted out, down to be first on his bus. So hustling the boys together, I chased after him.

Returning to the room after seeing the boys to their rides, I found Jadie still standing back by the counter. Pushing in the chairs around the table as

I approached her, I said, "I'm glad you stayed, because I need to talk to you."

Jadie glanced up, her expression guarded.

"Do you want to go in the cloakroom or are you comfortable here?"

"I don't think I can stay," she said warily. "My mom's taking me and Amber to get new shoes tonight."

"Yes, okay, this'll just take a few minutes."

Jadie looked down at the floor. "My mom's going to get us them kind of shoes that got dinosaurs on them."

"Well, what I wanted to say was that I think you're going to be seeing a psychiatrist at the mental health clinic. That same clinic in Falls River where you used to go when you were littler. Do you remember?"

Jadie leaned back against the counter and lifted up one foot. She caught it with her hand and fingered the stitching of her running shoe.

"Sometimes our feelings get sick, just like our bodies do, and when that happens, we go to a special doctor called a psychiatrist, who tries to make our feelings well again."

"I'm going to get high-top shoes. Amber wants them, too, but my mom says she can't have them, 'cause she can't tie bows yet. She's got to get the kind with Velcro fastenings."

"Mr. Tinbergen and Mrs. Peterson aren't entirely happy with the way we're getting on in here. They don't think I've been quite as much help as you need, and they think it would be better if you went to see someone who understands more about the kinds of troubles you've been having. This isn't a punishment or anything. This lady's really nice and she understands kids, and I think it's the right idea, too. You'll still be here for school, of course, but she'll help us out on this other matter."

"I like them shoes, 'cause they leave dinosaur footprints. Looks like a dinosaur's been walking there."

"*Jadie*. Are you listening to me?"

She had still been fingering the top of her shoe, but she stopped, her fingers going momentarily rigid. "Why should I?" she said in a disparaging tone and let her foot drop back down to the floor. "'Cause I can tell you never listen to me."

Chapter Twenty-Two

The first heavy snowfall of the winter came the Wednesday before Thanksgiving and turned the plains from buffalo-grass yellow to white. Looking out my window at breakfast time, it was as if the world beyond Pecking had disappeared. The jumble of rooftops was still there, but in the distance, the white prairie was indistinguishable from the white sky.

Fortunately, all my children made it to school, even Jeremiah, who lived the farthest out, and he, as usual, was full of weird and wonderful news.

"I seen you on TV last night," he announced, as we settled down for morning discussion.

"You did?"

"Yeah, we was watching this here movie and there was these two ladies wrestling. And this one lady, she looked just like you. I says to Micah, 'Hey, that there's my teacher!' But Micah said it probably wasn't."

Lowering my head slightly to disguise my smile, I managed a nod. "Micah was right. It wasn't me."

"It *looked* like you," Jeremiah said suspiciously. "Are you sure?"

"I'm sure, Jeremiah."

"Well, she was fighting this other broad. Then, just as she was getting her down good, WHAM! She pulls out this great big ol' knife and stabs her right in the heart. That one that looked like you, I mean. She stabbed the other one. And all this blood goes squirting everywhere. It was really good, man. You shoulda seen it."

"Mmmm."

"You *sure* it wasn't you?"

"Positive, Jeremiah. I haven't made any movies."

"I told Micah that was probably where you got so strong at. I said you were one strong broad. I *know.*" He grinned cheekily.

"Where exactly did you see all this?" I asked.

"On my TV. My mom's boyfriend's got this friend, see, and he gets stuff free sometimes. He's always bringing home these movies he gets for free."

"And you and Micah watch them?"

"Yeah. They're *good,* man," he replied enthusiastically.

"Do you think what happens on them is real?"

"You mean like when you was stabbing that other broad?"

I nodded.

Jeremiah paused. "Well, it's not real. But it's not *not* real, either. Those things could happen. It's sort of real, I think. I mean, some of the stuff they show on TV is real, like news and junk. And some of this stuff is sort of real, too. 'Cause I always think if it *could* happen, it could be real, and so maybe it is."

I glanced over at Jadie, sitting hunched, her head down. Jeremiah was a sturdy child, well-grounded in the world around him, and he clearly did not discern the reality of what he was watching easily. How easy would it be for a confused child exposed to violent, pornographic material to extrapolate it to real life?

For the most part, the day went well. The children were overexcited by the snow, the pageant, and the prospect of four days' vacation from school, so there was silliness on a monumental scale, but it was good-natured and not too outrageous. Philip and Jeremiah were the worst, egging one another on in the classroom, prancing around in their headbands, having a peeing contest up the wall above the urinal in the boys' restroom. Reuben caught the excitement of the day, but he and Brucie still found the disruption of routine more disconcerting than fun. Jadie, alone, was the odd one out. Although she now generally enjoyed a warm relationship with the boys during class time, particularly Philip and Jeremiah, on this occasion she kept separate. Badly bent over, her head lowered, her arms drawn up, she fought the rest of us off with irritable silence.

When afternoon came, we joined the other classes backstage and the excitement reached fever pitch, until finally, in a fit of laughter, Philip wet himself. This sobered the others considerably, and they gave their performance flawlessly. Afterward, we all retired to our individual classrooms, where the parents had been invited for cookies and punch. Everyone in my class had family there, except for Jeremiah, so I let him pass around the cookies and punch.

Jadie's mother came, accompanied not only by Sapphire but also Amber, who, being a kindergartner and attending mornings only, had no school in the afternoon. I found myself watching this little group furtively as I went about my task as hostess. There wasn't much conversation among any of them, but then conversation with Jadie in her bent-over position would have been difficult in any case. When Jeremiah came around, Mrs. Ekdahl accepted her cookies and punch from him graciously, gave a drink to Sapphire, who was sitting on the floor beside her, and then gave the toddler a cookie. From across the room, I studied her. Was this the face of Miss Ellie? Pam? Sue Ellen? Did she turn into some kind of monster behind closed doors, abusing her child so frightfully that Jadie's entire self had disintegrated?

I couldn't see anything. She'd made an effort to look nice, but there was an aura of pathos in the wildly out-of-date turquoise eyeshadow and streaky blusher. I'd always found Mrs. Ekdahl's well-intentioned but ineffectual efforts poignant, but now I couldn't dislodge the wariness. Repeatedly, I tried to sense even the slightest thing that might give substance to Jadie's stories.

After the children had gone, a festive mood remained in the school. Abandoning my room for the teachers' lounge, I joined the rest of the staff for coffee and sugar doughnuts. No one talked of pupils or lesson plans; all conversation revolved around Thanksgiving dinner, the holiday football games, and the diabolical weather.

Throughout the day, the snow had continued to fall, so when I left the school to go home, there was about eighteen inches on the ground. I got into my car and started the motor. A few cold, misty moments passed before the defroster cleared the windshield on the inside. In the meantime, I ran the wipers to knock the powdery snow off enough to give me a view. Then I shifted into reverse gear and went nowhere. A pause. I tried again and the all-too-familiar sound of spinning tires greeted me.

My car was hopeless at reversing in deep snow. It was too lightweight and it was front-wheel drive. Piqued because I had not had the foresight to reverse into my parking space, I knew the only solution now was to dig a bit of the snow away from the tires in order to get some traction. Pulling my gloves on, I got out again to get the shovel from the trunk.

Looking around the passenger side of the car from where I was standing beside the open trunk,

I was startled to see a bit of blond hair sticking out from under the front tire. I quickly went to see what it was but couldn't pick it up, because as I had been trying to reverse, the car had moved far enough back to run over it.

"What's that?"

Startled, I turned abruptly.

Lucy stood just beyond the other car. "What have you got there?"

"It seems to be a doll. One of my dolls, you know, those Sasha dolls from the classroom. Only it's trapped under the car. I was trying to back out, and now I'm going to have to move the car forward to release it."

"What the heck is it doing here?"

I'd already gone around the car and climbed back into the driver's seat. Pulling it forward, I moved the tire off the doll sufficiently for Lucy to pick it up. It was the doll with the long, blond hair, except that now, partially run over, it was no longer blond or long-haired. Gingerly, I touched its head, still intact but badly squashed.

"This is the doll Jadie had, isn't it? How do you expect it got here?" Lucy asked, her brow puckering. "That's an awful funny place for her to drop it."

I took the doll from her.

"I know she waits for you sometimes, but you wouldn't think she'd just drop it that way, would you? Kind of makes you think ... well, it sort of looks put there on purpose."

I felt a sickening tightness in my stomach.

"Kind of makes you think she wanted it to get run over."

Once home that evening, I was haunted by the doll. It had been lying perpendicular to the front tire on the passenger side, its head shoved right up against the tire, the rest of the body extending back under the car. There was no way I could, in ordinary circumstances, have avoided running over it. There was also no way, in my opinion, that it could have been dropped into that position accidentally. Someone had to have put it that way. But why? What purpose did it serve? In all likelihood, I would never even have known the doll was there, and thus, would never have realized I'd run over it.

The message behind this incident seemed clear enough to me. Everybody, myself included, had identified the doll as me, as my stand-in for Jadie when I was not physically there. To destroy it so dramatically was hardly a subtle hint about Jadie's feelings for me; and while such a nasty gesture didn't make me feel good, in and of itself it wouldn't have been too worrying. I knew I was a powerful figure in the lives of the children I worked with. The intensity of our relationship always made me a target for destructive feelings and many, many children over the years had made symbolic efforts to kill me. The fact that only the afternoon previously I had told her about the psychiatrist might have been ample stimulus for hate. Perhaps she felt I was abandoning her or giving up on her. Perhaps she felt betrayed, thinking that I might have told others about things she'd made me promise would stay between us. Perhaps she just felt I was getting too close for comfort. All were ample reasons for such intense hate. But still, that one thing did not make sense. Why position the doll so that I wouldn't know it had been destroyed? If this was a gesture of anger or defiance, what good was it, if I never knew it was made?

Thanksgiving morning, I rose early and in the predawn darkness, I set out for the city. Had things gone to plan, I should have gone up on Wednesday evening to stay with Hugh, so that we could drive over to the adjacent state in the morning to spend Thanksgiving with his sister and her family. Weather had prevented my going anywhere on Wednesday, and the way it was Thursday morning, I didn't think I could get into the city on time to make the subsequent journey to Annie's. Not wanting to chance ruining her Thanksgiving dinner by arriving late, I phoned Hugh and told him to go on ahead without me. I had a key to his apartment, so I said I'd just let myself in and be there when he got back.

The journey between Pecking and the city was, in a word, horrific. The snow had stopped, but the wind had picked up and the road was often lost in a ground blizzard. There wasn't a vehicle on the highway besides myself and the occasional snowplow. A couple of times a highway patrol car passed, and in both instances I expected to be pulled over and told the road was being closed. Valhalla and Harmony and all the other hamlets along the way had disappeared into the vast whiteness, their lumpiness no more distinguishable than that of trees or fence posts. The only way of marking progress was with the odometer and, since it steadily ticked over, I assumed I was still moving. But only just. I was seldom able to exceed forty miles per hour.

Despite the difficult driving conditions, I felt my mood lighten as the journey progressed. I'd always enjoyed driving and found long distances mentally relaxing. With the outrageous weather, I was forced to concentrate much harder than usual, but this, too, was beneficial. Preoccupied with the road conditions, I had no time to think about what I'd left behind.

When I came up to Hugh's apartment, I discovered that he, also, had not gone to his sister's.

"Not worth it in this weather," he said as he helped me in with my duffel bag. "And me there, you here—not a sensible arrangement, is it?" He grinned.

I laughed.

"Besides, I've cooked us our own Thanksgiving dinner."

"What? Now? How did you know when I'd be in?" This I was going to have to see, as Hugh's cooking skills were not renowned.

"Didn't I tell you about that Cordon Bleu course I was taking?" And with that, he tossed me out the box from a microwave dinner. "We got four more minutes 'til the bell rings. You hungry? You ready for the big gorge?"

Hugh and I got along far better when we only saw one another every few weeks. The arguments and agitations that had marred our relationship previously never arose during these short visits. We had the best of one another and made the most of it.

I spent the break in complete contrast to my normal habits. Hugh loved the honky-tonk bars down near the stockyards on the southern fringe of the city. He could play a pretty mean bit of guitar himself and enjoyed the smoky, crowded rooms and the country-western music. So we went bar-hopping every evening, staying well into the wee hours of the morning. The snow and the holiday had thinned the crowds, but there were still plenty of people left making good music and the dance floor was roomier.

I had desperately needed such a change, and it wasn't until early Sunday afternoon that my thoughts strayed back in the direction of Jadie and Pecking. Hugh and I had stayed out outrageously late the previous night and hadn't gotten up until after eleven. We'd then made muffins and bacon and taken these, along with a jug of orange juice, into the living room, where he sprawled across the couch and I across the floor, both absorbed in the Sunday papers. The sun had finally put in an appearance, and it shone brightly through the French windows, making the whole room pleasantly hot.

I'd already read the papers once and was lolling in the sun, browsing through the advertisements, when for no particular reason Jadie came to mind. "Is that occult bookstore open today?" I asked.

"Yeah, I suppose so. Why?"

"Do you think we could go down there before I have to leave? I'd like another look around."

"Still pursuing that issue, are you?" he asked.

"Yeah, sort of, I guess. I was thinking I'd like to talk to that girl again. You know. The witch."

"Hey, Brenda!" Hugh shouted as we came through the doorway of the bookstore. There were two or three other people amidst the crowded shelves in the tiny shop, and they all turned to see what the commotion was about.

"Hi, you guys," Brenda said cheerfully when she saw us. "How'd you like your books? Do the trick for you? Back for more?"

"Yes, they were okay. Pretty interesting," I said, then paused a moment, "but what I was really wondering was if I could have a quick word with you. I had something happen to me the other day; and I've been curious about it ever since. I was hoping maybe you could tell me if you'd ever heard of such a thing in connection with the occult."

"Yeah?" she asked, her eyes lighting up with interest.

"I mean, it might not be. It might very well be someone just acting silly, but ... well, I'm still kind of interested in this occult business, and I was just wondering ..."

I turned my head to see if the other customers had left yet. Hugh was browsing through the section on New Age material, but there was someone else around the corner still.

Brenda sensed my reluctance to talk there, in front of everyone. She jerked her head toward a curtained-off area behind the cash register. "Come back here," she said. "I can still hear from here, if anyone wants anything."

The place was narrow, no more than a walk-in closet, with a teapot, a couple of stools, and what appeared to be account books. It was heavy with the musty scent of sage tea.

Brenda pulled over one of the stools for herself and pushed the other in my direction. "Yeah, so what's going on?" she asked.

"I gave someone a doll," I said. "The doll does look somewhat like me. Certainly, the person concerned has used it to represent me, and I guess I did encourage that. It's a child we're talking about; she's got emotional problems, and I thought she'd be able to deal with them better if she had something to symbolize the stability of our relationship."

"Yeah?" said Brenda, curiosity brightening her expression. She leaned forward on her stool, putting her elbows on her knees.

"The other night after work, I went out to my car to go home. It had been snowing heavily, and the tires started spinning when I tried to back out of my parking space, so I had to dig it out some. As I was coming around to shovel out the front tire on the passenger's side, I found this doll I'd given to the little girl. It had been placed right under the tire, like so," I gestured, "so that when I backed the car out of my parking space, I would run directly over its head and break it."

Brenda's eyes widened, the pupils expanding.

"Now, I'm not exaggerating when I say this girl has emotional problems. She does, and I suppose the logical conclusion is that she put the doll there herself. Certainly, I feel positive it was placed there and hadn't fallen accidentally into that position, if for no other reason than that the snow would have kept it from rolling. But I guess what I'm wondering is if there might be an occult connection to all this. I'm wondering if perhaps someone else beyond this girl might be involved."

"I haven't heard of people doing that precisely, but I know what they're up to."

"What?"

Brenda paused and studied my face a long moment before continuing. "I'm not sure you're going to want me to say this. I mean, like, I don't even know you and I don't know what you're into."

"I'm not really into any of this on purpose, but if there is a definite satanic connection here, it would be very helpful for me to know."

"They're not wishing you well," Brenda said cautiously.

"I gathered that much myself. But is this satanic?"

"I don't know for sure who's doing it to you, but I do know what it is: black magic." A pause. Brenda scratched her head, then dropped her hands between her knees. Several moments passed, as she contemplated them. "See, I'm not really in that scene," she said at last. "Mine's white magic. I just want sort of to be one with the Mother Goddess and that kind of thing, you know? To be in tune with the earth. With the natural spirits. I don't mess with any of the black stuff."

"But it is definitely black magic? You know that? What kind? What does this mean?"

Brenda took a deep breath. "Well, see, they … *them* … well, in doing black magic … they're usually doing it for power. Power to get the things they want. Power to influence people. Power over their enemies. And part of getting the power means having to call up the forces of darkness. See, that's how we're different. In white magic, you never call upon the forces of darkness."

For a brief moment, I pulled myself back from this conversation and the absurdity of it struck me. Here I was, in some decrepit back room, having an earnest conversation with a witch over magic. *Me?* What immediately followed was the depressing realization that I wasn't dreaming. This was real life and I couldn't get out of it.

"In doing black magic, they're going to make sacrifices. That's all part of calling the dark forces, and if … well, if they have an enemy they want to get rid of, especially if the enemy is strong and has a lot of power, they're going to have to do a lot of magicking. They're going to need to make a sacrifice to get help ..." Brenda's voice faded and again she contemplated her hands. "There's this thing, see, about sacrifices," she said, her voice quiet. "A willing one gives you a lot more power than an unwilling one."

"You're saying this is sort of like a voodoo doll, aren't you?" I asked.

"Yeah, sort of."

I smiled reassuringly, because I could see she was uncomfortable telling me I was a victim of this kind of activity. "I think I'd already sussed that out, and it doesn't really bother me. It's not very nice to think about, but I don't believe in that stuff. They can't really frighten me with it."

A pause.

"There is one thing that bugs me, however," I said, "one thing I can't figure out. And that's the fact that the doll was placed with its head under the tire and its body back under the car. In ordinary circumstances, I would never have discovered it was there. It was only by chance that there was enough snow during the day for my car to get stuck. In any other instance, I would have simply driven away, smashing over the doll and being none the wiser for having done so. Was that just lack of sophistication, placing it there? Had someone just made a mistake? Because if they were trying to warn me off or frighten me, it would have made more sense to put the doll somewhere that I would have been sure to see it. The way it happened seems pointless to me."

"I don't think they were trying to scare you," Brenda replied. "Like, I suspect the doll was deliberately hidden. This is black magic, not just some game. The point of it was to get you to destroy the doll, which you wouldn't have done, if you'd known it was there."

"But why?"

"The doll's in your image, isn't it? If you destroy your own totem, you're destroying yourself. They will have put a very powerful spell on that doll. To invoke a willing sacrifice. They want you to commit suicide."

Chapter Twenty-Three

The drive back to Pecking on Sunday evening was a depressing one for me. I hadn't been totally honest with Brenda when I'd said I wasn't frightened by what had happened. I was. It was an insidious, creeping sort of fear, oozing into unoccupied corners of my mind; whenever I stopped actively thinking, I became aware of it. Four hours alone in the car made keeping it at bay hard work.

Did I believe in this kind of stuff? Might it be true? I could hardly ignore the fact of June Harriman's suicide the previous year, and, while there was in all likelihood no connection, it still made a chilling backdrop to the implications of the ruined doll. What I couldn't deny was the fact that a turning point had come for me. I could have accepted that Jadie had put the doll there; if she denied it, I could have even accepted that, knowing that if she was suffering from a multiple personality disorder, she might genuinely not remember having done it. What I couldn't accept was the obscure placement of the doll under the tire. It implied someone else. Even if Jadie had put it there herself, it implied someone else's instructions.

Over and over and over I pondered the various points of the case. It occurred to me that what I'd like to do was just keep driving, to go past Falls River, past Pecking, and on along the freeway to someplace different, someplace new. I had visions of reaching New Mexico, if I kept going long enough, emerging from the winter darkness into sunshine and heat.

Monday morning I took the blond-haired Sasha doll into school and carefully laid it out on one of the benches in the cloakroom. Jeremiah, the first to arrive, shrieked when he saw it.

"Wowie! Lady, come look at this!" he called from the cloakroom. "Some boog's come in here and fucked up one of your dollies. Come here, quick!"

"I know about it already, Jeremiah," I called back from the classroom.

The other children arrived then, clattering into the cloakroom with their schoolbags and lunch-boxes.

"It was *you!*" I heard Jeremiah say. "It was that girl!" He came running out to me in the classroom. "It's that boogy girl in there. You just ask her. She done it. You let her have that nice doll of yours, and just look what she done to it. Boy, bet you're sorry now. Bet you're never gonna let her have something nice again, huh? And it's gonna serve her right."

"Jeremiah, calm down."

"Man, lady," he said and leaned close to me, his eyes round, "what you gonna *do* to her?"

Reuben and Philip emerged from the cloakroom, their eyes huge with the drama of it all. Then out rolled Brucie, oblivious, as usual. But no Jadie.

"Time for morning discussion," I called. "Come on, everybody."

Still no Jadie.

"Coulda told you not to give her nothing. Coulda told you that girl's no good. Bet she's gonna say she didn't do it. Fucks up your doll and bet she thinks you're gonna believe her little pussy face, when she says she didn't do it."

"Jeremiah, please." I turned him physically around and pushed him gently toward the reading area, where we held morning discussion. Then I stalked to the cloakroom door. "Jadie? Come on, now."

Jadie wasn't in there. The doll remained, but the room was empty.

"Jadie?" I went into the cloakroom, then to the hallway door. I stuck my head out. No Jadie.

I returned to the classroom. "Was she here? Did you actually see her, Jeremiah?"

"Yeah, sure she was here. But when she seen what she done, she got the fuck outa here."

I held off morning discussion as long as I could, hoping Jadie would venture back, but she never did.

At recess I went down to Alice's room to see if Amber was there. Sure enough she was, but there was no sign of her sister. Had Jadie come to school this morning? I asked Amber. Yes, she apparently had. When lunchtime came and she was still missing, I reluctantly had to admit the need to call her home and let her mother know I'd somehow lost Jadie.

"Jadie's not there?" her mother said over the phone. "Well, no, she's home. Didn't she tell you? She got feeling sick, said she puked in the school toilets, so she came home. Didn't she say nothing to you first?"

I hung up the phone in dismay.

"I didn't do it."

Startled by the unexpected voice, I jumped. There, in the classroom door, stood Jadie. She wore no outer clothes whatsoever, only a saggy, well-washed jogsuit and bedroom slippers.

"Does your mom know you're here?"

"I didn't do it. I didn't hurt that doll. Cross my heart."

I closed my plan book. "No, I know you didn't. I did. Because I didn't see it there in the snow."

Closing the classroom door gently behind her, Jadie crossed the room to stand on the opposite side of the table.

"But I think you know how it got there. And why."

Jadie's mouth drew down, her face puckered with tears.

I sat, watching her. "So, what're we going to do about it?"

Jadie began to cry.

Rising from the table, I went into the cloakroom and picked up the doll. Then I returned to the classroom. Holding it out, I looked at it. "Well, what I think we ought to do is try to make it better."

Laying the doll on the counter beside the sink, I began to remove its soiled clothing. "It's only the head that's been damaged," I said. "There was a lot of snow and I think that acted as padding. I expect we could send her off to a doll hospital to be fixed."

Jadie, who had come back to stand beside me, watched my activities intently.

"Let's wash her off. You get the bottle of dishwashing liquid from under the sink. The dirt makes her look much worse than I think she is." I put the plug into the sink and began to fill it with warm water.

For several moments, Jadie, still tearful, made no effort to retrieve the bottle of liquid detergent. Then, hesitantly, she knelt and opened the cupboard door.

"When things go wrong," I said, "we try to make them better. Sometimes we can. Sometimes we can't. But trying gives us control over them, even if we fail."

I scrubbed the doll and then lifted it from the water. Strangely, it looked even more damaged clean than it had dirty. The broken face stood out in stark contrast to the smooth curves of its body.

Jadie leaned against the counter and watched as I took an old towel out and started to dry the doll. Cautiously, she reached a hand up and with one finger gently stroked the doll's arm.

"If I tell," she said, her voice soft, "will the policemen look for Tashee?"

I glanced over.

"Will they try and find her?"

"Do you want them to?" I asked.

"I always tried to take care of her. She wasn't as big as me. She was my age, but she was little. I tried to help her best I could ..."

I continued drying the doll, running the soft fabric of the towel over the smooth limbs.

"Would they believe me?" Jadie asked.

"We won't know if we don't try."

Jadie looked up. "Would you stay with me? If I told? If I did it now?"

I nodded. "Of course, I would. Shall we go talk to Mr. Tinbergen?"

Jadie took in a deep breath and then, at last, she nodded. "Okay."

Once again. The Story. Jadie wouldn't tell it. The moment we reached Mr. Tinbergen's office, she went stone silent, her head down protectively between her hunched shoulders, so I recounted all the private moments that had passed between us. Sitting on the hard plastic chairs, bathed in the bright fluorescent lights of Mr. Tinbergen's office, I reconstructed the world of the cloakroom.

Mr. Tinbergen's expression grew stricken as I talked. He paled. His eyes left my face, to wander restlessly around the perimeter of the room. He never looked me in the eye again that afternoon.

"What do you want me to do?" he asked, when I'd finished. His voice harbored a plaintive note I hadn't anticipated. Then again, he cast around the room, as if searching for something familiar he couldn't find. "I think I'm a little out of my depth on this one," he murmured. "We're going to need some help. This isn't a decision I'll want to make by myself."

I glanced at Jadie, beside me. Hunched down, doubled over, she had the constricted rigidity of a cerebral-palsied person, her limbs pulled back against her, her fingers twisted in to grip the material of her clothes. Her head was so far down, I couldn't see her face, but I didn't need to see it to know her mouth was clamped shut.

"You're sure about this?" Mr. Tinbergen queried, looking at Jadie. "You're sure she knows what she's talking about?"

"Yes."

"We're going to need help."

The first person Mr. Tinbergen called was Arkie in Falls River. Would she come down? Right now? he asked. After concluding the call, he paused a moment, the end of the receiver resting against his chin. Then he dialed Social Services. Explaining briefly that he had a case of suspected child abuse to report, he asked for a representative to come to the school.

Since both people coming were in Falls River, this meant a half hour's time lag before we could expect them to be in the office. I rose from my chair to go back to the classroom and get Jadie's school file and my own notes. Did she want to come with me? I asked Jadie, but she remained silent and immobile on the red plastic chair. She couldn't even manage a nod or a shake of the head.

I knelt beside the chair. "Do you think you can talk, Jadie?" I asked, bending low enough to see her face. I gently pushed her hair back slightly.

No response.

"I know this is frightening. I know you're scared, but do you think you can manage? I'll stay with you. I'll be right here."

No response.

"She's going to have to say something," Mr. Tinbergen replied.

She raised her eyes then to meet mine, although she didn't raise her head. With only a slight movement of her constricted arm, she pressed her fingers against her mouth.

Arkie was the first to arrive. "Well, you do know how to pick up live wires, don't you?" she said to me when we met out in the front office. I sensed a note of irritation. Perhaps she thought I was blowing this all out of proportion, that I'd let an overactive imagination run away with me, when we could have solved this in a calmer, more civilized fashion. Or perhaps she was simply tired and hungry, as I was, and annoyed to be pulled out when she'd have rather gone home.

The social worker was named Delores Verney. Short, overweight, and fiftyish, she wore a pair of huge, owlish glasses pushed up on top of her head. Her hair, dark at the roots and bright blond at the ends, was in a short, cropped style, now rumpled to stand up in a manner very similar to Jeremiah's, when he needed a haircut. Her smile, however, was broad and easy, and she shook my hand with a heartiness that intimated that we were old friends.

"I think we have to face the fact that a criminal offense may have been committed here," she said, as way of greeting. "From what I'm told, we well may have to take this child—and most likely all other children in the home—into care for the time being. The only way I can get a place-of-safety order at such short notice is in conjunction with the police, so I've gone ahead and phoned the station. We should be getting an officer out here in a few minutes."

This conversation, like the one with Arkie, was hissed in the front office, while Jadie remained with Mr. Tinbergen in his office. Both he and I realized immediately that the most serious problem facing us was not the abuse but Jadie's fear. Indeed, she had yet to say a word, even to Mr. Tinbergen. So he and I took it in turns to sit with Jadie or meet-and-greet in the front office, in hopes that Jadie would not be intimidated by a rush of new people. Thus, everyone was shuttling back and forth in what could only be described as organized confusion.

"I prefer to work with someone from our station in Falls River," Delores said to me. "I know we're going to need to go through the Pecking police to do anything, but there's only what? Two officers here? Three? I wouldn't trust them with a case like this. I wanted a woman officer—that's the usual procedure around here with child victims, if at all possible—and my girl in Falls River is experienced. One of the best in the state for child abuse. Now," she said, pausing for breath, "who's the one making the complaint?"

Heart long since sunk into my shoes, I knew, like Pandora, I had opened the box and was never going to get the lid back on again.

The policewoman's name was Lindy. She was much younger than I'd expected, perhaps no more than thirty, and startlingly attractive. Large brown eyes and glossy, well-cut hair framing her face gave her the look of a Hollywood starlet, not a midwestem police officer; her appearance was further enhanced by stylishly casual clothes rather than a uniform.

Lindy had worked with Delores on several child abuse cases and seemed competent and confident. I took heart from this. On the other hand, the officer from the Pecking station seemed ill at ease. Unless there was concrete evidence, he kept saying, it was just going to be this girl's word against her parents. Gotta find semen, else there wasn't going to be a case.

Unexpectedly, I once again found myself downplaying the occult connection. In the heat of the first few moments with Mr. Tinbergen, it had been easy to mention the broken doll, the Black Mass symbol, and other aspects of Jadie's bizarre tales that indicated ritualistic abuse; however, as time wore on and more and more professionals joined us, I found myself disinclined to go beyond the obvious. Yes, I said, there were definite indications of abuse, particularly sexual abuse. Yes, I said, there was the possibility of more than one person being involved. But I couldn't make myself go out on a limb and say I thought we were looking for a coven or something like that. When Lindy turned to me and asked who, precisely, I thought was abusing Jadie, I paused. Who, indeed? I sputtered and tried to explain that she used some kind of code name for them. At this point Arkie jumped in to say Jadie appeared to be suffering from a dissociative disorder and that either she, herself, was disintegrating into an assortment of personalities or she had splintered her abuser or abusers into multiple personalities. Possibly both. Of course, Arkie said, sexual abuse was commonly implicated in dissociative disorders. I fell silent at this point and didn't add anything to Arkie's statement. I'd be grateful just to get Jadie out of the home, I thought. That was the main objective.

Jadie, herself, was no help at all. Despite her initial agreement to talk about the abuse with Mr. Tinbergen, she clammed up the moment she went into the office and had not said a single word since.

She managed an occasional nod and that was all. Hunched over, drawn up, every muscle rigid, she appeared to have been turned to stone by fear.

We stayed in the school office until almost 7:15 in the evening, discussing among ourselves the type and extent of abuse suspected, the possible perpetrators, Jadie's psychological makeup and that of other family members. It was decided that Jadie, Amber, and Sapphire would be taken immediately into the care of Social Services on an eight-day place-of-safety order, during which time the police would examine the case.

The time then came to adjourn to the police station, and it was decided that Mr. Tinbergen, Arkie, and I had probably made our contributions to the proceedings for the evening and didn't need to go along. They had our statements and that was all we could give. It went out of our hands from this point onward. Despite my emotional involvement, I could appreciate this, but I mentioned my concern for Jadie. Would she be comfortable going alone in the police car with Lindy and Delores, or would she be better with one of us along? Lindy pointed out the extreme care now needed to keep from inadvertently biasing anything Jadie might say. It might be better if we kept contact to a minimum. And Jadie seemed to accept this next step. She disappeared through the door of the school, her hand in Lindy's, and didn't give a backward glance.

About 9:15, Lindy phoned me from the Pecking police station. They'd brought the Ekdahls in, she said. Mom and Dad seemed completely bewildered by all of this. Amber, who had been interviewed separately from Jadie or her parents, denied all knowledge of abuse. Jadie refused to talk to anyone about anything. There hadn't been a word out of her since she'd arrived. Lindy didn't need to mention the amount of frustration she was feeling because of Jadie's silence; it echoed clearly in her voice, but she made it plain how damaging this attitude was going to be. She explained that she'd already called Arkie, and Arkie had told her to phone me. I was the one would could make mutes talk.

At the police station, I was met at the front desk, let through a heavy door with an electronic lock, and taken down a long corridor to a large back room. The place was alive with people, mainly from Social Services in Falls River, but also with additional police personnel.

Lindy greeted me. "We've put a place-of-safety order on the girls, and Delores has managed to find a short-term foster home in Red Circle that'll take all three of them for the week. That's super, because it means they'll be close enough to continue attending school here. I think that's best. It's going to be a disruptive enough week as it is. Mind you, we still haven't got anything out of Jadie, and, heck, Torey, the whole works'll fall right through the floor if this kid keeps it up. I'm praying to God you're going to be able to make her see sense."

"One won't talk, one won't shut up," Delores muttered. "I was trying to explain to the six-year-old that they'd be staying with another family for the week, and she's gone hysterical on me. Absolutely hysterical."

"It's going to be difficult," I said.

"Why's that?" Delores asked.

"They're a closed-in family. The mother told me they've never left the girls with anyone for any length of time. Not even a babysitter for the evening."

"Oh Jesus, are you joking?"

I was led down the hall to one of the interview rooms, and the door was opened. There sat Jadie, alone. I came in and the officer shut the door behind me and left us.

It was a small room, not even as large as the cloakroom at school. The walls were lined with corkboard to ensure privacy. There was a switch by the door to turn on a red light outside so others in the hall would know when they should not interrupt. The room had no windows and was furnished with only a metal-legged table, three plastic chairs, and a file cabinet.

Jadie was sitting on a chair that had been pushed up to the table. She was bent over so far that her head touched the tabletop.

"This is proving a long night, isn't it?" I said and came over. Pulling out one of the other chairs, I sat down. "Are you tired?"

She nodded.

I was tired. The evening had been so emotionally exhausting that I found I had almost no feelings at all as I sat there. I felt a deep form of sympathy for Jadie, almost maternal in its strength, and I wanted to catch her up in my arms and protect her, but that was all I felt. Certainly, I had no inclination just then to carry on with what I'd been sent in to do.

"Have they told you what's going to happen next?" I asked. "Lindy says they're going to let your mom and dad go pretty soon, but they're thinking it would be better if you and your sisters didn't go home just at the moment. Just until this thing is sorted out. So the three of you are going to stay at a place in Red Circle. A foster home. Rather like Philip has got, with a special foster mom and dad to take care of you while you're there."

Jadie put her elbows on the table and propped up her head with her hands. She gave little indication of listening to me. Both of us, I think, were so far past exhaustion as to be numb.

"You'll still come to our class. We'll still see each other."

On the table beside Jadie lay two rag dolls, one dressed in man's clothing, the other in woman's. A girl doll lay a little farther along. Stretching across the table, Jadie reached for the girl doll. She held it up in front of her and stared at it.

"Jadie, it's not going to help at all if you don't talk to them."

"Did you tell them about Tashee?"

"You're expecting me to do all the work here, Jadie, and I can't. *You* tell them about Tashee.

You're the one it happened to, not me. You're the one who knows."

"I can't."

"You can. And you must."

"I can't. There's spiders here. I seen 'em. They're going to hear. They're going to tell Miss Ellie what I done."

"That's over with, lovey. We're putting an end to it right now."

"It's not over with," she said mournfully. "The spiders are watching."

Exhaustion overtook my patience. I sighed in desperation. "Look, Jadie, what can I do? Would a can of Raid help? If I spray the place myself, will you *talk* to them?"

Close to tears, she looked at me. "No, please, you got to tell them for me."

When I finished with Jadie, one of the social workers came and took her into another room where Amber was. A small box of old, well-worn toys was provided, although both girls looked so tired as to be beyond play. I then went down to the room where Lindy and Delores were to discuss the difficulties we were going to encounter if Jadie failed to speak. About ten minutes later, we heard the sound of doors opening and closing. Voices filtered through to us from the corridor.

"That'll be Mr. and Mrs. Ekdahl leaving," said Delores, and she pushed back her chair. "I'd better go get the girls, so they can say good-bye."

I stepped cautiously out into the corridor after everyone had passed. Uneasy about being the one to cause so much trouble, knowing I was the one to destroy this family, and still not sure that I'd pointed the finger at the right people, I was reluctant to be seen; but at the same time, I was curious to see them. Both looked dazed. Mr. Ekdahl, small and wiry, his thinning hair rumpled, stood back as Amber came running down the corridor.

"Mommy! Mommy!" she screamed at full volume. "Take me with you! I wanna go home!" Mrs. Ekdahl, a bedraggled-looking figure in saggy clothes, clutched her young daughter to her.

There was nothing in their demeanor that set the Ekdahls apart from any other of millions of midwestern families. I think, as I stepped into the corridor, I was praying I'd see something to clinch the matter in my mind. I think I wanted to at least sense evil in them, if nothing else, and come away secure in the knowledge that somehow these people were guilty of what I was accusing. There *had to* be abuse. Even if the occult connection could never be proved, even if Jadie was found to be severely disturbed and capable of fantasizing the worst of what she spoke of, I did feel certain something terrible was at the root of it. But I stood in abject terror of accusing the wrong persons.

The crowd had clustered just before the electronically locked door, where Amber was clutching frantically at her mother's clothing and crying. No one noticing me, I slipped down to the room where Jadie and Amber had been. Jadie was still there, still sitting on the floor beside the box of toys, a decrepit-looking Barbie doll in her hands.

"Your parents are going now. Do you want to come say good-bye?"

"Look here at how long the hair is this doll's got," Jadie remarked. "I got Barbies at home, but none of mine gots hair like this."

"I said, your parents are going now."

"It don't got no clothes, though. I got some clothes. I wish I could have this Barbie."

"Jadie ..."

At last she lifted her head and looked up at me, her thick hair tumbling back over her shoulders. "You just tell 'em good-bye for me, okay?"

Taken aback, I regarded her. "You won't be seeing them for quite a while. Amber's gone to say good-bye. Don't you want to come, too?"

"No, I'm busy playing," she replied, the emotion in her voice unreadable. "You say good-bye for me."

At the far end of the corridor, Amber was being prized off her mother's leg. I stayed well back, embarrassed to be seen, frightened by what I'd done this evening. Finally, the door unlocked with an electronic buzz, and a policeman opened it to let the Ekdahls out into the front part of the station. The door closed automatically, giving a loud, long sigh, and then the lock snapped audibly back into place when it was completely shut. Amber, still sobbing, was carried by in the arms of a social worker.

In the silence that followed, Jadie appeared in the corridor. She scuttled past me and down to the door. Coming up against it, she tried to open it. Delores, who'd seen her go back, hurried after her. "They've already gone, sweetheart," she said.

Jadie jiggled the handle of the door.

"Oh, sweetheart, I am sorry. They've already gone."

Jadie tried it again. "I just wanted to see if the door was locked."

Chapter Twenty-Four

Jadie didn't come to school the next morning, a result, I suspect, of the long night before. When she did show up the following day, she looked like a different child. Literally. Her mass of dark hair, which had always been loose and often uncombed, was now parted smartly on the side. The thicker section was pinioned back from her face with a wide white clip and the rest was done into long corkscrew curls. These had been gathered into two pigtails and tied with red bows. The effect was both quaint and peculiar. To complete the transformation, Jadie was wearing a garishly checked red-and-white dress with ruffled sleeves, which I doubted was hers.

"Whoooeeee!" Jeremiah cried, when he saw her. "Look at that girl, man! Ain't she a piece of cake?" And he ran after Jadie, smacking his lips.

"Get away," Jadie replied irritably.

"Jeremiah, sit down, please."

"Yeah, but look at them curls, man. Trying to drive a guy wild, that's what she's doing with them curls." He paused a moment in thought. "She's a foam fattal, that's what she is."

"Oh, just ignore him," Jadie replied in a thoroughly disgusted voice.

She seemed happier. Her posture was not quite so rigid; her movements were freer. She tolerated Jeremiah's attentions; she allowed Philip to work with her; she acknowledged Reuben and Brucie's existence for the first time in ages. But during math, when she had gone to take her folder back and put it on the window ledge, I caught her pausing to gaze out the window toward her house.

"Do you miss being home?" I asked softly, touching her shoulders.

"Amber does."

"What about you?"

She chewed her lip a moment and then slowly nodded. "Yeah, I do. I miss my mom, mostly. I miss her kissing me at night. I miss my Barbie dolls. I don't hardly got any of my own toys, and I keep wondering what's happening to them. Mostly, I miss things being the way they were."

At lunchtime, Jadie joined the others in the cafeteria, the first time she'd ever eaten lunch at school. After seeing the children down to the lunchroom, I headed back to my room to collect my sack lunch before going to the teachers' lounge. However, just before the bell had rung, I'd been using some homemade modeling dough with Brucie and could now feel the salt from it on my hands. So, I detoured into the girls' rest room to wash them before collecting my lunch.

There were several younger children in there, using the toilets and washing their hands, and they finished quickly at the appearance of a teacher, leaving me alone. However, when the last of them had gone out the door, I had the sense I was still not entirely by myself. Turning my head, I looked around. There, just inside the door, stood Amber.

Like Jadie, she had been considerably tidied up. Her hair had never been as ungovernable as Jadie's, but she'd still always looked a little wild. Now, however, her long blond hair had been brushed carefully and the sections around her face had been pulled back and tied with a bow. Like Jadie, she wore a slightly out-of-date outfit suggestive of donation clothes.

"Hi," I said.

"What you done to my mommy and daddy?"

"I haven't done anything to them," I said, not sure that was completely true.

"Then how come we can't go home?"

"If things all come out fine, I'm sure you will be able to go home again. But the people from the police and Social Services need a little time to make sure things are fine."

Amber cocked her head slightly. "You're listening to what Jadie tells you," she said, her voice soft, almost hoarse.

"We only want to make sure everything is all right for you girls."

"Jadie can't help the way she is. She got borned wrong and she don't know what she's saying. She can't help it; it's not her fault, but you shouldn't oughta be listening to her."

At recess in the afternoon, Jadie came to stand with me. It was a cold, gray December day with a bitter wind sifting snow off the tops of the heaps where it had been cleared back from the playground. I took shelter in the lee of the building to watch the children. Jadie stood next to me.

"I'm not going to be able to talk to you anymore," she said, after several moments had elapsed in silence.

"Why's that?"

"'Cause me and Amber are coming by taxi now. I won't be able to stay after school, like I done before. You'll have to take me down to my ride now, just like you do with the boys." There was a note of pride in her voice. I think she enjoyed being like the others.

"If you want to talk, we'll always find time for it, somehow."

Jadie leaned closer as the wind gusted. Snow eddied around our boots. "Have you told them about Tashee yet?" she asked quietly.

"Have you?"

A pause, then she shook her head. "They won't believe me, if I tell 'em. You tell 'em, okay? You're grown up. They'll believe what you say."

I looked down at her. "I've told them what

I know, but that's the best I can do. It didn't happen to me."

"They brought them dolls out. They got holes in them, them dolls. Did you know that? You know, poop holes. And they got hair under their arms. Yeeuch," Jadie said, smiling and making a face. "The man one's got a dicky. And so does the little boy."

I nodded. "That's to make it easier for you to let them know what's happened."

"Amber, she don't want to touch them. They make her scared. They're like the dolls J.R. makes. His dolls got dickies on them too and they're big and hard. Amber gets nightmares about them dolls."

"Have you said this to the social worker?"

Jadie didn't answer.

"You *have* to talk to them, Jadie. I'm not kidding. I can back up what you're saying, but I can't be the one who says it all, because I wasn't there. When I tell it, I might tell it wrong, and it's very important that we don't get anything about this wrong. We need it all to be true."

She pressed against me as the wind blew.

"I mean it, Jadie. You have *got* to talk to them. You need to tell them in your own words what's going on. It's not going to be good enough, coming from me, if you don't talk, too."

"Amber don't like you anymore," she muttered in response.

"I know."

"She hates you."

"Yes, I can pretty well imagine."

"I said you was doing good, that you were going to get us out of this. I said she ought to like you, 'cause you were God. But she said no. She said you ain't."

"She's right, there."

Jadie shrugged good-naturedly.

"I'm not God. The time's long since come for you to stop thinking I am."

"I don't care."

"And it's all right for Amber to feel angry with me," I said. "A lot of frightening things have happened very suddenly."

Jadie tilted her head slightly, making the sausage-shaped curls tumble down over her shoulder. "Tashee still likes you, though."

"She does?"

"Tashee says Amber don't know. Amber's too little, but I got to take care of her. I got to take care of Sapphire, too, 'cause she's littlest of all." A pause. "I don't think Sapphire hates you. She's too small to understand anything."

Concerned, I looked at her. "How does Tashee tell you these things?"

Jadie shrugged. "She just does. See, what I think happened is that when Tashee died, her ghost got inside me, so I could talk for her. I listen and then I think about her, and that way I can hear her. I think what she wants and how I can make her happy and then that's what I try to do."

My heart sank.

Chapter Twenty-Five

The week went by in a disconcerting jumble of meetings, phone calls, and disjointed conversations. On two occasions, social workers came to the school with their dolls and equipment to interview Jadie and Amber. The police appeared, combed through Jadie's school files, and talked individually first with me, then with Mr. Tinbergen, and then with Alice Havers, who had had Jadie for two of her years at the school. Time and again, we saw the police cars parked across the street in front of the Ekdahls' home.

Very little information on the investigation filtered through to us in the school, which I found disconcerting in the beginning and then downright distressing. Despite being integral in bringing the case to the attention of the police and Social Services, I was now very much on the periphery of the investigation, and my fear that they were acquiring no substantial evidence mounted as the week progressed.

More difficult were the stark warnings to me about talking with Jadie. While I was told to carry on as normal in the classroom, I was instructed not to encourage any in-depth conversations between us alone, for fear that I might ask leading questions that would prejudice the case were it ever to come to court. Indeed, as the week went on, I had the horrible sense that the lawyers now representing Mr. and Mrs. Ekdahl were going to try to prove that I had planted many of these ideas in Jadie's fertile imagination.

All of this made me more and more reluctant to stand behind my accusations of occult involvement. With Jadie refusing to talk, with only skimpy evidence of any abuse, much less abuse by a large group of people, and with the police lawyers repeatedly suggesting that if the defense discovered I had gone several times to the occult bookshop and consulted with a person claiming to be a witch, they could be well down the road to proving the occult connection came from me. I wanted only to extricate myself, career intact.

In the quiet of Lindy's office, I did talk at some length with her about my suspicions. Couldn't it be, for instance, that Jadie was familiar with the old video machine I'd brought in the previous year because she'd come in contact with one before? I'd asked. What if the abuse sessions were filmed? Could that account for the number of times Jadie had asked me if I'd seen them on my TV? Perhaps she'd seen them played back in private and assumed they were being broadcast. Perhaps this was why everyone was referred to by "Dallas" character names. Wouldn't that be a perfect ploy to keep from being identified? With the reference to being on TV, outsiders would naturally conclude it was all a child's fantasy.

Jadie's continual reference to being given Coca-Cola was another example, I told Lindy. In one of the books on satanism I'd gotten from the occult bookstore, there had been mention of putting Valium or similar drugs into soft drinks to make the victims of the ritual assaults more compliant. While admittedly it sounded a bit farfetched to me, Jadie had mentioned Coke as an integral part of her times with Miss Ellie and the others too many times for me to dismiss it out of hand. Certainly, that would account for Jadie's hazy recollection of specifics during these occasions.

Lindy appeared to take these points seriously and was particularly interested in the doll incident; she felt, as I did, of all the occurrences, it was the most likely to indicate the involvement of someone other than Jadie. On the other hand, she felt the same kind of professional leeriness.

She said, "I think it's just going to muddy the water, if you bring in all these heebie-jeebie things, don't you? What we've got to do is get these kids safe. From what you've said, from the way this oldest girl acts, I feel fairly definite about the fact these girls have been abused, and I'd hate to see them go back home. But if you get in there talking about ghosts and witches and all that, Torey, we're going to be asking for it. Their defense is going to shred us. Know what I mean?"

I did. Still unable to convince myself beyond the shadow of a doubt that Jadie's terrible stories were factual, I didn't know what kind of witness I would make. Mortified at the thought of what it would do to my professional credibility, embarrassed that I might be thought a crackpot or worse, it was only too easy to agree that unless concrete evidence to the contrary came up over the course of the investigation, I would not make a major issue out of the satanic business.

I came home from the meeting with Lindy to fall wearily into the chair in front of the TV. I didn't bother to make myself a meal. I didn't even bother to take off all my outer clothes. Feeling overwhelmed, I flicked the TV on and just sat, staring vacantly at it.

The doorbell rang.

Not wanting to answer it, but not daring not to, given all that was going on, I pulled myself up from the chair. Opening the door, I found Lucy.

"Hi," she said nervously, glancing around. "Am I interrupting anything?" Despite the amount of time we had spent together in the summer, she had almost never been over to my apartment, and I think she continued to harbor fantasies about the grand city lifestyle I must be carrying on. She looked vaguely disappointed to find it empty.

"Come on in." Then, suddenly aware I was still wearing my jacket, I pulled it off. "I just got here myself."

"I didn't mean to bother you or anything. It's just that I was nearby, and I haven't been seeing much of you at school ..." Lucy looked over at me and the moment's hesitation became a full-blown pause. "Are you okay, Torey?" she asked softly. "I guess that's what I wanted to know. I mean, we're all aware of what's going on. It's all anybody talks about in the teachers' lounge ..."

"Sit down," I said and smiled. "You want something? A soft drink? Coffee?"

"No, I was just stopping by. But how is it going?" She settled into the other armchair. "Are you all right?"

Sitting back down myself, my jacket still in my hands, I told her. She already knew a good deal about Jadie's strange other world, but I told her now about the seamy stuff, about my concerns for something deeper and more horrific than straightforward sexual abuse, but at the same time, I mentioned all my doubts. I spoke of the problems Lindy and her officers were encountering, of the complexity in reporting something of this nature. Lucy listened silently, chin braced in her hand.

I hadn't meant to include Lucy in all of this. I liked her very much and, indeed, she was as close to a confidante as I had in Pecking. In quiet moments together at school, we'd shared much of ourselves with one another. We cheered each other on in the good times and cheered each other up in the bad.

But there remained an innocent and naive side of Lucy that had kept me from sharing everything. She loved her world of white weddings, potluck suppers, and sleighbells in the snow. I didn't like to be thought of as cynical, because I didn't think I was, but my brand of realism didn't marry well with Lucy's world. Yet, there I was, tired, frightened, and very much in need of a sympathetic ear. So Lucy got all of it.

She listened thoughtfully, not saying a word until I'd finally fallen silent. "Do you really think that's going on? That ritualistic stuff? Do you really think some little girl's been murdered?"

"To be perfectly honest, at this point I don't know what I think. I'm so jumbled up, even in my own mind."

"But Jadie thinks there is?"

I nodded.

"What have the police found?" Lucy asked.

"They haven't told me very much. The worst part of this whole deal is the lack of communication. I'm not supposed to be talking to Jadie, in case I inadvertently ask leading questions. The police aren't talking to anybody. Social Services are going their merry way, not feeling obliged to tell me anything, which they aren't, of course. I'm just the teacher. And Jadie ... Jadie's not saying a word to anyone." I sighed. "It's going to fall through, I just know it. They're not going to come up with any hard evidence. I've been involved in other, just ordinary abuse cases and, believe me, the kind of evidence the police need to prosecute ... we're going to get all this way and it's going to be thrown out. I just know it is."

Actually saying that, hearing myself say it, brought me to the brink of tears.

Lucy looked over. "I think you're doing the right thing."

"But what if they don't find anything? What if Jadie ends up going back home? What if Jadie never says a thing, and I'm stuck here with this big story about murdered children and voodoo dolls?"

"Well, just because she didn't tell them, Torey, doesn't mean she didn't tell you. Just because they don't find anything doesn't mean it didn't happen. You got to listen to yourself. If it's crazy-sounding, it's crazy-sounding, but that doesn't mean it couldn't be real."

"But this is Pecking," I muttered,

Lucy grinned. "I ought to be saying that, not you."

I smiled.

"I guess what you've got to be asking," she said, "is why *not* Pecking?"

At the end of the week, Arkie appeared in the doorway of my classroom. "We've got an appointment today. Did you hear about it?"

I nodded. "Rumor of it, yes."

"Lindy wants us in the police station in Falls River at 4:30. Can you manage that? They've got to decide which way they're going. Delores says she can get a twenty-eight day extension on the place-of-safety, but I haven't heard what the police are going to do. If they're not going to prosecute, I'd expect the kids to go back with their parents."

"What do they want with us?"

Arkie shrugged. "Just tying up loose ends, I suppose."

I regarded her. There'd been distance between us in the last week. I sensed Arkie still did not approve of my insistence that Jadie's claims might be true, and I knew she was deeply afraid of the exploitive media attention this sort of case would garner. That remark she'd made to me last time we were out to dinner, the one about "good-bye *New York Times*, hello *National Enquirer*" stuck in my mind. I'd diminished myself professionally in Arkie's eyes and it upset me.

"What do you want to see out of this?" I asked.

Arkie gave a slight lift of her shoulders. "Justice to be done, I guess."

The Christmas season refused to stay at bay, despite my distinct lack of mood for it. Decorative lighting was strung from the street lamps and through the small trees along the downtown sidewalks of Falls River. An ectomorphic Santa Claus with black hair sticking out from under his cap stood on the corner outside the police station and dolorously rang his bell. The sound merged with the piped carols as we entered the building.

"Hi, you guys," Lindy said, coming to the front desk to meet us. "Come on back."

I'd been expecting a whole crowd at this meeting, as I'd assumed it would be a summing-up of the week's findings, but in fact, there were only Lindy, Arkie, and myself. Lindy must have picked up on my surprise, because she said, "This is just an informal invitation. I thought we could make one last stab at getting the facts straight."

Arkie and I nodded.

We were in a small, gray-painted room with a large table. Arkie and I pulled out chairs and sat down. Lindy, who held a set of file folders, sat across from us. She laid the files out on the table.

"I'll have to confess this is proving a pretty hard case," she began. "I wish I could give you good news, but ..." She rifled through the papers. "We've had a good look at the girls and there's nothing to support any kind of physical abuse, other than perhaps that circular scar on the six-year-old's abdomen. While maybe not as clean as they could be, otherwise the girls were all in good physical condition.

"In terms of sexual abuse, well ... the hymen's been broken in all three girls. This happens naturally in many instances and, of course, this is what the parents maintain. That's feasible in the two older girls' cases, but it is rather unusual in an eighteen-month-old. However, we could hardly build a case for sexual abuse on that alone. The eldest girl and the baby also show evidence of anal dilation. This may mean anal penetration, but then again, it may simply indicate constipation—very common in girls of both ages. Otherwise, there has been no evidence of semen, seminal fluid, blood in the underclothes, vaginal irritations or infections. In short, we haven't got a good case for sexual abuse based on the hard evidence."

Lindy shifted papers and picked up another file. "Our psychologist has had three extended play periods with the girls, two individually and one with all three together, each time using the anatomically correct dolls. Nothing significant occurred with the younger two. With the eldest—that's your Jadie—it's obvious she's sexually aware. She quite openly demonstrated vaginal intercourse, anal intercourse, and fellatio, but we do have to keep in mind she's nearly nine.

"Dr. Denning, from the mental health clinic, has assessed the two elder girls for stability and overall functioning. Both are of normal intelligence, from what he can tell, although Jadie refused to participate in the verbal parts of the test. Neither appears wildly stable, according to him; neither was wildly cooperative, however. So goodness knows how helpful these data are.

"Regarding your comments, Torey, about the possibility of occult involvement or a porn ring or something similar, we took a search warrant and went through the house. We didn't come up with much. A handful of *Playboys* stuffed down the back of the sofa, two books on astrology, one on numerology, a small box full of bones, which the path lab has identified as coming from small animals, and six boxes of white candles."

"What are their explanations for those last two items?" I asked.

"Mr. Ekdahl says the bones are some he's collected out in the field. He says he likes to reassemble skeletons as sort of a hobby. Says he'd always wanted to be a taxidermist but couldn't afford to pursue it, so he goes out walking on the weekends and collects the bones. He was able to substantiate all this insomuch as he had two completed skeletons, one of a squirrel and one of a cat." Lindy wrinkled her nose. "They were rather nauseating, really, because he's glued them up in these coy little poses. We did bring the two skeletons in, but I must confess, I could hardly imagine anyone performing black rites around a squirrel sitting on a little red bench with its legs crossed and a newspaper in its paws.

"As for the candles, they're just ordinary penny candles, which they say they keep in case of winter power cuts. Six boxes do seem a bit much, but Mrs. Ekdahl claimed they were on sale when she bought them. So ..." Lindy paused.

"That's not really going to be enough, is it?" I asked.

"Not to prosecute, no."

"But what about these characters from 'Dallas'?" I asked. "She talks so realistically ..."

"No, *she* doesn't," Lindy replied. "That's the whole problem. *You* talk realistically. She doesn't talk at all. I have never yet heard this kid utter a word. And while we've tried to follow up some of the things you've said she's said, unless you can give us something more specific, what are we supposed to do? A plain example: when you talk about these characters, you're talking about five or six or more suspects, *all* involved in serious sexual abuse. At best, we've got two suspects. Where are the other ones? Who are they?"

"I think we have to face the possibility that these people simply may not exist at all," Arkie said, her voice soft. "I know it's hard for Torey. She's closest to the child; she has the girl's confidence, and certainly the girl can be remarkably vivid when she does talk. But irrespective of whether abuse has occurred or not, Jade is a seriously disturbed child. There is a hearty chance we're chasing moonbeams."

I looked over at Arkie in dismay.

"Torey, you've *got* to accept this."

"But why can't you accept it could be real?"

"Because it can't. Because she's disturbed. Because I don't want to see a replay of the Salem witch hunt right here on my own turf. That's what that was, wasn't it? Hysterical children accusing innocent adults. Human nature hasn't changed, and I just don't want to be a party to destroying these people's lives. These are *people,* Torey. This is a *family* we're talking about here, and they're never going to be the same because of this. You and I and the police and everyone, we'll walk out of it. The Ekdahls won't. I'm scared shitless by this talk of witches and Satan and stuff, not because of what it is, but because of what it can do. It's exciting, *interesting,* something to liven up a dull police report and a bunch of dull lives. I'm so frightened we're going to forget these are people and we're destroying them."

I fell silent. Indeed, we all did, the silence weighing down on us in the small room. Lindy shuffled through her papers for a moment, but the silence remained.

Finally, Lindy looked over at me. "What do you think? Do you really believe she's telling the truth?"

A depressing weariness overtook me. "I don't know. I really don't. But ... it's not so much what she says when she's talking about the abuse, it's the little things. Like how she talks of Tashee always being cold. Or how Tashee was short for her age. Or like the other week, just before Thanksgiving. One of my boys is Sioux and he got to talking about a headdress and some other Indian articles his father has, when Jadie mentioned that Tashee had a pair of genuine moccasins. Then she scooted back and showed this boy how the moccasins came up around the ankles. That incident struck me, because it wasn't Tashee she was talking about and it wasn't me she was talking to. It was the moccasins and it was to him. From her description, she was clearly referring to real Indian moccasins, because they do look so different from what gets fobbed off on the tourists. Such a casual, minor reference. It'd take considerable skill to lie like that, and I'd find it unusually complete, if it's the result of some kind of psychopathology."

"But it could be," Arkie replied. "Maybe *she* wanted those moccasins. Then it'd be only natural that she'd put them on Tashee."

Lindy pursed her lips. "So, basically, we're not a whole lot further along than we were at this time last week."

Chapter Twenty-Six

"So, what we gonna do in here, man? You gonna get us a Christmas tree or what?" Jeremiah demanded. We were only half an hour or so into the morning on Tuesday, all sitting together around the table, supposedly working, but nobody was. Brucie was in deep conversation with his crayon, flipping it before his face and saying "Bwah, bwah, bwah" to it. Reuben had done his first math problem, to which the answer was "12." So taken by the sight of "1" followed by "2", he felt compelled to continue on, writing "3", "4", "5", and so on, covering his paper with minute numbers. I'd already stopped him twice and reoriented him, but he reverted the moment I turned my attention away and was now up to 736. Philip had drawn a gigantic Christmas stocking on his paper and was decorating it with stars. Jadie just sat.

"I think we have plenty of time to worry about Christmas trees in the weeks ahead, Jeremiah. Now is the time for numbers."

"Fuck numbers. We gonna have a party?"

"We'll discuss it another time. Now we work."

He slammed his pencil down on the table, grabbed his chair, and slammed that down as well. Then he saw Philip's paper. "Look at him, lady. Look at what that little boog's doing. Hey, baby boogs, what's Santy Claus gonna bring you, if you been a good boy? Put in your itty, bitty stocky?"

"Jeremiah, please sit down." I reached a hand behind me to the bookcase. "And here, Phil, here's *another* math sheet." I removed the decorated one.

"I don't hang up a stocking no more," Jeremiah announced. "I'm too big. That's what my mom says. Says I won't get nothing in it." He shrugged. "But don't matter, 'cause what I want don't fit in a stocking anyhow. Know what I want?" He flung himself down on his back on the tabletop, his face right under mine. "A BMX."

Deciding to ignore him, which wasn't easy, as he was nearly lying in my lap, I stretched across to reorient Brucie.

"What you gonna get, girlie?" he asked Jadie, as he rolled across everyone's work on the table to come face to face with her.

"Go stick your head in a toilet, okay?" Jadie replied.

Rising, I took hold of Jeremiah's shirt collar and belt and lifted him bodily off the table. I placed him upright in his chair.

"Hooeeee! Did you see that, guys? That is one strong broad there. Lifted me up just like that. Man, better mind what she says. Better do what this dame wants. Man, lady, you know how to treat a guy."

"Jeremiah, *work.*"

About twenty seconds' silence reigned before Jeremiah looked up. "I know what. Let's make Christmas wishes."

"You've already told us about your bike. Now, go back to math, please."

"No, not that. Wishes. Like peace on earth and stuff. Like what you'd wish for—not for yourself, man—for everybody."

The idea caught my fancy. "Okay, Jeremiah, what would your Christmas wish be?"

"That people with brown skin don't get picked on no more. That it don't matter that you got brown skin or black skin or anything, that nobody gets beat up, just 'cause they're different."

"Well, that's a very good wish, Jeremiah. Wouldn't it be lovely, if it came true?"

"What do you wish for, girlie?" he asked Jadie.

Jadie thought a moment, then shrugged, and I didn't think she was going to answer. Finally, however, she did. "No more fighting, I guess. That everybody in the whole world could be happy."

Philip jumped up and down excitedly. "Mhhheeee!"

"Okay, you. Your turn," I said. "What do you wish for?"

"Hhhhhaann huhhh," he said and gesticulated wildly, a grin on his face. He pointed to Jadie.

"I'm sorry, we can't quite understand you. Can you use your signs?" I asked, because Philip now had quite a wide vocabulary of sign-language gestures.

He signed wildly and leaped from his chair again. "Hhhaann hhuuuuhhhhh!"

"Stand up?"

Still grinning broadly, he pointed at Jadie and signed elaborately.

"You want Jadie to stand up?"

Further signs and gestures.

"Your Christmas wish is that Jadie would stand up ... straight?"

Happily, Philip nodded.

"Hey, that's cruel, man," Jeremiah cried. "Don't you know better than to go around making people feel bad for the way they are? She can't help being crippled no more than you can help being a dumb fucker."

I reached a hand out to touch Jeremiah's arm, but it was Jadie who interceded. "I'm not crippled, Jeremiah. I can do it," she said quietly.

He looked over at her.

"I can stand up straight." Then, with the same creaking slowness she'd first exhibited in the cloakroom with me, Jadie put her hands on the table and pushed her body upright in the chair. Once that far, she took a deep, shuddery breath and then shoved her chair back. With what appeared to be a tremendous effort, she rose to her feet, erect.

Philip appeared so pleased I feared he'd swoon. "Hhhuhhh! Hhuhhh! Hhhuuuuhhhh!" he cried, although none of us knew what he was saying.

Jadie pressed both hands across her stomach.

"What's the matter? Are you feeling sick?" I asked.

"No," she replied, her voice perplexed. Arching her back slightly, she pressed the area around her navel. "I don't hurt?"

All of us watched her.

"I don't hurt there," she said, amazed.

Jeremiah finally recovered his voice. "Hey, man," he said with admiration. "You're really standing up."

Jadie looked over at him.

"You're standing up, Jadie, just like you was normal."

When the recess bell rang and the others scampered off to the cloakroom to get their jackets, I caught Jadie by the arm. "Do you suppose we could have a little chat? Mrs. McLaren is going to take the boys down, so we won't be interrupted. I want a moment alone with you."

She looked up at me.

"You know what today is, don't you? Eight days since you and your sisters moved out to Red Circle."

She nodded slightly.

"Has anyone talked to you about what's going to happen next?"

Jadie shrugged. "People been coming out, if that's what you mean. This doctor keeps coming out and looking up our butts. And there's that lady with those dolls."

"Yes, but I mean about the future. Has anyone said what's going to happen from here on?"

"We're going to a new foster home? That's what Mrs. Verney says. She says me and Amber are going to get to go home for our toys, and then we'll go somewhere else, 'cause we can't stay in Red Circle. They only take kids for short times there."

"Has anyone mentioned the possibility of going back to your parents?"

Jadie looked up. She hadn't been able to maintain her erect posture and was bent forward again. Catching hold of the back of the chair, she kept herself from folding over farther.

"What would you think of returning home?"

When I said that, her eyes filled immediately. "I wanna go back." A tear escaped and she caught it with her fingers. "That's my Christmas wish, my real one. I miss my room and my toys. And I just wish my mommy would hold me."

Knowing that in all likelihood the girls were going to be returned to their parents, I had been intensely worried about Jadie's reaction to this news and had anticipated an awful confrontation. Now, hearing her talk like this, immense relief washed over me. A whole morning's tension dissolved so rapidly as to leave me weak-kneed. "So, you'd like to? Oh, I am happy to hear that."

"Except that I can't."

"My news is pretty good. Because what I wanted to tell you was that I think you can. I was down at the police station last night and as long as they feel everything is okay at your house, they'll probably send you and Amber and Sapphire home instead of to a new foster placement."

Jadie raised her head abruptly to look at me, her eyes widening. All the color in her cheeks vanished, leaving her skin a whitish gray, like forgotten pastry dough. "But everything *isn't* okay," she said in a choked whisper.

"They've looked things over pretty well—"

"It *isn't* okay." Her breathing grew shallow. Clutching at her face, she looked rapidly from side to side, as if anticipating invasion. Then her hands came up to cover her eyes a moment.

At last she looked over at me. "It was just a *wish,*" she wailed. "Didn't you know that? Didn't you understand? I didn't mean really doing it, when I said I wanted to go back. I *can't* go back."

I regarded her.

"Miss Ellie'll be there. After what I done, if me and my sisters go back now, Miss Ellie'll *kill* us."

Stricken, I just stood. There was nothing I could say. I couldn't reassure her she wouldn't go back, that I could keep her out, that I would rescue her, because there was nothing I could do. Throughout this entire situation, I'd never made any promises to Jadie about what would happen if she came forward. While not often, I still had experienced other instances in which a child's accusations of abuse had been unsubstantiated and the child had been returned home, so I knew enough not to make promises I couldn't fulfill. Technically, I suppose, I was in the clear. On a human level, however, I felt absolutely wretched.

A discouraging silence enveloped us. All sorts of wildly unrealistic ideas were stampeding through my head, visions of snatching Jadie and running off with her, leaping in the car and just driving off, but I knew them to be fantasies even as I had them. Nothing workable came to me.

Wearily, I pulled out a chair at the table and sat down. Jadie continued to stand. Her eyes wandered, fleetingly met mine, then we both looked away. She sighed. The silence deepened.

At last Jadie pulled out a chair on the opposite side of the table and sat down too. "I'm not going back," she said, her voice soft but final. She said nothing else.

What could I do? A jumble of nonsense was in my brain. Did I defend myself? Defend the police actions? Did I try to make it sound as if it wasn't really so bad? Did I point out how nice it was going to be to sleep in her own bed and play with her own toys again, even if it did mean the occasional rape? Did I offer to run off to Mexico with her? Did I promise to become her crusader to fight her parents, the police, and City Hall, if necessary? Did I say I'd never give up? Did I offer comfort? Did I say I understood, although in no imaginable or unimaginable way was it possible that I did?

Jadie, across the table from me, picked at her arm. Her left hand resting palm upward on the tabletop, she tweaked the skin of her wrist, making it go white. I glanced up at the clock and prayed Lucy would keep the boys out of here if I ran over the allotted time for recess.

"You know what?" Jadie murmured, her voice low but calm, conversational. "Them there, know what you can do with them?" She touched the veins in her wrist. "You can take a knife, and if you cut there, all the blood in your body runs out. It runs out so fast you die."

Shaken sharply from my thoughts, I looked over.

"Dead's not so bad," she said softly. "It's dying that hurts. But being dead ... that's all quiet-like. I reckon it's like when you go to sleep. Except there's no dreams."

As I realized what she was talking about, my mouth went dry. "Jadie, don't think like that."

She looked up then, meeting my eyes. "Why not?"

"Because it's not going to solve anything."

"Why not?"

I didn't know why not. I didn't know what to say anymore. For lack of a better response, I reached out across the table to her and saw my hand was shaking. Jadie let me touch her, but she didn't respond. Instead, she just sat, fingering the veins of her wrist.

"I'm not going back," she said at last, lifting her eyes to meet mine. "I don't care what you say, what any of them say. I'm not going back. I'm never going back."

"You know what would be a better idea than that?" I asked.

She looked up again.

"To tell them about Tashee. To tell them everything."

"I already have. They don't believe me."

"You haven't, Jadie. You haven't said a word. You've made me do the talking and who they don't believe is me. *You* tell them. You *know.* So, you tell them, because if they hear things from you, the way you've told me, they'll have to believe you. Nobody can hear those things and not believe."

Jadie went back to fingering the vein.

"Why won't you at least try?"

No response.

"Are you frightened? Is that it? What of? Miss Ellie? Her spiders?"

Jadie shrugged.

"What if the police came here? To the school? If I called Lindy from the police station, she'd come out. You could go in the cloakroom and lock the doors, just like you and I've done. Would that make it easier? Could you talk then?"

Jadie looked up, and for the first time I could sense her wavering.

"What if I go call her now?" I asked. "Right this minute? She could come out this morning, before anything happens about your going back home. If you told her, Jadie ..."

"I can't."

"If you don't want to go back, they need to know why. That's the only way they can stop it."

"I can't." She lowered her head.

"You want to cut your wrist? Is that what you're thinking about? But then what's going to happen to Amber and Sapphire?"

Tears came to her eyes.

"Just think what it'd be like for them, if you weren't there."

"I can't."

"You *can.* If you can stand upright as you just did, because you wanted to enough, then you can talk."

"But ghosts don't have mouths," she whimpered.

"Maybe ghosts don't, but you're a girl, Jadie. You've got a mouth. You *must* talk. Please."

"I can't," she murmured, doubling over until her head was almost on the tabletop.

"You *can.*"

"You tell them for me."

"I've told them all I can. It's your turn now."

She began to cry.

"Sit up, Jadie."

Laboriously, she pushed herself back into an upright position. A minute passed, perhaps two, then finally she looked at me. She nodded. "Okay."

Chapter Twenty-Seven

Lindy came immediately, arriving at the school about 11:15. The children and I were sitting around the table when the door opened. Upon seeing her, Jadie rose without prompting. Silently, she led Lindy into the cloakroom. The door went shut and the snick of the lock echoed in the classroom.

"Who's that lady?" Jeremiah asked. "What's she doing with our girlie?"

"She's just come to talk with her."

"How come?"

"Jadie's having some problems at home," I replied, "and that lady's come to help."

"Whew," Jeremiah said softly, "that dame sure is a looker. Ain't our girlie lucky?"

"Maybe so."

The lunch bell rang and the others clattered out to join Lucy's horde, while I remained in the classroom. There was no sound from the cloakroom. This building was old and the walls thick, so very little passed between rooms. Consequently, I couldn't even discern whether Jadie was talking to Lindy. Filled with anxious curiosity, I was tempted to go nearer the door, but I didn't. My concern was that I might have brought Lindy out on one more wild goose chase, and they were closeted in there, face to face, once more weighted down by Jadie's immutable silence. On the other hand, they'd been in there so long, I assumed Jadie must be talking. Had she finally found the courage?

What worried me most was what would become of Jadie if she didn't talk. Recalling her at recess time, her child's wrist turned upward, her fingers over the veins, I knew her talk of suicide was not idle. Whether her eight-year-old mind comprehended death in those terms, I did not know, but she certainly understood dying. Sitting alone at the table, waiting, I tried to think of what else I could do.

Mr. Tinbergen entered the room about noon. "They're still in there?" he asked, nodding his head toward the cloakroom.

"Yes."

Nearing the table, he sat down. We didn't speak. We just sat.

When they emerged from the cloakroom, it was 12:35. Jadie, pale but fairly erect, came out first. She looked exhausted, as if what she needed most was sleep, but there was a weary calm about her.

"Would you like some lunch, Jadie?" Mr. Tinbergen asked. "I think they've saved you some." Rising from his chair, he extended a hand to her.

Lindy, appearing even paler than Jadie, pulled out Mr. Tinbergen's vacated chair across the table from me and fell into it. She watched as the door closed quietly behind Mr. Tinbergen and Jadie.

"I think I'm going to be sick," she murmured, her eyes still on the closed door.

"Jadie talked?"

"I'm not joking," Lindy replied. "I think I'm going to throw up."

Perhaps she wasn't joking. Her face had gone gray; she clutched the edge of the table with one hand, her fingertips going white from the pressure. I glanced around quickly for some way to be of help. "I'll get you a glass of water."

"I've been in this business six years now," Lindy said, as I returned from the sink, "and I have never in all my born days heard anything like that." Taking the water from me, she sipped it. "Did she tell you about that little girl? About what ... those people ... are supposed to have done to her? How they killed her?"

I nodded.

"I've come across plenty of blood and gore in my day. You get it in this job. You get *used* to it. But when a child, a little child starts to tell you these things ... That knife. The blood. Tasting the blood." Lindy shuddered. Then she looked over. "I feel unclean. Know what I mean? I want to go home and have a shower. Scrub myself. Throw away my clothes. Burn them. I feel dirty just from having been in there, talking about those things."

A small pause came as Lindy and I sat. The lights were out in the room, casting it in daylight gray. From beyond the closed windows came the muted laughter on the playground.

"That, about the cat, was the worst," Lindy said. "She was telling how they laid the cat on her chest and then they pulled it apart ... literally took its legs and *pulled* it to pieces on top of her." Lindy grimaced. "... And the blood ... smearing their hands in the blood of the cat, rubbing it all over Jadie's face and body ..." She paused and pressed her fingers against her mouth. "And then she was saying how ... how they licked it off ... how they performed ... subjected Jadie to cunnilingus with the blood of the cat still on her body."

Lindy's face suddenly went white. She looked over, her eyes wide. "Cat," she murmured. "Cat skeleton. That's it, isn't it?"

"I think we ought to have Christmas music," Jeremiah said.

"I think you ought to get your work done," I replied. "You still have half a sheet of math and all your reading left from this morning."

"Shit, man, you never let us have any fun."

"*Work,* Jeremiah."

"Gotta sharpen this here pencil first."

"Use mine," and I quickly slapped one down in front of him.

Peace reigned for about two minutes before Jeremiah raised his head again.

"Listen," I said before he had a chance to open his mouth, "we've had a difficult, disruptive morning. People have been coming in and out, things have been out of the ordinary today. Now, no one has managed to finish what's in their folders and we've only got forty minutes until going-home time. If everyone knuckles down, we can probably get done in half an hour. That'd leave enough time for me to read you another chapter from our book. How about that?"

"Aw, come on, lady, whatcha say we have just a little bit of Christmas music? It's Christmastime, for Pete's sake. Let's get ourselves in the mood."

"If I put a record on, will you actually work?"

"Yeah, sure, man," he answered graciously. "What kind of boog you take me for?"

So I rose and selected a record of Christmas carols. Gentle, familiar music filled the room, soothing all of us. At last, everyone worked.

The record was still playing when the knock came. Jeremiah jerked up, startled, and was on his feet instantly. I looked over.

Mr. Tinbergen was visible through the window in the door. He beckoned me out into the hallway. When I opened the door, I found Delores there, as well.

"I've come to take Jadie," she said. "Like Lindy promised her."

I looked questioningly.

"The police have decided to pursue the case further. Apparently there's been an order issued to dig up the Ekdahls' garden or something like that. Anyway, I've just been over to the house and collected the girls' belongings, because the police have sealed it. Looks like things are hotting up." She nodded toward the classroom. "Anyway, we thought it would be better if we took Jade and Amber now, from school, rather than have them ..." She didn't finish the sentence.

"Are they still going to be able to attend school here?" I asked.

Delores shook her head. "I know you and Jade have a good relationship, and we've tried to take that into account in placing her, but it didn't seem like a good idea for her to stay here. Lindy has told me a little bit about all this ... you know ... and we've decided to get them right out of the immediate area. God forbid the media should get wind of this, but you just can't be too careful. And with the house right across the street from the school ..."

I nodded.

Opening the door, I looked at my five, all still at the table, the strains of "Silent Night" filtering around them. Reuben, his eyes on us, was mouthing the words of the carol.

"Jadie?"

She rose and approached us.

"Mrs. Verney is here. She's come to take you and Amber to your new foster home."

Jadie looked at her, then me. Her posture, although not completely erect, was still upright. "Is it going to be in Red Circle?" she asked.

"No," I said, voicing Delores's shake of the head. "I think you'll be a little farther away, and I think this means you won't be coming back to our class, because it'll be too far."

"Never?" Jadie asked, her voice surprised. "Where am I going? Will I be in a real class? Will I be in third grade?"

"Well, we'll see," Delores replied with a smile. "Maybe you will."

"What?" shrieked Jeremiah, leaping up from his chair. "Where's our girlie going? Why you letting them take her away?"

"I'm going someplace you can't come," Jadie retorted, a note of pride in her voice I hadn't anticipated.

"How? Where? What d'ya mean?" Jeremiah protested. "What does she mean, lady? Is she going to be in a real class? How come? What she done to get outa here?"

Jadie had gone to her cubby to collect her few belongings.

"What'cha mean, a *real* class?" he cried, running after her. "We're real. This here class is real. Are you *going?*"

"Yeah," said Jadie.

He paused, stunned.

"I'm going to my new home, Jeremiah," she said and disappeared into the cloakroom to get her things.

Jadie was a long time in the cloakroom, and when she finally emerged, her arms were loaded with coat, boots, her pencil box, crayons, notebooks, and artwork. Coming over to us in the doorway, she paused and looked up at me. I gazed into her blue eyes, their clearness so sharp that they appeared faceted like crystals.

"Good-bye, lovey," I said. "I'm sure we'll see each other again soon."

"Here. This is for you." She inclined her head toward the armful of things, and I saw sticking out between her fingers a small piece of folded notebook paper. I took it from her.

"Is she *really* going?" Jeremiah asked. He peered through the door at Delores. "You really taking her somewhere?"

"I don't mind," Jadie said, then slipped by Mr. Tinbergen and out into the hallway. The three of them turned and headed away.

Jeremiah remained with me in the doorway, his shock at Jadie's sudden departure almost palpable. "Hey, lady!" he finally cried out, just as Delores, Jadie, and Mr. Tinbergen were reaching the stairs. "Hey, lady, stop! I wanna tell you something."

Delores paused and looked back.

"Did you notice, lady? Did you see our girlie can stand up?"

Back in the classroom a pall of silence descended. The record had ended. No one moved, no one spoke. Back and forth we looked, from one to another. It had all happened so quickly, so completely, that none of us knew what to do next.

Then Reuben, in a soft, breathy, schoolboy soprano, began to sing "Silent Night." Jeremiah, and then Philip, ran to the window. I crossed the room to join them.

Below us, the front door of the school opened and Delores emerged with Jadie and Amber. They started down the long walk toward Delores's car, parked at the curb.

"I want her to turn around and look at us," Jeremiah whispered, his breath fogging the glass. "Ain't she even going to turn around? Come on, girlie. Give us a wave."

Then, just as she reached the end of the walk, Jadie paused. Still holding Delores's hand, she turned and looked over her shoulder toward the classroom window.

"Hey! She sees us! Jadie! Jadie! Bye! Bye-bye, Jadie!" Jeremiah shouted against the windowpane. Both he and Philip waved wildly. A smile touched Jadie's lips and she waved back.

Leaving the boys to clamor against the glass, I turned back to the classroom. In my hand, I still had the small piece of paper Jadie had given me. Carefully pulling it open, I found two words. *Thank you.*

Epilogue

The drama of Jadie's case continued for several months after she left my class, during which time the police, who took Jadie's accusations very seriously indeed, conducted an intensive investigation, which included, among other things, excavating the Ekdahls' yard and dismantling their garden shed in search of Tashee's remains.

Throughout this time the question that divided us all continued to be discussed and occasionally argued: were the episodes Jadie had told me about real-life experiences? Or were they the creations of a seriously disturbed child?

There was a strong basis for believing Jadie's stories weren't real. First and foremost, she had a long history of bizarre psychological behavior, which, while it had never previously included hallucinations, did indicate quite serious pathology.

Additionally, many of the aspects of her stories are common to the phobias, obsessions, and hallucinations of disturbed children. A fear of being watched or spied on by insects, a fear of spiders in general, a fear of blood and visions of it dripping down or onto the body are all psychological experiences which I, myself, have encountered many times in my work with psychotic-type children, and in virtually all these cases I knew beyond a shadow of a doubt they were mental phenomena and had no basis in reality. Similarly, such acts as carving the symbol on Amber's stomach or even killing Jenny could conceivably have been done by Jadie herself. In fact, if she were as seriously disturbed as the nature of her stories would indicate, such mutilations and abuse would be within the realm of anticipated behavior.

Rejecting the face value of Jadie's stories did not rule out the possibility that Jadie was genuinely abused. Indeed, based on the circumstantial evidence in the case, the professional conclusion was that Jadie had probably been subjected to serious abuse, most likely sexual, at some point in her life and that this had contributed significantly to her mental state at age eight. Her mutism resulted perhaps from a fear that if she talked, she would tell about the abuse. Her deformed posture was an effort perhaps to physically keep the story in and/or protect the vulnerable genital area. Following this line of thinking, Tashee became comprehensible, not as a real little girl, but as a fragment of Jadie's own self, perhaps the genesis of a multiple personality disorder or as a depersonalization of what Jadie found good and whole in herself, separated out to be kept safe from the degraded self. Jadie's constant need to protect and care for Tashee and her frequent reports of "talking" to Tashee, as if Tashee were near at hand, were understandable acts in this context. Similarly, the characters of "Dallas" took on some meaning. If the abuse was committed by her father, that would be difficult enough to bear, but if her mother joined in, or perhaps simply knew and did nothing to stop it, Jadie may have found it necessary to create an evil persona in the form of Miss Ellie, which would leave the kind, loving person Jadie knew as her mom unsullied. If ethereal strangers, materializing out of the television, did all these things, then Jadie could still feel safe with her parents.

Throughout the many weeks of police investigation and the endless meetings with social workers and mental health personnel, this psychological explanation of Jadie's experiences became the increasingly accepted point of view. On numerous occasions, I found myself in accordance, feeling that yes, this was the only comprehensible conclusion that could be drawn. It provided answers for the most difficult questions; it made acceptable sense; and it brought Jadie's case into line with what we already know about the human mind. And yet ... The big questions *were* answered by this explanation, but the small things continued to niggle at me. For instance, why was Jadie so frightened of having her picture taken? Where had she gained knowledge of video recorders and video cameras in an era when they still weren't commonplace in people's homes? Why did she speak of Miss Ellie and the others "putting their faces on" and wearing "ghost clothes"? And what about Jadie's symbol, the cross within the circle, which she had made so many times for me in so many ways? In the end, speculation on this concurred with the psychiatric opinions voiced at the Sandry Clinic the previous summer, that the circle was representative of the vagina, and the cross ("X marks the spot") was a sort of "I was violated here" message. But why, then, would Jadie have made it on Amber's stomach? And on a more subtle level, why had Jadie been so curious about my work with other elective mutes? Why had her questions about my work always centered around whether they talked to me in the end and when they did, had I believed what they said? And had I helped them?

The only other alternative, of course, is to assume that the events Jadie told me about were true, that she was not a psychotic child in a sane world, but the other way around. In this explanation of her behavior, one realizes that her world would have to have taken on horror-film madness, and she was thus reacting with understandable terror to a situation she had no control over.

Taking Jadie's stories fully at face value brings us indisputably to ritual child abuse, meaning that she and her sisters and most probably other children were being abused in a predetermined ceremonial fashion by an organized group. Given the nature of many of the things she told us, the obvious conclusion is that it was related to practices of the occult, or more specifically, satanism.

Satanism is not the nonbelief in God, but rather the antithesis of standard Christianity, and the majority of satanic practices revolve around defamation of Christian practices. In reversing the credo of love toward others, it becomes a selfish cult, centered on what individuals can get for themselves. This emphasis on personal power is what gives satanism much of its appeal, particularly to weak and unsuccessful personalities. Its further appeal comes from its creative side. There are no rules and no restrictions governing the practice of satanism. One of black magic's most flamboyant exponents, Alistair Crowley, had great influence on the development of modern satanism, and his "'do what thou wilt' shall be the whole of the law" has provided the justification for fulfilling many abnormal sexual or violent urges.

Certainly, there was a strong satanic flavor to much of what Jadie referred to. The Black Mass is symbolized by an encircled cross, although the drawings of it I've seen in books do differ slightly from Jadie's. Jadie's was simply a quartered circle. The traditional Black Mass symbol is a cross with bars at each end, like two crossed capital I's, which then have a circle around them. However, Jadie did also make several other strange symbols, although less frequently than the circled cross. One of them, an inverted T with a small circle just above the crossbar, is remarkably similar to a satanic curse mark. The others we never found interpretations for.

The Black Mass itself is a perverted form of the Catholic Mass. Apparently, there is vast variation in the practice of this ritual, but the main components appear to include an altar and numerous altar artifacts, which usually include among them candles, inverted crosses, incense, daggers, bones, types of jewelry, bells, gongs, chalices, and bowls containing herbs or salts. Most of these items are black, white, or made of silver. The participants are generally cloaked in black, white, or red and/or wear face and body paint. In the Catholic Mass, according to dogma, the communion elements of bread and wine become the body and blood of Christ. The Black Mass is a travesty of the Catholic Mass, which uses bodily products, usually urine or semen and feces in place of bread and wine, to represent the carnal spirit of Satan. In further satisfying the carnal nature of this deity, sexual activity is often a major part of the religious ceremony. Pain is also an important factor and masochism is common. And as a further perversion of the Christian practices with their emphasis on life, death plays a significant role in satanic ceremonies. The presence of a coffin is common, with members lying in it or engaging in sexual activities in it.

Many satanists see themselves as simply practicing a chosen religion and no more, a right everyone is guaranteed under the American Constitution. They eschew the darker images of animal mutilations, bloodletting, and human sacrifice, and say that most of what is reported about them in the press is the work of practical jokers, horror-fiction writers, and propagandists from the fundamental religious groups. Others, among them many members of the police departments in major American cities, such as Chicago, San Francisco, and St. Louis, disagree. Animal sacrifice as a regular part of satanic rituals is well reported, as is blood drinking. Ritualized child abuse and human sacrifice still linger in the shadowy netherworld between fact and fiction, as police investigators have virtually never been able to turn up sufficient evidence that the rumored homicides occurred. On the other hand, a considerable number of children over the past ten years have reported startlingly similar experiences. Among these are being given drugs, either legal ones, such as muscle relaxants, or illegal ones, by means of drinks or injections; participating in chanting to call up the devil or demons and to put themselves into an altered state of consciousness; being urinated upon or having excrement wiped over them; being made to eat insects or being told that the insects were messengers of Satan and would report back everything the child did when not with the group; engaging in a wide variety of perverted sexual acts; being placed in coffins and having the lid shut; being tortured by snakes; and being tied to or suspended from upside-down crosses. Several of the children claim to have witnessed other children being sacrificed, in all instances by stabbing through the heart, slitting the throat, or being tied to an upside-down cross and set alight. Reported instances of animal sacrifice have included members of the group physically pulling the animal apart. These reports are not only quite consistent among even very young children, but they are widespread, occurring in vastly separated parts of the United States, as well as Canada, Great Britain, and continental Europe. Because much of what is reported is of a criminal nature, it has been the police departments who have accrued the largest number of these cases. However, the medical community, particularly from the children's hospitals, such as Cardinal Glennon Children's Hospital in St. Louis, have also contributed their knowledge to the understanding of these reports, as have such groups as the National Child Assault Prevention Project. Indeed, both the Federal Bureau of Investigation and the United States Department of Justice have received detailed summaries of these findings during the course of the 1980s, Consequently, despite the elusive nature of "concrete evidence," a large body of people have chosen to believe these children.

In spite of this official involvement, it still takes an unusually open mind to encounter such information and not dismiss it immediately. Even to me, now, much of what Jadie said and of what the children above reported seems too farfetched, like a nasty mix of Stephen King and *National Enquirer.* This made this particular explanation of Jadie's stories the most difficult for all of us to deal with. I, myself, knew nothing of the darker side of occultism when all this began, other than the usual lurid media accounts of the Manson Family and of a particularly nasty murder which had taken place near my hometown in the seventies. My firsthand experience was limited to the Ouija board and tarot cards as part of a fairly standard rites of passage through adolescence. As a consequence, it was pure coincidence that we made the first connection between Jadie's behavior and satanism, because if Hugh hadn't been waiting near that occult bookshop during his lunch hours, I doubt I would have ever related the encircled cross to satanism. In fact, if I'm honest, I don't think I would necessarily have made the connection when Jadie started talking about the cat and the blood. Part of this was due to innocence. I simply didn't *know* and it is hard to see things one is ignorant of. Part of this was due to a certain amount of blindness. I was accustomed to seeing all disturbed behavior in psychological or psychiatric terms, and it was thus easy not to see other alternatives. And part was undoubtedly resistance. I didn't *want* to see it. Like UFO's, abominable snowmen, and the Loch Ness monster, the lighter sides of occultism are a part of modern folklore, real in the way that they speak consistently to a secret side in every one of us. They are the trolls and fairies of urban society. However, it takes a brave soul to admit to believing in such things. Even when matters became fairly advanced between Jadie and me, I was reluctant in the extreme to acknowledge something so far outside the ordinary could account for her experiences. I was fairly young, not long established in my career, and terribly vulnerable to the pressures of "being professional." Consequently, I found it difficult to jeopardize my status by espousing ideas usually reserved for the lunatic fringe.

None of this was helped by the fact that at the time it was virtually impossible to find any concrete information on occultism in acceptable, mainstream sources. Brenda and her bookstore were my only outlets during the course of my time with Jadie, and I found myself wholly suspect in seeking out information in such a location. As the years have gone by, I have acquired considerably more knowledge from considerably more respectable sources, but even today the basic knowledge has to come from the fringe.

With added knowledge, I must admit that, incredible as it all sounds, there is no way to deny the similarities of some of Jadie's stories to those of other reported cases of occult abuse. Jadie often talked about Miss Ellie and the others "having their faces on" or wearing "ghost clothes," which may have referred to face paint or masks and robes. It may also account for her not recognizing any members of the group. Perhaps the omnipresent soft drinks that she reported Miss Ellie always administered at the beginning of these sessions contained drugs, which may have further enhanced her inability to recall precise details. Her fear of spiders may have been a psychological scare tactic to keep her from revealing what was going on. Perhaps "the stick" Jadie referred to her sisters and herself "going upside down on" was an inverted cross. And her talk of eating feces, the sacrifice of Jenny, and, of course, the voodoo doll are all in close concurrence with very well documented Satanic practices. Perhaps most convincing of all for this theory, however, is that much of her distress and the reported abuse coordinated quite closely with important dates on the pagan calendar, with, most notably, Jenny's death occurring near April 30th, or Beltane, the second most important sabbat, or celebration date, and Tashee's reported murder and Sapphire's first molestation occurring near or on Halloween, the most important sabbat.

This brings us, of course, to the question of Tashee. Looking at Jadie's stories in this light, this means, of course, Tashee would have been a real child, and Jadie may have witnessed her murder as part of a ritual sacrifice. In fact, much of Jadie's account fits within the framework of occult ritual. Six, Tashee's age, was recognized as being important within the group and as giving power. Six is considered an important number within witchcraft and other magic-based groups, as it is a multiple of three and therefore more highly endowed with magical power. It is also highly regarded among satanists as part of the number 666 or the mark of the beast, generally taken to mean Satan. Jadie also reported Tashee's throat to have been slit with a crescent-shaped, elaborately carved dagger, which implies a weapon of ceremonial design. And, of course, there was the blood. Moreover, Jadie made frequent reference to "the power" the group would bring on themselves by sacrificing a six-year-old child.

The police in Pecking and Falls River took Jadie's allegations about Tashee's death seriously and did a very thorough job of searching the area in and around the Ekdahls' home and also in a wooded area not far from Pecking. However, nothing was found. They also tried to establish Tashee's possible identity, although no child of Tashee's age or description had been reported missing from the Pecking or Falls River area. As the investigation continued, they cast their nets wider to include the city, and, as the months passed, eventually the entire United States. They sifted through information on thousands of missing children, but Tashee was never identified. This does not, however, necessarily disprove her existence. A lot of corpses aren't found for many reasons and that may be sufficient answer. As to precisely who Tashee might have been, if she was a real child, that's harder to answer. Looking at it from the satanic perspective, perhaps she was the product of a "brood mare," young women in the group who have been made pregnant solely to provide a child for sacrifice and whose resulting baby is born at home and the birth not registered. If that assaults common sense too severely, perhaps it would be easier to find her among the thousands of faceless missing children, abducted maybe years earlier, perhaps even by a family member, and the police simply failed to identify her.

Like the psychological explanation for Jadie's stories, the occult explanation is fairly complete and, if one can cope with the incredibility factor, it makes acceptable sense of the information. Yet, like the former theory, I still find myself with unanswered questions. Once again, I find the issue of cameras and video recorders not satisfactorily explained. This is a fairly mundane matter in comparison to some of the others, but it figured with great frequency in Jadie's accounts. In no literature have I found reference to photography or video recording as an integral part of occult activity. Indeed, the stress on secrecy inherent in such counterculture behavior seems to rule out such a permanent and easily interpreted kind of record. Another hole in the satanic theory was the simple fact that Jadie never once, neither with me nor with the police, mentioned Satan, the devil, the master, or any of the other common references to the deity. It is possible, of course, particularly in light of the fact that the group appears to have been led by a woman, that this group was not purely satanic but a type of black magic coven, but even here Jadie did not attach significance to such things as pentagrams and other commonly used symbols of witchcraft.

This leaves us with only one other possible explanation for Jadie's accounts and that is that someone was using the girls for pedophilic purposes, most likely to make pornographic films, and the occult activities were used either as a pretext to frighten the children and keep them in line, or else as a part of the content of the films themselves. Or perhaps both.

The cameras and video recorders become self-explanatory in light of this possibility, as does

Jadie's intense fear of having her picture taken. The soft drinks she spoke of in all likelihood would have contained drugs, in particular, muscle relaxants like Valium. This would be necessary, not only to ensure the child's cooperation, but also to make sexual intercourse and other, more perverted, acts appear easier and more naturally occurring. And if occult-inspired scare tactics were being used, a child under the influence of drugs would not be as alert to the sleight-of-hand activities used to provide the special effects.

If child pornography were the explanation for Jadie's experiences, it seems probable that at least one of her parents would have been directly involved, although not necessarily in committing the actual abuse. Their part may simply have been to allow the girls to be used, and this may account for Jadie's poor recollection of where her parents were during the sessions with Miss Ellie and the others. As an organized, working group intent on turning out a product, they would not necessarily have been structured in the way Jadie perceived them. Miss Ellie may have been an actress, possibly the star, and her behavior may have been in line with the film format, rather than anything directed personally toward the girls. Or perhaps it may have been. Perhaps her sadistic inclinations were enlisted to help keep the children in line while others got on with the business of making the film.

The use of the "Dallas" character names becomes comprehensible as well in that major police departments have documented the use of cartoon character names in connection with both ritual abuse cases and pedophilic cases. Used as code names among the group, it deters discovery by making it likely that if any child involved attempts to tell an outsider, her story is more likely to be dismissed as a television-inspired fantasy. Certainly, this explanation would be a good fit in Jadie's instance.

Much of the content of Jadie's stories can be substantiated as typical of hard-core child pornography. Horror and occultism crop up regularly in films that combine sex and violence. The torture of children and small animals or both together is disconcertingly popular in this bleak underworld, particularly when it culminates in a sexual act. Jadie's account of Jenny's death and the subsequent sexual activity fulfill all these requirements. Other aberrations in sexual taste, including the use of bodily products, is also a fairly common feature of some seamier films.

As with the satanic explanation, in this theory Tashee would have to be regarded as a real child. "Snuff" films, where an individual is actually killed on camera, are mercifully uncommon, although they are regarded as the pièce de résistence for many hard-core pornography viewers. Consequently, it seems less likely in this instance that Jadie witnessed an actual murder. More likely, the murder was staged for filming purposes, and Jadie was either made to believe it genuinely happened so that her own performance would be more real, or else, as a child of six and possibly under the influence of drugs, she was unable to discern it was only acted.

This explanation would give better insight into why Jadie occasionally mentioned seeing or talking to Tashee after she was supposedly murdered, because if Tashee was still alive, this would be understandable. In a similar vein, it would obviously account for the lack of criminal evidence in the police search. As to who Tashee actually was, however, that still remains firmly within the realm of speculation. Again, as in the satanic theory, she may have been an abducted child or a runaway. More likely, she would have been, like Jadie, a child willingly provided to the group.

It must be acknowledged that if hard-core pornography was responsible for Jadie's horrific stories, those involved did have a fair insight into the darker aspects of occultism. Whether or not this contributed significantly to the content of the films is a moot point, but there is no doubt it was used to wield considerable psychological control and those using it understood the power of their subject matter. Young children, particularly those between about four and ten, are strong believers in magic. This is the age of Santa Claus, fairy tales and all the good luck/bad luck superstitions that rule childhood, and anyone who has spent much time with children of this age is only too aware of the intensity with which they believe. It is a normal developmental stage, but it is easily exploited. Adults can be terrifying enough on their own, but coupled with scary images and intimations of supernatural powers, this would be enough to ensure cooperation from the most stalwart child.

Over the course of the months that followed Jadie's revelations, all three of these theories—the psychological, the satanic, and the pedophilic—received a good deal of attention from the professionals. Interestingly, acceptance of one explanation or another seemed to follow professional groupings, with social workers and those from mental health almost uniformly sticking to a psychological explanation, while the police and medical community tended to prefer something more concrete. The police, in particular, stuck by the satanic theory and the possibility that Tashee was a genuine murder victim.

And me? What did I believe? I don't know. I wish I did. Some ten years on I still find this the single most harrowing case I've been involved with, in part because it still persistently controverts all efforts to close it. As I write the book, I so wish I could draw the kinds of satisfying conclusions that would elevate it from the inelegant real-life situation it is. Certainly, I realize a clear-cut climax and resolution would make it a much better book. Unfortunately, it would also make it fiction.

Having spent all those afternoons listening to Jadie talk in that quiet, matter-of-fact manner of hers, I find it impossible to discount all reality behind her stories. Intuitively, I feel those people must have been there in some form and must have committed at least some of those acts. However farfetched the accounts were, they *felt* real. On the other hand, all three theories assault my common sense on some level. The last, that Jadie was a victim of organized pedophiles, provides the most comprehensive answer for me. Even so, I cannot fully accept this nor fully discount the others.

What was never in doubt, however, was the fact that something *was* wrong, something serious enough to create emotional disturbance, not only in Jadie, but also eventually in Amber. It was obvious that in spite of confusing information and lack of substantial evidence, something had to be done. My loyalties, of course, lay with Jadie, and my first concern was to see her and her sisters in a safe environment. On the other hand, it was equally paramount at the stage when the girls were taken into foster care that the rights of all parties be protected, most especially in light of the fact that we had no direct evidence that the people we were accusing were the perpetrators.

One of the most difficult problems we had in dealing with this case was the potentially sensationalistic nature of much of the information. This made the media's, and ultimately the public's, voyeuristic curiosity a major threat, because while we, as professionals, may have been overly reluctant to acknowledge the possibility of occult-related abuse, the media was overenthusiastic. This had a twofold effect. First, it tended to frighten the more conservative professionals into rigidly maintaining their view that satanism belonged in the realm of bad novels and horror films and could not possibly turn up as the explanation of a real-life situation. Concerned particularly with the increase in right-wing, fundamentalist attitudes, they feared we would be seeding dangerously fertile grounds if, as professionals, we were seen to discuss such a topic seriously, and this could have long-term effects on the public's perceptions of mental illness. Second, the presence of a voracious media brought fear to all of us regarding a witchhunt, not only figuratively, but literally. Jadie's parents deserved the inalienable right of innocence until proven guilty, and, equally important, a fair trial. However, in the black-and-white world of reporting, good copy is everything. So is reader/viewer draw. Bias often isn't. A young, physically attractive child full of gory tales of torture, murder, and sex is irresistible prey. So, while Arkie and I had parted ways in our thinking on Jadie's case, I continued to respect the vehemence with which she defended Jadie's parents. Sensing the potential for hysteria, Arkie was terrified that we could create a new Salem, and I feel her fear was well justified.

The investigation into Jadie's disclosures continued actively for well over six months, during which time the police pursued all lines open to them. Social Services arranged for both Jadie and Amber to be seen on a regular basis by Phyllis Ruiz, the child psychiatrist from the Falls River mental health clinic, and eventually, both girls were hospitalized on a children's psychiatric unit in the city to allow for further assessment in an effort to better understand their situation. I returned to my class in Pecking, although I too continued to see Jadie regularly out of school hours.

Jadie stuck by her stories. While hospitalized, she formed a close relationship with one of the therapists on the children's unit and told this woman almost verbatim several of the incidents she'd told me. Amber, on the other hand, deteriorated during the course of the hospitalization. Confused and extremely unhappy, Amber seemed to suffer more than either of her sisters in the aftermath of Jadie's disclosures. She coped by blocking out much of what was unpleasant to her, which made working with her at the time difficult, and has resulted in her having virtually no recollection of that period. One is left to wonder, of course, how much else she has chosen to forget.

Despite their efforts, in the end the police were unable to turn up any hard evidence to support Jadie's accounts. Such things as the cat skeleton, which Lindy and I and several others had come to regard as "Jenny," could be considered only circumstantial evidence, as there was no way to link it to the cat Jadie had talked about. Mr. Ekdahl maintained he'd found the cat run over in the road, and there were enough broken bones in the skeleton to support this. While the idea of collecting a dead cat in such circumstances, then taking it home, cleaning the bones and reassembling the skeleton struck most of us as a highly unsavory pastime, it was hardly illegal.

Understandably, this outcome left many of us feeling deeply frustrated. In believing a crime had been committed, and I think all of us did, whether it was straightforward child abuse or something more sinister, the desire to see justice done was strong. However, life often doesn't work out according to how we think it should, so we needed to be satisfied with smaller gains. Still, we *did* gain. Through our efforts, all three girls were removed from the home, and, we hoped, removed from further trauma. Jadie, in particular, blossomed while in foster care, becoming more open and settled, which enabled her to return successfully to a regular school program. When the Ekdahls petitioned to have Jadie returned to them eighteen months later, Social Services felt it would be unwise to disrupt her newfound stability and stated it would be better if Jadie remained in foster care. The Ekdahls did not challenge this. A few years later, our actions were further justified when Mr. Ekdahl was arrested and convicted of molesting an eight-year-old schoolgirl near his home. He is now in prison. Jadie, Amber, and Sapphire all now live in permanent foster homes.

Whatever the past, Jadie is now doing admirably. Almost twenty, she has been living for more than six years with her current foster family and this she considers her home. By choice, she has no contact with either of her natural parents, although she does remain close to her two sisters, who both live in separate foster homes nearby. By the time Jadie had joined her current foster family, she was attending school with no special education support whatsoever. An able student, she soared academically, going through high school in the top ten percent of her class. She is now attending a large Eastern university and plans to eventually pursue an academic career, most likely in English literature. An unusually attractive young woman with her dark hair and blue eyes, she shows no indication of her former physical problems, other than a slight stoop. Indeed, when I look at her now, it's hard to remember the shrunken, silent Jadie of long ago. If the wind catches her hair, which is still long and still a bit unruly, I'll see the ghost of her, but that's all. The real Jadie's far too busy getting on with her life.

One Child

Sunday Times No. 2 Bestseller

Sheila was a deeply disturbed six-year-old when she came into Torey Hayden's life, yet over the course of five remarkable months, this dedicated special-education teacher profoundly touched the life of this unique little girl, helping to free her from a hellish inner prison of rage and silence.

ISBN 0 00 719905 8
Available now in all good bookstores.

Read more about Sheila and Torey's first encounter in this extract from *One Child*, Torey Hayden's bestselling book.

One Child

I should have known.

The article was a small one, just a few paragraphs stuck on page six under the comics. It told of a six-year-old girl who had abducted a neighborhood child. On that cold November evening, she had taken the three-year-old boy, tied him to a tree in a nearby woodlot and burned him. The boy was currently in a local hospital in critical condition. The girl had been taken into custody.

I read the article in the same casual manner that I read the rest of the newspaper and felt an offhand what-is-this-world-coming-to revulsion. Then later in the day it came back to me while I was washing the dishes. I wondered what the police had done with the girl. Could you put a six-year-old in jail? I had random Kafkaesque visions of the child knocking about in our old, drafty city jail. I thought about it only in a faceless, impersonal manner. But I should have known.

I should have known that no teacher would want a six-year-old with that background in his or her classroom. No parent would want a child like that attending school with his or her child. No one would want that kid loose. I should have known she would end up in my program.

I taught what was affectionately referred to in our school district as the "garbage class." It was the last year before the effort to mainstream special children would begin; it was the last year to pigeonhole all the odd children into special classes. There were classes for the emotionally disturbed, classes for the physically handicapped, classes for the behaviorally disordered, classes for the learning disabled, and then there was my class. I had the eight who were left over, the eight who defied classification. I was the last stop before the institution. It was the class for young human refuse.

The spring before I had been teaching as a resource person, supplying help to emotionally disturbed and learning disabled children who attended regular classrooms part of the day. I had been in the district for some time in a variety of capacities; so I had not been surprised when Ed Somers, the Director of Special Education, had approached me in May and had asked if I would be interested in teaching the garbage class the next fall. He knew I had had experience with severely disturbed children and that I liked small children.

And that I liked a challenge. He chuckled self-consciously after saying that, aware of how contrived the flattery sounded, but he was desperate enough to try it anyway.

I had said yes, but not without reservations. However, I longed for my own classroom again with my own set of kids. I also wanted to be free of an unintentionally oppressive principal. He was a good-hearted man, but we did not see things in the same way. He objected to my casual dress, to my disorderly classroom, and to my children addressing me by my first name. These were minor issues, but like all small things, they became the major sore spots. I knew that by doing Ed the favor of taking this class, allowances would be made for my jeans and my sloppiness and my familiarity with the kids. So I accepted the job, confident that I could overcome any of the obstacles it presented.

My confidence flagged considerably between the signing of the contract and the end of the first day of school. The first blow came when I learned I was to be placed back into the same school I had been in and under the same principal. Now not only did he have to worry about me but also about eight very peculiar children. Immediately we were all placed in a room in the annex which we shared with the gymnasium and nothing else. We were totally isolated from the rest of the school. My room would have been large enough if the children had been older and more self-contained. But for eight small children and two adults, plus ten desks, three tables, four bookcases and countless chairs that seemed to mate and multiply in the night, the room was hopelessly crowded. So out went the teacher's desk, two bookshelves, a file cabinet, all but nine little chairs and eventually all the student desks. Moreover, the room was long and narrow with only one window at the far end. It had originally been designed as a testing and counseling space, so it was wood-paneled and carpeted. I would have gladly traded all that grandeur for a room that did not need lights on all day or for a linoleum floor more impervious to spills and stains.

The state law required that I have a full-time aide because I was carrying the maximum load of severely disturbed children. I had been hoping for one of the two competent women I had worked with the year before, but no, I received a newly hired one. In our community, which had in close proximity a state hospital, a state prison and a huge migrant workers' camp, there was a staggering welfare list. Consequently, unskilled jobs were usually reserved for the unemployed listed with Social Services. Although I did not consider my aide position an unskilled one, Welfare did, and the first day of school I was confronted with a tall, gangly Mexican-American who spoke more Spanish than English. Anton was twenty-nine and had never graduated from high school. Well, no, he admitted, he had never worked with children. Well, no, he never especially wanted to. But you see, he explained, you had to take the job they gave you or you lost benefits. He dropped his gargantuan frame onto one of the kindergarten-sized chairs, mentioning that if this job worked out, it would be the first time he had ever stayed north all winter instead of following the other migrant workers back to California. So then we were two. Later, after the school year started, I acquired a fourteen-year-old junior high school student who devoted her two hours of study hall to coming over and working with my class each day. Thus armed, I met the children.

I had no unusual expectations for these eight. I had been in the business long enough to have lost my naiveté. Besides, I had learned long before that even when I was shocked or surprised, my best defense was to never show it. It was safer that way.

The first to arrive that morning in August had been Peter. Eight years old and a husky black with a scraggly Afro, Peter had a robust body that belied the deteriorating neurological condition that caused severe seizures and increasingly violent behavior. Peter burst into the room in anger, cursing and shouting. He hated school, he hated me, he hated this class and he wasn't going to stay in this shitty room and I couldn't make him.

Next was Tyler, who startled me by being a girl. She slunk in behind her mother, her dark curly head down. Tyler was also eight and had already tried to kill herself twice. The last time the drain cleaner she had drunk had eaten away part of her esophagus. Now her throat bore an artificial tube and numerous red-rimmed surgical scars in ghoulish testimony to her skill.

Max and Freddie were both hauled in screaming. Max, who was a big, strapping, blond six-year-old, carried the label of infantile autism. He cried and squawked and twirled around the room flapping his hands. His mother apologized because he always acted so unpredictably to change. She looked at me wearily and let the relief to be free of him for a few hours show too plainly in her eyes. Freddie was seven and weighed 94 pounds. The fat rolled over the edges of his clothing and squeezed out between the buttons on his shirt. Once allowed to flop on the floor, he ceased crying, ceased everything, in fact, to lie lifelessly in a heap. One report said that he, too, was autistic. One stated that he was profoundly retarded. One admitted not knowing.

I had known Sarah, age seven, for three years. I had worked with her when she was in preschool. A victim of physical and sexual abuse, Sarah was an angry, defiant child. She had been electively mute throughout the previous year when she had been in a special first grade class at another school. She had refused to talk to anyone except her mother and sister. We smiled upon seeing each other, both of us thankful for a familiar face.

A smartly dressed, middle-aged woman carried in a beautiful, doll-like child. The little girl looked like a picture from a children's fashion magazine, her soft blond hair carefully styled, her crisp dress spotless. Her name was Susannah Joy, she was six, and this was her first time in school. My heart winced. To be placed in my class upon entrance to school was not a hopeful sign. The doctors had told the parents that Susannah would never be normal; she was a childhood schizophrenic. She apparently hallucinated both visually and auditorily, and spent most of her days weeping and rocking her body back and forth. She rarely spoke and even when she did, seldom meaningfully. The mother's eyes implored me to perform the magic ritual necessary to turn her fairy child back to normal. My heart ached seeing those pleading eyes, because they signified nonacceptance. I knew the pain and agony that lay ahead for those parents as they learned that none of us would ever have the type of magic they needed for Susannah Joy.

Last to come were William and Guillermo. Both were nine. William was a lanky, pasty-faced boy haunted by fears of water and darkness and cars and vacuum cleaners and the dust under his bed. To protect himself, William engaged in elaborate rituals, compulsively touching himself or chanting little spells under his breath. Guillermo was one of the countless Mexican-American migrants who came to work in the fields each year. He was an angry boy but not uncontrollable. Unfortunately, he was also blind. At first I was stymied that he had been placed in my class, but was informed that the classes for the blind and partially sighted did not feel equipped to deal with his aggressive behaviors. Well, I thought, that made us even. I did not feel equipped to deal with his blindness.

So, then we were ten, and with Whitney, the junior high student, we were in all eleven. When first I surveyed this motley bunch of children and my equally motley staff, I felt a wave of despair. How would we ever be a class? How could I ever get them doing math or all the other miracles that needed accomplishing in nine months? Three were not toilet trained, two more had accidents. Three could not talk, one wouldn't. Two would not shut up. One could not see. Certainly it was more of a challenge than I had bargained for.

But we managed. Anton learned to change diapers. Whitney learned to get urine out of the carpet. And I learned Braille. The principal, Mr. Collins, learned not to come over to the annex. Ed Somers learned to hide. And so we became a class.

By Christmas vacation we belonged to one another and I was beginning to look forward to each new day. Sarah had begun to talk regularly again; Max was learning his letters; Tyler was smiling occasionally; Peter didn't fly into rages quite so often; William could pass all the light switches in the hallway to the lunchroom and not say one charm to protect himself; Guillermo was begrudgingly learning Braille. And Susannah Joy and Freddie? Well, we were still trying with them.

I had read the newspaper article in late November and had forgotten it. But I shouldn't have. I should have known that sooner or later we would be twelve.

Ed Somers appeared in my room the day after school resumed following Christmas vacation. He came early, his kind face swathed in that apologetic expression that I was beginning to realize meant trouble for me. It was the expression attached to things like not getting a special tutor for Guillermo, or yet another hopeless report from the newest doctor Susannah's parents had found. Ed wanted things to be different; I believe he genuinely did, which made it impossible for me to be angry with him.

"There's going to be a new child in your class," he said, his face mirroring his hesitance to tell me.

I stared at him a long moment, not comprehending. I already had the state-allowed maximum and had never anticipated having another child. "I have eight now, Ed."

"I know, Torey. But this is a special case. We don't have any place to put her. Your class is the only option we have."

"But I've got eight kids already," I repeated dumbly. "That is all I can have."

Ed looked pained. He was a big bear of a man, tall and muscular like a football player but padded with the extra softness of middle age. His hair was nearly gone and what was left he had carefully combed across the shiny dome. But above all, Ed was gentle and I was amazed that he had ever made it to such a high position in education, a profession not known for its kind treatment of gentle people. But perhaps that was his secret, because I never failed to soften when he looked so hurt by what he was having to do to me.

"What's so special about this kid?" I asked tentatively.

"This is that girl who burned the little boy in November. They took her out of school and made arrangements to send her to the state hospital. But there hasn't been an opening in the children's unit yet. So the kid's been home a month and getting into all sorts of trouble. Now the social worker is beginning to ask why we aren't doing anything for her."

"Can't they put her on homebound?" I asked. A number of my children had been taught by homebound, a term referring to the practice of sending a teacher into the home to teach a child when for some reason he could not attend school. Often, severely disturbed children were handled in this manner until appropriate placement could be found.

Ed frowned at the floor. "No one is willing to work with her."

"The kid's six years old," I said in surprise. "They're scared of a six-year-old?"

He shrugged, his silence telling me more about this child than words could have.

"But I already have all the children I can handle."

"Choose a child to be transferred. We have to put this child in here, Torey. It will just be temporary. Until a place opens up at the state hospital. But we have to put her in here. This is the only place equipped to handle her. This is the only place she'll fit."

"You mean I'm the only one idiotic enough to take her."

"You can pick whom you want transferred."

"When is she coming?"

"The eighth."

By that point the children were beginning to arrive and I had to prepare for our first day back from vacation. Sensing my need to get to work, Ed nodded and left. He knew that, if given time, I would do it. Ed knew that, for all my bravado, I was a pushover.

After telling Anton the news, I looked over the children. As we went through the day I kept asking myself who should go. Guillermo was the obvious choice, simply because I was least equipped to teach him. But what about Freddie or Susannah Joy? Neither was making progress of much note. Anyone could lug them around and change their pants. Or maybe Tyler. She wasn't so suicidal now; she hardly ever spoke of killing herself anymore; she no longer drew those black-crayoned pictures. A resource teacher could probably handle her. I looked at each one of them, wondering where they would go and how they would make it. And how our room would be without them. I knew in my heart none of them would survive the rigors of a less-sheltered class. None of them was ready. Nor was I ready to give them up, nor give up on them.

"Ed?" I clutched the receiver tightly because it kept slipping in my sweating hand. "I don't want to transfer any of my kids. We're doing so well together. I can't choose any one of them."

"Torey, I told you we have to put that girl in there. I'm really sorry. I hate to do it to you, but there isn't any other place."

I stared morosely at the bulletin board beside the phone with all its proclamations of events my children never could attend. I was feeling used. "Can I have nine?"

"Will you take nine?"

"It's against the law. Do I get another aide?"

"We'll see."

"Does that mean yes?"

"I hope so," Ed replied. "But we'll just have to see. Will you need another desk?"

"What I need is another teacher. Or another room."

"Will you settle for another desk?"

"No. I don't have any desks. There wasn't room for the first eight. So we just sit on the carpet or at the tables. No, I don't need another desk. Just send me the kid."

Twilight Children

Two children trapped in a prison of silence and a woman suffering in the twilight of her years—these are the cases that would test the extraordinary courage, compassion and skill of Torey Hayden, and ultimately reaffirm her faith in the indomitable strength of the human spirit.

ISBN 0 00 719819 1

Available now in hardback in all good bookstores.

In paperback October 2006

ISBN 0 00 719820 5

Read more about Torey's encounter with Cassandra, Drake and Gerda in this extract from *Twilight Children*.

Twilight Children

She was a small, fine-boned girl with a pointed pixie chin and unusually distinct cheekbones. Her hair was a soft black, straight and shoulder length, but it had been rather raffishly cut, as if perhaps done by another child. Her eyes, however, defined her face. Enormous, protruding slightly, and fluidly dark, like shadowed water, they overpowered her other features. She wasn't what I would call a pretty girl, but she was striking in a faintly unreal way, so that when she lifted her hand to push hair back from her face, I half expected to see elfin ears.

"Hello," I said and pulled out the chair at the table.

She hunched forward, hands down between her knees so that her chin was almost on the tabletop. Her eyes, however, remained on me. She smiled in a manner that was rather self-conscious, yet friendly enough.

"What's your name?" I asked.

"Cassandra."

Ah, a mythical name. It fit the fairy-tale looks.

"How old you are, Cassandra?"

"Nine."

"My name's Torey, and you and I are going to be working together each day." I pulled out a chair adjacent to hers and sat down. "Can you tell me why you've come to the unit?"

Her dark eyes locked on mine, and for a moment or two she stared intently, as if she expected to find the answer there. Then she shook her head faintly. "No."

"What about your mom? What did she tell you about why you were coming here?"

"I don't remember."

"Okay," I said. I bent down and opened my box of materials. Taking out plain paper and a smaller cardboard box, I laid them on the table. "Most of the children I work with come to the unit because they have problems that make them feel bad. Sometimes, for example, they have problems in their family. Maybe someone in the family is really unhappy and it makes them do hurtful things. Maybe there's been a divorce. Maybe there's lots of fighting at home. For some of the children who come here, it's other things. Maybe they've been in an accident or a really scary situation, or they've been very ill. Some have been treated or touched in a way that felt wrong, or people tried to make them keep secrets that hurt. And sometimes ... sometimes kids don't even know the reason they have troubles. They just feel angry or worried or scared all the time. So these are some of the reasons children come to the unit."

Cassandra watched me with unusual intensity, as if she were really trying to take in what I was saying, trying to absorb it, almost. Nonetheless, there was an oddly blank quality to her stare, almost as if she were listening so carefully not for the content of what I was saying but rather because I was speaking to her in a foreign language she didn't quite understand.

"Hearing about reasons for other children coming to the unit," I said, "do you think any of those describe you?"

"I don't know."

"Okay. Well, I'll share with you some of the things other people have told me about you. You can then say if you think they are true or not.

"Your mom, for instance, tells me that you had a scary thing happen to you when you were five. She says that she is divorced from your dad and that you and your sister were supposed to live with her and not see him. Then one day your dad came to school and had you get into his car, even though that was against the rules. He drove off with you and wouldn't bring you back, and he wouldn't phone your mom to tell her that you were safe, and he wouldn't let you phone your mom. She says you were gone a long time—about two years—and during the time you were with your dad, some very scary things happened to you. Is that right?"

Cassandra nodded. Her demeanor was pleasant, cheerful even, as if I'd said no more than "Your mom says you are in third grade."

"Your teacher tells me that you like school, that you can be very enthusiastic about what is happening in class. She says you are quite a smart girl and can do really well sometimes."

Cassandra smiled.

"But she also tells me that at other times you have lots of problems. You can get very angry and have a hard time following the rules. Occasionally when you are at school, you get *very* upset and then you stop talking. Mrs. Baker says there are sometimes days and days when you don't want to say anything to anyone, and this makes it difficult to do your work in class. But she tells me while these are bad problems, they aren't the biggest problem. She says the biggest problem is that you very often don't tell the truth. You make up stories about people that get them into trouble, and you often talk about things that aren't really happening at all."

I paused. "What do you think? Do *you* think these things have caused trouble for you?"

Cassandra shrugged. It came off as almost a comical gesture, the way she did it. She brought her shoulders way up and rolled her eyes in an exaggerated fashion that was tinged with tolerant good humor, as if to say, "Silly grown-ups, who make mountains out of molehills."

"These are the reasons the grown-ups have given me, when I asked, 'Why is Cassandra Ventura on the unit?' "

Cassandra rolled her eyes again, then looked up to the right, then up to the left, then back to the right.

"What do you think?" I asked. "Do these things seem like problems to you?"

"I don't know."

"I'm interested in your thoughts. There isn't a wrong or right answer to my questions. We're just exploring."

"I don't know," she repeated.

"You don't know?"

"I don't remember."

"You don't remember what? If you do those things? If people think those are problems? Or you don't remember what I just said?"

Again she shrugged and rolled her eyes.

I pushed one of the plain pieces of paper in front of Cassandra, then I opened the small box. Inside was an assortment of marking pens, pencils, and crayons. "I want you to draw me a picture of your family."

She hesitated. "I'm not a very good draw-er."

"That's okay. They can just be stick figures, if you want. You can make them any way that's easy for you."

"Like bubbles? Instead of sticks, can I draw them round, like bubbles?"

"If that's what you want."

"Fish!" she said with sudden animation. "I draw really good fish. I figured out this way. Let me show you." She picked up an orange crayon. "See? You make a circle. Then you draw a little triangle on one end with the point sticking against the circle and that's the tail. See?" She made several more fish along the side of the paper. "Can I make them fish?"

"You decide," I replied.

But she didn't make fish. And she didn't make stick figures. Instead, Cassandra dropped the crayon and took a pencil. She began to draw very small, very carefully proportioned people. First a man, then a girl, then a smaller girl, then a woman. A pause. Cassandra considered the picture. Then she added another figure next to the mother. This was a second man. Then she added a third man. Another pause.

Everything thus far had been done in pencil. Indeed, she'd chosen a very sharp, hard-lead pencil and so the drawings were quite faint. She then put the pencil down and reached over for the box, pulling it closer. Looking through, she picked out different crayons and set about placing her family in a pleasant scene of grass, blue sky, and bright sunshine. She worked carefully, coloring in the grass after drawing the lines and then the sky. She assiduously avoided coloring over the orange fish so that it looked almost as if they were balloons in the air. She pressed hard when making the sun, turning it waxy yellow, many of the rays extending out over the crayoned blue of the sky.

While Cassandra had been careful not to color over her fish at the edge of the paper, she had had no such compunctions about coloring over the family. They were hardly visible through the blue she'd used for the sky.

"There," she said, then paused to regard the picture. "No, wait." She reached out and took up a black magic marker. Carefully she penned in a smiling face on the sun. "That's better. That's a happy picture now, isn't it?" Then she continued with the black marker and drew a strange little blobby shape in the sky not far from the sun. It had three protrusions, making it look rather like a clover leaf without the stem.

"You've worked hard on that. Can you tell me about it? Who are these people in the family?"

"Welllll," she said in a slow, drawn-out voice, "that's my dad." She pointed to the first faint figure. "That's my sister Magdalena. And that's my sister Mona. And that's my mom. And that's Daddy David. And that's Uncle Beck."

"And where are you in this picture?" I asked.

"I'm not in this picture. Am I supposed to be in this picture? I thought you said you wanted a picture of my family."

I nodded.

"You wanted me in the family?" she asked.

"Well, if you wanted to draw everyone in your family, it might include you, mightn't it? ... but then again ... however you see it, that's good. There isn't a right or wrong way of doing it."

"Everyone? You wanted everyone? I didn't know you said everyone. I didn't know you meant everyone."

Cassandra reached over and picked out an assortment of crayons—red, yellow, blue, green. Down in the right-hand corner of the picture she began to draw several small snakes, all with smiley faces. She made about ten of them of different sizes.

"This is becoming quite an intricate picture," I said. "Can you tell me about these?"

"This is Mother Snake and this is Father Snake and these are the kid snakes. And this is Minister Snake. And this is Cowboy Snake. And this is Fairy Snake. They're my brothers and sisters, these ones. He's my brother and he's my brother and this one's my sister."

"Ah," I said. "Your mom only told me about your sisters Mona and Magdalena."

"These are my other brothers. In my other family. From when I was abducted. I lived in a whole other family then, and these are my brothers and sisters from there. I called them 'Minister' and 'Cowboy' and 'Fairy' because that's how they liked to dress up. Well, not him. He really was a minister. He was a grown-up. Like seventeen, I think. But Cowboy and Fairy were my age. Well, Fairy was younger. She was three. I took care of her."

"I see. Your mother didn't mention your other family."

Cassandra grinned then. It was an openly saucy expression. "Maybe she doesn't know."

Or maybe I don't know, I was thinking. There was something too playful about her behavior, making it feel manipulative to me. I was getting a sense of smoke and mirrors about Cassandra, that she was astute at giving what she surmised I wanted so that I never noticed what wasn't being offered.

"And that's me, there," she said and pointed to the clover-shaped blob in the sky.

"Ah," I said, "so you are in the picture now?"

"Yup." She looked up at me and smiled. "But I'm up there 'cause I'm an alien."